When the Waves Ruled Britannia

How did a rural and agrarian English society transform itself into a mercantile and maritime state? What role was played by war and the need for military security? How did geographical ideas inform the construction of English – and then British – political identities? Focusing upon the deployment of geographical imagery and arguments for political purposes, Jonathan Scott's ambitious and interdisciplinary study traces the development of the idea of Britain as an island nation, state and then empire from 1500 to 1800, through literature, philosophy, history, geography and travel writing. One argument advanced in the process concerns the maritime origins, nature and consequences of the English revolution. This is the first general study to examine changing geographical languages in early modern British politics, in an imperial, European and global context. Offering a new perspective on the nature of early modern Britain, it will be essential reading for students and scholars of the period.

JONATHAN SCOTT is Professor of History at the University of Auckland. His previous publications include *England's Troubles: Seventeenth-Century English Political Instability in European Context* (Cambridge 2000) and *Commonwealth Principles: Republican Writing of the English Revolution* (Cambridge 2004).

When the Waves Ruled Britannia

Geography and Political Identities, 1500–1800

Jonathan Scott

CAMBRIDGE
UNIVERSITY PRESS

CAMBRIDGE UNIVERSITY PRESS
Cambridge, New York, Melbourne, Madrid, Cape Town,
Singapore, São Paulo, Delhi, Tokyo, Mexico City

Cambridge University Press
The Edinburgh Building, Cambridge CB2 8RU, UK

Published in the United States of America by Cambridge University Press,
New York

www.cambridge.org
Information on this title: www.cambridge.org/9780521152419

First published 2011

Printed in the United Kingdom at the University Press, Cambridge

A catalogue record for this publication is available from the British Library

Library of Congress Cataloguing in Publication data
Scott, Jonathan, 1958–
    When the waves ruled Britannia : geography and political identities,
    1500–1800 / Jonathan Scott.
        p.   cm.
    ISBN 978-0-521-19591-1 (hbk.) – ISBN 978-0-521-15241-9 (pbk.)
    1. Great Britain – Politics and government – 1558–1603.   2. Great
    Britain – Politics and government – 1603–1714.   3. Great Britain –
    Politics and government – 1714–1820.   4. Great Britain – History,
    Naval.   5. Great Britain – Historical geography.   6. Great Britain –
    Foreign relations.   7. Great Britain – Economic conditions.
    8. National characteristics, British.   I. Title.
    DA355.S36 2011
    941–dc22   2010051880

ISBN 978-0-521-19591-1 Hardback
ISBN 978-0-521-15241-9 Paperback

For John Morrill, a fishy tale

There was a man who was born in Yen but grew up in Chu, and in old age returned to his native country. While he was passing through the state of Jin his companions played a joke on him. They pointed out a city and told him: 'This is the capital of Yen.'

He composed himself and looked solemn.

Inside the city they pointed out a shrine: 'This is the shrine of your quarter.'

He breathed a deep sigh.

They pointed out a hut: 'This is your father's cottage.'

His tears welled up.

They pointed out a mound: 'This is your father's tomb.'

He could not help weeping aloud. His companions roared with laughter. 'We were teasing you. You are still only in Jin.'

The man was very embarrassed. When he reached Yen, and really saw the capital of Yen and the shrine of his quarter, really saw his father's cottage and tomb, he did not feel it so deeply.

The *Liezi*
Quoted in Kuriyama Shigehisa, ' "Between Mind and Eye": Japanese
Anatomy in the Eighteenth Century', in Charles Leslie and Allan Young
(eds.), *Paths to Asian Medical Knowledge* (Berkeley, 1992)

Contents

List of figures   *page* viii
List of maps   ix
Preface: Geography and the sea   xi
List of abbreviations   xvii

Introduction: Britain's island idea   1

1 Community of water   11

2 Queen of Sparta   31

3 The discipline of the sea   54

4 Ark of war   73

5 Blowing a dead coal   92

6 The British empire in Europe   116

7 The world in an island   137

8 Anti-continentalism   153

9 What continent?   173

   Conclusion: floating islands   194

Appendix: Duck Language (1724)   198
Bibliography   200
Index   222

Figures

1 Cover page of volume I of Richard Hakluyt, *The Principall
   Navigations, Voiages and Discoveries of the English Nation.*
   Reproduced by kind permission of the Syndics of
   Cambridge University Library.   *page* 49
2 The River Thames with St Paul's Cathedral on Lord Mayor's
   Day, *c.*1747–8, by Canaletto.   135

Maps

1 The sixteenth-century grain trade   *page* 12
2 The chief cities of Europe in the first half of the
   sixteenth century   32
3 The early modern Atlantic world   74
4 The southern North Sea and the narrow seas   94
5 European empires in 1750   158
6 British voyages in the South Pacific, 1699–1775   184

Preface: Geography and the sea

This study began as a trickle and swept me out to sea. It remains a limited vessel navigating more than one large body of knowledge, but I hope it is seaworthy. I began by reading voyage narratives, most, though not all, maritime. These included the journals of Cook and the frequently hair-raising accounts by early British settlers of their voyages to New Zealand. The travellers were always seasick, there were always storms, and amid the sharks, seabirds, red shrimps off Argentina, and many other creatures and events, life went on: birth, eating, drinking and death. Most travellers arrived. '[W]e could see the smoke rising from several fires on shore. The coast was by what I could see rocky and steep ... we hauled a fine white fish weighing about 40 pounds like our cod and called by the natives harbouker [hapuka, grouper] ... Fine night dead calm the harbour like a mirror reflecting all the lights from the little shops that ran along the beach.'[1]

This starting point owed something to the work of J.C. Beaglehole, and not only to his famous editorial labours (those footnotes still hold good, and he was an extremely sound judge of south-east Asian tropical fruit). Beaglehole also wrote about seventeenth-century England, gave a brilliant inaugural lecture called 'The New Zealand Scholar', and produced his lip-smacking first book, *The Exploration of the Pacific*, while a semi-unemployed doctoral graduate trained in an entirely different historical area.[2]

Several of the preoccupations informing this study are characteristic of New Zealanders, including, and perhaps especially, expatriates. They include maps, geography, islands, and the mental contemplation

[1] ATL, MS Papers 0495, Diary of G. Darling, November 1842, entries for Tuesday 1st and Thursday 3rd at New Plymouth, New Zealand, p. 16.
[2] J.C. Beaglehole, 'On the Place of Tasman's Voyage in History', in J.C. Beaglehole (ed.), *Abel Janszoon Tasman and the Discovery of New Zealand* (Wellington, 1942); J.C. Beaglehole, 'The New Zealand Scholar', in Peter Munz (ed.), *The Feel of Truth: Essays in New Zealand and Pacific History* (Wellington, 1969); J.C. Beaglehole, *The Exploration of the Pacific* (3rd edn, London, 1966); Tim Beaglehole, *A Life of J. C. Beaglehole: New Zealand Scholar* (Wellington, 2006) pp. 152, 211–12.

of distance in space as well as time. When my father died in 1960 a collection of essays was published in his memory called *Distance Looks our
Way* because for New Zealanders that was the case.[3] This project engages
with English and then British thinking about space, at a time when the
spatial and cultural parameters of European experience were being revo-
lutionized. It reflects how closely the texts in question intertwined space
and time: no geography without history, or vice versa; no voyage without
clockface, and eventually chronometer, as well as compass (and stars). It
was partly because history informed politics, and geography history, that
geography belonged within the political realm.[4] Contemporaries read
Thucydides and Livy map in hand.

In the words of Nathaniel Butler, 'as geography without historye
seemeth a carkasse without motion, so history without geography wan-
dereth as a vagrant without certaine habitation'.[5] Whether in Camden or
Hakluyt, although for different reasons, textual navigation aimed to ori-
ent the reader in space and time. For the former, the point of departure
was part of the context for explaining the place of arrival. For the latter,
voyaging had a chronology essential to the pressing of territorial claims,
and the charting of a voyage had to show not only where a traveller had
been, but how a reader might get there, vicariously or in practice.

This book has two scholarly purposes. One addresses the early modern
English and then British political use of geographical language.[6] Here
I have drawn upon the work of historical geographers and scholars of
English literature as well as that of historians. I have not mastered the
field of early modern geography. What I suggest is that geography has
been a relatively neglected component of the history of political ideas.

[3] Keith Sinclair (ed.), *Distance Looks our Way: the Effects of Remoteness on New Zealand* (Auckland, 1961). The title came from Charles Brasch's poem 'The Islands': 'Everywhere in light and calm murmuring/Shadow of departure; distance looks our way;/ And none knows where he will lie down at night.' (*Collected Poems*, (ed.) Alan Roddick (Auckland, 1984).)
[4] Robert J. Mayhew, *Enlightenment Geography: the Political Languages of British Geography, 1650–1850* (Houndmills, 2000) p. 33.
[5] Quoted in Alison Games, *The Web of Empire: English Cosmopolitans in an Age of Expansion* (Oxford, 2008) p. 11. Compare Peter Heylyn, *Cosmography in Four Books. Containing the Chorography and History of the Whole World: And All the Principal Kingdoms, Provinces, Seas, and Isles thereof* (London, 1677) reversing the formula on p. 17: ''Tis true *Geography* with-out *History* hath life and motion, but very unstable, and at random; but *History* without *Geography*, like a dead carcass, hath neither life, nor motion.' Mayhew, *Enlightenment Geography* p. 33. For a recent discussion of this disciplinary relationship see Alan R. H. Baker, *Geography and History: Bridging the Divide* (Cambridge, 2003).
[6] 'English and then British use' here refers to a temporal sequence. This does not relate to the user, implying that English people became British, or excluding the Scots and the Welsh. It refers to the thing described, the English and then British state (the latter estab-lished in 1707). Most writers discussed happen to have been English or Scottish.

While historical geographers examine the politics and religion of early modern geography, and historians of political thought examine constitutional and moral languages, there has been no general attempt to map the changing *geographical* language of English and then British politics, despite its crucial role in creating an image of the state.[7] While there have been important literary analyses of the national content of early modern texts, including travel writing and geography, this study attempts to understand the geographical components of early modern British political thought, sub-national, national, regional and imperial.[8] Its subject is the geographical articulation of political identities, particularly as these concerned the relationship of land to sea.[9]

My second and related focus is upon how a rural and agrarian English society transformed its government in a mercantile and maritime direction under the extreme pressure of war. This process took centuries, infinite ingenuity, blood and treasure, and remained highly incomplete. Yet as a process capable of being analysed historically it raises the question: what happens to politics when you add water? Although this society depended upon both fresh and salt water, the emphasis in early modern political writing, for reasons of economic and military security, was increasingly upon the challenge posed by the sea. Here I draw upon historiographies concerning state formation, empire, and maritime and naval history. Having previously worked with the first, I am, however, newer to the others.[10] Water is now hot, and in particular '[t]he history of the sea has become so complex, so multidimensional, that its potentialities may be lost'.[11] This huge topic cannot here be treated systematically. However, it is an inescapable context for understanding the construction of early modern England's and Britain's political and geographical self-image. Related themes include trade and the history and consequences of trade; what contemporaries called the discipline of the sea; and what became the idea of an island nation and empire.

---

[7] Note, however, David Armitage, *The Ideological Origins of the British Empire* (Cambridge, 2000).

[8] Richard Helgerson, *Forms of Nationhood: the Elizabethan Writing of England* (Chicago, 1992); Andrew Hadfield, *Literature, Politics and National Identity: Reformation to Renaissance* (Cambridge, 1994) pp. 2–15; John Kerrigan, *Archipelagic English: Literature, History and Politics 1603–1707* (Oxford, 2008).

[9] See relatedly Colin Kidd, *British Identities before Nationalism: Ethnicity and Nationhood in the Atlantic World 1600–1800* (Cambridge, 1999).

[10] Jonathan Scott, *England's Troubles: Seventeenth-Century English Political Instability in European Context* (Cambridge, 2000).

[11] Glen O'Hara, '"The Sea is Swinging into View": Modern British Maritime History in a Globalised World', *English Historical Review* 124, 510 (2009) p. 1130. On fresh water see Michael Cathcart, *The Water Dreamers: the Remarkable History of our Dry Continent* (Melbourne, 2009).

Both of these topics develop earlier work. My *England's Troubles* discussed contemporary political imagery deploying images of the natural world to depict a tempest-tossed ship of state.[12] *Commonwealth Principles* looked in more detail at some maritime components of English republicanism, in writing and practice.[13] Both set these themes in a European, and particularly Anglo-Dutch, framework. This book is a sequel to *England's Troubles* which investigates articulations of early modern England's European identity from the perspective of geography rather than religion. It examines what English and Scottish writers made of a geography as characteristically European as their religion, and which embroiled them no less inescapably in the sanguinary affairs of Europe locally, regionally and globally. It is a successor to *Commonwealth Principles* in being a study in the history of ideas focused upon primary texts, in this case manuscript as well as published. Returning once more in this context to Anglo-Dutch history is not to suggest that it has been neglected. However, the duration, multifaceted nature and cumulatively transformative impact of Dutch upon early modern English history remains underexplored. The situation is serious: even cricket was a Flemish import.[14]

Geography and the sea come together here in the figure of the island. Although islands have become another preoccupation of New Zealanders, long before that English and then British people came to describe themselves as islanders.[15] An island for early modern Europeans was not what it is for New Zealanders now. While contemporaries never failed to distinguish between water and land, they had an almost endless analytical repertoire for dealing with each, and with their relationship to each other. This book examines development of the idea of Britain as an island nation, state and then empire. For this the sources are voluminous, left by a society whose religious and political debates were saturated with images of the natural world, and whose imperial experience was intertwined with the ambitions and observational practices of natural philosophy. They include works of polemic, counsel, poetry, drama, satire, geography, history, natural philosophy, maritime treatises, political philosophy and travel writing.

[12] Scott, *England's Troubles*, Cover and chs. 1–2.
[13] Jonathan Scott, *Commonwealth Principles: Republican Writing of the English Revolution* (Cambridge, 2004), Cover and pp. 98–105, 143–50, 261–72.
[14] 'O lorde of Ipocrites/Nowe shut upp your wickettes/And clape to your clickettes!/A! Farewell, kings of crekettes!', John Skelton on immigrant Flemish weavers in 'The Image of Ipocrisie', 1533. 'Belgians Invented the Game of Cricket', *Television New Zealand News*, Wednesday 4 March 2009 (online resource).
[15] Ken Lunn and Ann Day, in 'Britain as Island: National Identity and the Sea', in Helen Brocklehurst and Robert Phillips (eds.), *History, Nationhood and the Question of Britain* (Houndmills, 2004), note this but do not analyse or explain it.

This book, largely written at the University of Pittsburgh, bears the imprint of that Department of History in several ways. It had a powerful Atlantic history programme, and some of that salt water rubbed off on me. More generally, Pittsburgh is a department committed to transnational and global graduate training in history. Although this book is not a global, or even transnational history, I benefited enormously from my interaction with students and faculty comparing many parts of the world. Those students included Catherine Balleriaux, Tania Boster, Roland Clark, John Donoghue, Niklas Frykman, Chris Magra, Jake Pollock and Kate Sorrels, all of whom have contributed to this project, or at least tolerated my going on about it (what choice did they have?). My resource base has been especially fortified by Jake, who is working on a related topic. Faculty to whom I am indebted include Reid Andrews, Bill Chase, John Cooper, Pinar Emiralioglu, Alejandro de la Fuente, Janelle Greenberg, Jim and Peggy Knapp, Patrick Manning, Lara Putnam, Evelyn Rawski, Bruce Venarde and Jen Waldron. Paul Millett, John Morrow, Andrew Neill, John Reeve, Jonathan Sawday, Andrew Sharp and Michael Witmore all drew my attention to material I would otherwise have missed. This book could not have been written without the support of the University of Pittsburgh and the resources available there to the Carroll Amundson Professor of British History. These made possible the trips to London and elsewhere for archival work, and time for reading and writing.

Not for the first time I am indebted to Colin Davis, Martin Van Gelderen, Mark Kishlansky and Markku Peltonen. John Morrow, with whom I edited another volume while writing this, read an early draft, discussed, understood and supported the project while scooting across Auckland harbour aboard *Swift*, amid many other notable acts of friendship. I am most grateful to the two anonymous referees for Cambridge University Press.

During my own graduate education I was exceptionally lucky to fall under the lash of John Morrill. The first-rate *Morrill* now has many hands, a lot more sprightly around the rigging than myself. John's command of the period, of its reefs, winds and currents, is only one of the qualities of a remarkable citizen of the republic of life. This book is a miserly return for everything he has done for me. For this reason I have added, at least, some servings of fish, which I offer freshly caught and plainly seasoned with warm affection and gratitude.

When, in Pittsburgh, I began this New Zealand-like study of an aspect of British history, I considered myself to be living in the middle of a world-spanning bridge of English language connecting the three countries. Now that I have moved to Auckland, the book reads like a bridge leading me home. But one of its implications is that home is not a place, but a process. In any case history, if not kept under the strictest supervision, will govern the historian: 'The young [and not so young] are mastered by the Dead.'[16] I am more grateful than I can say to Anne, Sophia and Thomas for being part of our process; for learning their own lessons beside mine.

[16] James K. Baxter, 'Summer 1967', quoted in Jonathan Scott, *Harry's Absence: Looking for my Father on the Mountain* (Wellington, 1997) p. 10.

Abbreviations

ATL   Alexander Turnbull Library, Wellington, New Zealand
BL   British Library, London
NMM   National Maritime Museum, Greenwich, London
PL   Pepys Library, Magdalene College, Cambridge

Introduction: Britain's island idea

The fact that British influence – measured by the standards ... of ancient Greece or China – is a relatively recent ... phenomenon only adds to its interest. It is part of ... the history of western Europe's Atlantic-side peoples ... the land we inhabit is the sump into which Eurasian history has drained ... the spread of farming and metallurgy and Indo-European languages; the colonizations of Phoenicians and Greeks ... the migrations of Jews in antiquity, and the coming of Christianity ... the arrival of oriental mathematics, science and technology; the invasions of Germanic, Slavic and steppeland peoples; Ottoman imperialism ... Many of these movements created their refuse ... who ended up on the Atlantic shore ... unable to get any further west, as if pinioned by the winds. The great problem of their history is not why they took to the sea and spread over the world, but why they took so long about it.

Filipe Fernandez-Armesto, 'Britain, the Sea, the Empire, the World'[1]

Human beings have always exploited water. Intensive agriculture developed on irrigated flood plains; the first complex urban cultures (Sumerian, Egyptian, Indian, Chinese) made use of coastal as well as river and caravan transport. In Song China, as later in the Netherlands and then Britain, commercial societies developed by linking rivers with canals.[2] In the early modern period the whole globe was made one 'water world' by the startling accomplishments of long-range Portuguese, Spanish and other European cannon-carrying seafaring.[3]

Yet there have been few maritime civilizations. Since the development of agriculture and until late industrialization most people have worked the land and been bound by its produce, limits and seasons. Maritime economies and cultures developed around the edges of the Assyrian,

---

[1] In David Cannadine (ed.), *Empire, the Sea and Global History: Britain's Maritime World, c. 1760–c.1840* (Houndmills, 2007) pp. 7–8.

[2] W.H. McNeill, *A History of the Human Community: Prehistory to the Present* (4th edn, Englewood Cliffs, N.J., 1993) chs. 1–6; J.R. McNeill and William H. McNeill, *The Human Web: a Bird's Eye View of World History* (New York, 2003) chs. 1–3.

[3] McNeill and McNeill, *The Human Web*, p. 179.

Roman, Byzantine, Chinese, Ottoman and Iberian empires, in Tyre, Athens, Carthage, Venice and Amsterdam.[4] They were, that is to say, the product of cities, rather than of states. However, sometimes cities created states. In the late sixteenth century this occurred in the northern Netherlands, where the driving forces behind the United Provinces were Amsterdam, Utrecht, Haarlem, Leiden, Delft.[5] A century later, following a successful water-borne Dutch invasion in 1688, the United Kingdom of Great Britain (1707) was created by and through London, however stylish Edinburgh came to look at the party. It was created by the capital as a political power, and through it as a national, regional and imperial entrepot.[6]

In the ancient world the development of maritime Greek culture exploited the geography of the eastern Mediterranean, but was not created by it. It owed something to earlier Egyptian, Cretan and Phoenician example. Like their neighbours, most Greeks by 600 BC had developed an agricultural and pastoral economy, and an aristocratic/warrior society. Change came for three reasons. One was that two of the agricultural products concerned, wine and olive oil, were highly tradable. Another was the dispersed Greek pattern of polis settlement, first in Ionia (Asia Minor) and then in colonies from the Black Sea to the western Mediterranean.

The third development was the decision of Athens to invest in maritime military as well as economic power, and to integrate both into politics. The result was a democratic system capable, militarily, of stopping Persia (though not, as it turned out, Sparta). One result was an Athenian empire distinct from the colonies which had preceded it. Although this maritime culture never replaced agriculture, it integrated with it, shaped it, and occasionally displaced it within Attica in particular.

In the analysis of 'Pseudo-Xenophon': '[In Athens] it seems just that the vulgar, the poor and the people are given the preference to the distinguished and rich people, for the simple reason that the people is the motive power in the navy and gives the state its strength ... much more than the heavy-armed infantry.'[7] In early modern England also, military

[4] J.H. Elliott, *Empires of the Atlantic World: Britain and Spain in America 1492–1830* (New Haven, 2007) p. 18; Pinar M. Emiralioglu, 'Cognizance of the Ottoman World: Visual and Textual Representations in the Sixteenth Century Ottoman Empire (1514–96)', unpublished PhD dissertation, University of Chicago, 2006.
[5] Jonathan Israel, *The Dutch Republic: Its Rise, Greatness, and Fall 1477–1806* (Oxford, 1998) p. 114.
[6] In *Web of Empire* Alison Games brings together the histories of migration, trade, and religious and political travel to suggest that this empire was shaped around and through, rather than by, London. For the web as a metaphor for empire see also Tony Ballantyne, *Orientalism and Race: Aryanism in the British Empire* (Houndmills, 2002) pp. 13–17.
[7] Hartvig Frisch (ed.), *The Constitution of the Athenians: a Philological Analysis of Pseudo-Xenefon's Treatise De Re Publica Atheniensium* (Copenhagen, 1942) p. 13.

need eventually brought about political, economic and social change. The military extremity which led, in 1645, to the creation of the New Model Army helped to unleash a religious and political revolution. No less important, though less examined, was the creation of a new and unparalleled English republican naval power with a distinct social philosophy and social structure.[8]

In terms of its speed and scope the only early modern transformation comparable to the ancient Athenian one occurred in the northern Netherlands (a fact later remarked upon by the Scottish Enlightenment writer James Dunbar). Here, too, the rise of a mercantile, maritime economy exploited regional geography, between the Baltic and the Mediterranean, and at the intersection of three major rivers and the sea.[9] Dutch economic development not only imitated Portuguese example, but appropriated Portuguese possessions. Unlike Portugal, however, and like Athens, late sixteenth-century Holland and Zeeland imported their grain. Along Athenian lines the United Provinces became a highly cultured and prosperous urban product of large-scale migration. As in Athens the society which resulted was not only post-royal but significantly post-aristocratic. As in Athens, without the struggle for survival against a neighbouring empire (in this case the Spanish Habsburg) these developments might never have occurred.

Unlike Athens or the United Provinces, sixteenth-century England was a rural, aristocratic and monarchical grain-growing society. Yet, beset by military necessity imposed by Spain, the United Provinces and then France, it was driven during the following two centuries to acquire components of a maritime economy, government and culture. Although these developments were initially peripheral, they came to involve social and political change. To England came, eventually, mercantile republicanism, commercialized aristocracy, parliamentary monarchy and global empire. By the eighteenth century the British state had become sufficiently powerful to impose its fiat upon mighty commercial trading companies, and trade had become integrated with agriculture and manufactures to an extent which would help to make industrialization possible.[10] Whereas during the Elizabethan period maritime voyaging

---

[8] The authority remains Bernard Capp, *Cromwell's Navy: the Fleet and the English Revolution 1648–60* (Oxford, 1989). As Capp acknowledges, however, this navy was not Cromwell's, in origin at least, for the importance of which fact see chapter 4 below.

[9] Israel, *The Dutch Republic*; Jan de Vries and A. van der Woude, *The First Modern Economy: Success, Failure, and the Perseverance of the Dutch Economy, 1500–1815* (Cambridge, 1997).

[10] Philip J. Stern, '"A Politie of Civill & Military Power": Political Thought and the Late Seventeenth-Century Foundations of the East India Company-State', *Journal of British Studies* 47 (April 2008) pp. 282–3.

was sponsored by a coalition of gentlemen and merchants operating with permission of the crown, and whereas the Dutch economic miracle was achieved by the mercantile political marginalization of landed gentry, only in Britain from 1660 to 1800 did aristocratic and mercantile culture achieve a political and social coalescence capable of determining, and being determined by, government policy.

As the culmination of a long-term process of imitation and adaptation in agriculture, trade, maritime culture, political economy and government this was not a development in one country.[11] Key to the process was war: calamitous military failure as well as success, and therefore experience of what was necessary to fight war successfully.[12] This study emphasizes the social and political impact of this experience. As the co-operative necessities of hoplite warfare created the Greek polis and (building on classical example) the Dutch military revolution created a republic, rather than a monarchy, so in eighteenth-century Britain the relationship of economic, political and military structures was the outcome, not of a single event in 1688–9, but of more than a century of Dutch-informed trial and error. Within this long-term international relationship and process, this study identifies three striking 'moments' of Anglo-Dutch political proximity, in 1584–5, 1649–54 and 1688–97. Each entailed elements of rivalry and even conflict intertwined with alliance, emulation and attempted union. These were opposite sides of the same coin.

In the Netherlands water, fresh and salt, was everywhere. The United Provinces was a phoenix risen around, and within, a complex delta. In Holland and Zeeland, in particular, economic life, including the acquisition and retention of dry land, required continual hydraulic activity. In England, by contrast, though the country was well watered by rain and rivers, geography, economy and society were all different. This was so despite a component of internal geography in Lincolnshire and Cambridgeshire by locals 'very properly call'd *Holland*, for 'tis a flat, level, and often drowned Country, like *Holland* itself; here the very Ditches are navigable, and the People pass from Town to Town in Boats, as in *Holland*'.[13] It was so despite natural harbours, in depth and

---

[11] Jonathan Scott, 'What the Dutch Taught Us', *Times Literary Supplement*, 16 March 2001 pp. 4–6; Charles Wilson, *England's Apprenticeship 1603–1763* (2nd edn, London, 1984) Part 1; David Ormrod, *The Rise of Commercial Empires: England and the Netherlands in the Age of Mercantilism 1650–1770* (Cambridge, 2003).

[12] Scott, *England's Troubles*. See also John Brewer, *Sinews of Power: War, Money and the English State 1688–1783* (London, 1989); Linda Colley, *Britons: Forging the Nation 1707–1837* (New Haven, 1992); Michael Braddick, *State Formation in Early Modern England c.1550–1700* (Cambridge, 2000).

[13] Daniel Defoe, *A Tour Thro' the Whole Island of Great Britain*, (ed.) G.D.H. Cole (2 vols., New York, 1968) vol. II p. 424.

in relation to the prevailing westerly winds, greatly superior to those on the other side of the channel. As one Elizabethan commentator complained:

Whereby it plainly appeareth, That as the Excessive Expence of the Low Countryes bestow'd on *Havens*, hath not Impoverish'd, but the clean contrary, greatly Enrich'd them by Incomparable Wealth and Treasure, with number of Rich, Fair and Populous Towns; So our Sparing Mind, or rather greedy Getting, Gaining and Enriching Land from your Majesty's *Havens* and Navigable Channels, hath utterly Destroy'd and Spoiled many good *Havens* by nature left us, and thereby wrought very Beggary, Misery and Desolation on these your Frontier Towns.[14]

In the United Provinces a maritime economy (including political economy) had improved harbours and coastal towns, while English agricultural activity degraded them. For England, embracing the ocean would require mastery of a new element. It was not until 1675 that John Seller, Royal Hydrographer, produced the first English maritime atlas. ''Till Seller fell into it', commented Samuel Pepys, 'we had very few draughts, even of our own coasts, printed in England.'[15] Meanwhile, English mariners used Dutch maps, printed books and loan words, and studied Dutch shipbuilding and trade.[16] Dutch engineers, investors and immigrants transformed the internal landscape, draining the Fens, introducing Dutch methods of animal husbandry and crop rotation, and establishing market gardening so that in 1699 John Evelyn could report that there were now enough English-grown ingredients to make a salad.[17]

Other important cultural resources included reverence for antiquity (humanism) and Protestantism. This helps to explain why, despite the importance of Portuguese and Spanish technology, knowledge and example the most important maritime models for England were ancient Athens during the Elizabethan period, the United Provinces during the seventeenth century, and Phoenicia/Carthage during the eighteenth. This was so despite the fact that Athens had been a democracy, and Carthage and the United Provinces were republics. From Homer, Plato, Herodotus, Thucydides, Xenophon and Polybius English writers learned

---

[14] 'A Memorial of Sir *Walter Raleigh* to Q. *Elizabeth* Touching the Port of *Dover*' in Sir Walter Raleigh, *A Discourse of Seaports; Principally of the Port and Haven of Dover* (London, 1700) p. 2.

[15] John Seller, *Atlas Maritimus* (1675) discussed, with quotation from Pepys, in Martin Thompson, 'Images of an Expanding World', *Cam: Cambridge Alumni Magazine* 50 (Lent Term 2007) p. 31.

[16] John J. Murray, 'The Cultural Impact of the Flemish Low Countries on Sixteenth- and Seventeenth-Century England', *The American Historical Review* 62, 4 (July 1957).

[17] John Evelyn, *Acetaria: A Discourse of Sallets* quoted in ibid. p. 852; Keith Wrightson, *Earthly Necessities: Economic Lives in Early Modern Britain* (New Haven, 2000) p. 161.

to re-imagine the North Sea as the eastern Mediterranean, and Catholic Spain (and then France) as Persia. From contemporary Dutch practice, English politicians, administrators and merchants learned an array of secrets of economic, fiscal and military modernity.

Within the historiography of the nineteenth and twentieth centuries it is increasingly appreciated that nations and states wrote themselves not only in speeches and on paper, but upon landscapes and waterways.[18] This is no less true of the early modern period. In England as in Ireland, much of the 'ideology and, indeed, central values of the culture were wrapped up in the landscape – its occupation, its use, its names, stories and legends'.[19] When the United Kingdom of Great Britain was eventually created, a long fought for and complex cultural achievement (economic, social, political and military) was explained as a natural fact. The general claim was of a special relationship to the ocean. As an Erskine Childers character put it in 1903: 'we're a maritime nation – we've grown by the sea and live by it ... We're unique in that way, just as our huge empire, only linked by the sea, is unique.'[20] The specific claim was that Britain was an island nation.

To use the terminology of Daniel Defoe in the Appendix to this volume, this was an aspect of the duck language by which residents of Britain persuaded foreigners, or themselves, that their country was elementally unique. For humans, though not for ducks (according to humans), this informed a moral argument, since the languages of politics remained moral and indeed primarily confessional. To the extent that this argument was nationalist these writers were also quacking through their tailfeathers. The purpose of duck language, Defoe dramatically observed, was to '*kidnap*' and betray foreign ducks. This is not to say that Britain developed a sense of self which was exceptionally exclusive, xenophobic, or anything other than a recognizably local version of European nationalism. It is to say that, within this historical formation, the tropes of island, island nation, oceanic destiny and empire were central.[21]

[18] Thomas M. Lekan, *Imagining the Nation in Nature: Landscape Preservation and German Identity, 1885–1945* (Cambridge, Mass., 2004) p. 5; David Blackbourn, *The Conquest of Nature: Water, Landscape and the Making of Modern Germany* (New York, 2006); Stephen Daniels, *Fields of Vision: Landscape Imagery and National Identity in England and the United States* (Princeton, 1993).
[19] William J. Smyth, *Map-making, Landscapes and Memory: a Geography of Colonial and Early Modern Ireland c.1530–1750* (Notre Dame, Ind., 2006) p. 3.
[20] Childers, *The Riddle of the Sands* quoted in O'Hara, '"The Sea is Swinging into View"' p. 1132.
[21] Brendan Simms, *Three Victories and a Defeat: the Rise and Fall of the First British Empire, 1714–1783* (London, 2007), Introduction.

This built upon a series of developments.[22] These included the Anglo-Scottish dynastic union achieved in 1603, the brief political and military unification of Albion by Oliver Cromwell, and the creation of the United Kingdom of Great Britain in 1707. These events underwrote the creation of a modern English, and then British, military-fiscal state. Crucial to the process was development of an empire, European, Atlantic and global. The relationship between English and then British state and empire formation, in particular militarily, has been a powerful theme of the historiography of both the seventeenth and the eighteenth century.[23] 'The motif of the island' has been asserted to be '*the* theme of British colonialism'.[24]

Britain's island idea came to encapsulate all of these claims: internal unity; military security; global mobility and reach. Above all it implied separation. To this day the United Kingdom stands upon the threshold of its future, distracted by an idea about its past. That idea is Britain's separateness from the rest of Europe. In the 1930s, the origins of this believed fact were traced by G. M. Trevelyan to the Elizabethan emancipation of the 'national and patriotic genius' from 'that obedience to cosmopolitan orders and corporations which had been inculcated by the Catholic church and the feudal obligation ... In the heat of that struggle, English civilization was fused into its modern form, at once insular and oceanic, distinct from the continental civilization of which the Norman Conquest had once made it part.'[25]

By the mid-eighteenth century this insular 'Britannia' claimed to rule the waves. This claim signified independence not only from external power, but within historical time. In relation to a series of features of modernity the suggestion became, not only that Britain was free, but that it had been first.[26] In 1940 Winston Churchill spoke of 'our long island

---

[22] Brian P. Levack, *The Formation of the British State: England, Scotland and the Union 1603–1707* (Oxford, 1987); Colley, *Britons*.

[23] For the seventeenth see Armitage, *Ideological Origins*; Braddick, *State Formation*; Brewer, *Sinews of Power*; Nicholas Canny, *Making Ireland British 1580–1650* (Oxford, 2001); Games, *Web of Empire*; Scott, *England's Troubles*. For the eighteenth century Colley, *Britons*; C. A. Bayly, *Imperial Meridian: the British Empire and the World 1780–1830* (London, 1989) pp. 81–6; P. J. Marshall, '*A Free though Conquering People*': *Eighteenth-Century Britain and its Empire* (Aldershot, 2003); Kathleen Wilson (ed.), 'Introduction: Histories, Empires, Modernities', in Wilson (ed.), *A New Imperial History: Culture, Identity and Modernity in Britain and the Empire 1660–1840* (Cambridge, 2004); Simms, *Three Victories*.

[24] Diana Loxley, *Problematic Shores: the Literature of Islands* (New York, 1991) p. xi. Empire and islandness is a theme in Kathleen Wilson, *The Island Race: Englishness, Empire and Gender in the Eighteenth Century* (London, 2003).

[25] G. M. Trevelyan, *History of England* (2nd edn, London, 1937) p. 323.

[26] For contemporary versions of this story see Roy Porter, *The Creation of the Modern World: the Untold Story of the British Enlightenment* (New York, 2000); Alan Houston and Steven Pincus, *A Nation Transformed?* (Cambridge, 2001).

history ... and the long continuity of our institutions and our empire ... we shall prove ourselves once again able to defend our island home, to ride out the storm of war, and to outlive the menace of tyranny ... we shall fight on the beaches, we shall fight on the landing grounds'.[27] This claim to island identity was defended decisively by 1945, and again in 1982, when the Thatcher government fell back upon images of '*This Sceptered Isle*' and of a globe-spanning 'island race'.[28] Viewed from another part of the world island identity might have a different meaning (for instance small, or universal). Visiting his childhood home of Trinidad (still a British colony) from England in 1956, V. S. Naipaul reported: 'Trinidad is a funny place. It has a population less than Nottingham's yet, while Churchill calls England an island, they call T'dad a country. And really it is hard to feel while you are here that Trinidad really is small. Jamaica is even worse. Jamaica is the world for Jamaicans.'[29]

In his *History of the English-Speaking Peoples* Churchill stated the geographically embodied British claim to separateness moderately. The island was 'not widely sundered from the Continent' and

very accessible to the invader, whether he comes in peace or war, as pirate or merchant, conqueror or missionary. Those who dwell there are not insensitive to any shift of power, any change of faith, or even fashion, on the mainland, but they give to every practice, every doctrine that comes to it from abroad, its peculiar turn and imprint.[30]

It is no longer acceptable to make such claims to distinctness in cultural or racial terms. One interesting consequence is that the dependence of British historians upon geographical language has deepened. Following John Pocock's 'Atlantic Archipelago' and Hugh Kearney's *The British Isles*, a study by Norman Davies is simply called *The Isles*. Linda Colley, despite setting its history in European and imperial contexts, refers to Britain as 'these islands'.[31] In 2005 *The Economist* celebrated republication of H. E. Marshall's *Our Island Story* (1905), arguing that its 'brave mix of truth and myth' once again looks 'cutting edge'.[32]

---

[27] Quoted in Angus Calder, *The Myth of the Blitz* (London, 1991) pp. 28, 38.

[28] Loxley, *Problematic Shores* Appendix p. 170.

[29] Quoted in Patrick French, *The World is What it is: the Authorised Biography of V. S. Naipaul* (New York, 2008) p. 171.

[30] Winston S. Churchill, *The Island Race* (New York, 1964), an abridged version of *A History of the English-Speaking Peoples*, from which these words are taken.

[31] Linda Colley, *Captives: Britain, Empire and the World 1600–1850* (New York, 2002) pp. 4–5, 17, 46.

[32] 'Notes on a Small Island: an Old Approach to History is New Again', *The Economist*, 20 August 2005. See also Stefan Collini's review of the *Oxford Dictionary of National Biography* under the title 'Our Island Story', *London Review of Books*, 20 January 2005.

In fact it was a conspicuous English failure to fight on the beaches, or anywhere else, which helps to account for the fact that the process which created the modern British state was not English, but Anglo-Dutch. The extent to which a massive foreign invasion of England remains unrecognized by British and other European public conciousness is surely remarkable.[33] In November 2009, *The Guardian* newspaper battled an anti-Low Countries backlash in the wake of the appointment of Herman Van Rompuy as the first president of the European Union. 'Before deriding the statelets of north-western Europe', an editorial warned, 'English chauvinists should recall the hand the great British patriot, Lord Palmerston, played in settling the map. These countries have been overrun militarily more than any others, but so many different invaders have now left their mark that the culture is now one of metropolitan tolerance.'[34] The Dutch republic was uniquely tolerant before it overran England militarily in 1688. If tolerance were a by-product of invasion William III would have encountered flower power, Beatles records and gay matrimony in Torbay. Before 'settling the map' of others, early modern Britain had to settle the map of itself. If, thereafter, the United Kingdom became a maritime power, that was not because it was an island. Other such powers (Athens, the United Provinces, the United States) had not been islands, although all contained many;[35] other islands (Crete, Sicily, Ireland) had not been such powers. 'They are an island people, maritime by instinct, proud, valiant, dogged.' It is no accident that these words were penned in England shortly after the Second World War, though in fact by a New Zealander writing about Crete.[36]

By comparison to New Zealanders English people do not evince any remarkable interest in islands as such.[37] Far from poring self-consciously over maps of archipelagos in the Aegean or South Pacific, they are rather simply more or less securely possessed of their sense of otherness in

---

[33] Despite a considerable scholarly literature in the wake of Jonathan Israel's pathbreaking 'The Dutch Role in the Glorious Revolution', in Israel (ed.), *The Anglo-Dutch Moment: Essays on the Glorious Revolution and its World Impact* (Cambridge, 1991) pp. 105–62. For references see Scott, *England's Troubles* chs. 9, 20–1; Lisa Jardine, *Going Dutch: How England Plundered Holland's Glory* (New York, 2008) pp. xi–xiii and ch. 2.

[34] *The Guardian*, Monday, 23 November 2009, p. 22.

[35] Sir William Temple described Holland as 'an Island made by the dividing-branches of the ancient *Rhyne*, and called formerly *Batavia*'. Temple, *Observations Upon the United Provinces of the Netherlands* (London, 1673) p. 6.

[36] Dan Davin quoted by Keith Ovenden, *A Fighting Withdrawal: the Life of Dan Davin* (Oxford, 1996) p. 145.

[37] Allen Curnow, *Early Days Yet: New and Collected Poems 1941–1997* (Manchester, 1997) pp. 86, 191–3, 217–19, 222–4, 226–9, 235–6; J. G. A. Pocock, *The Discovery of Islands: Essays in British History* (Cambridge, 2005). New Zealand has one literary journal called *Islands* and another, *Landfall*, which has just published an 'Islands' special issue.

relation to the rest of Europe. That this has been packaged geographically is secondary, though it is to the history of that packaging that we are about to turn.

Nations are products, not of nature but of culture.[38] As David Armitage has written:

Because Britain's maritime destiny seemed compelled by nature, it was by definition beyond historical analysis; similarly, because Britain's natural situation divided it physically from the rest of Europe, its history could be seen as unavoidably exceptional. A fact so stubborn could hardly be historical; a history so exceptional was inassimilable to other European norms. British naval mastery came to be seen as [as] inevitable as the expansion of the British empire, and each would be subject to the same complacent amnesia. If the myth indeed had a history, it would become more contingent and hence less inspiring.[39]

If this myth had no history, nor was it a statement about geography. It was the deployment of a geographical trope to project a new, and modern, military reality.[40] England was not an island; early modern islands were not divided from the rest of Europe; and British geography was not exceptional in European terms. However, to follow Armitage in replacing politics with history, and inspiration with perspiration, we must begin not with any assertion of empirical reality, but with a reconstruction of the relationship between geographical and political perceptions as they existed and changed over time.

---

[38] Wilson, *Island Race* pp. x, 5; Benedict Anderson, *Imagined Communities: Reflections on the Origin and Spread of Nationalism* (2nd edn, London, 1991). The question of whether 'nature' is itself 'culture' is visited briefly in chapters 1 and 9 below.

[39] Armitage, *Ideological Origins* p. 101.

[40] John Reeve, 'Britain or Europe? The Context of Early Modern English History: Political and Cultural, Economic and Social, Naval and Military', in Glenn Burgess (ed.), *The New British History: Founding a Modern State 1603–1715* (London, 1999) pp. 291–3; Loxley, *Problematic Shores*.

1   Community of water

> The Hyrkanian or Caspian Sea is enclosed on all sides by the land, like an island in reverse.
>
> Ptolemy, *Geography* Book 7[1]

> No man is an *Iland*, intire of it selfe; every man is a peece of the *Continent*, a part of the *maine*; if a *Clod* bee washed away by the *Sea*, *Europe* is the lesse, as well as if a *Promontorie* were ... Any mans *death* diminishes *me*, because I am involved in *Mankinde*; And therefore never send to know for whom the *bell* tolls; It tolls for *thee*.
>
> John Donne, *Devotions Upon Emergent Occasions, Meditation XVII*

John Donne wrote the above famous passage in 1624. This was the year when, at a time of profound danger for European Protestantism, England entered the Thirty Years War. Therefore, as Brendan Simms has argued, Donne's must be understood as not simply a moral but also a geopolitical rumination.[2] Donne's point, however, was not simply that England, one of the clods which could be washed away, was part of Europe, its continent and maine. Europe's geography was continent *and* islands in complex relationship. Donne, while using geographic language, was not talking about geography. The 'maine' of which islands, promontories and continents were all part was 'Mankinde'. At a time of religious crisis 'No man' could escape his fate as a creature of one God, or therefore doubt for whom the bell tolled.

Early modern writers using geographical language frequently turn out to be talking, not about geography, but about politics, history or religion. Nor have modern historians of England subjected to much questioning an idea of an island nation which could be mistaken for a geographical fact. In the *Faerie Queene*, a literary fiction constructed for religious and political purposes, Edmund Spenser's 'first step ... was to articulate the geographic nonsense that England was an island and Queen Elizabeth

---

[1] *Ptolemy's Geography: an Annotated Translation of the Theoretical Chapters*, (eds. and trans.) J. Lennart Berggren and Alexander Jones (Princeton, 2000) p. 109.
[2] Simms, *Three Victories* pp. 9–10.

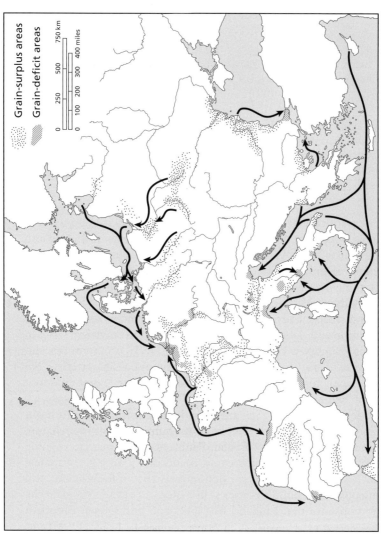

Map 1 England was no more outside a European geography of islands and peninsulas, plains and mountains, rivers, oceans and inland seas than was Scandinavia, Iberia or Sicily. Map based on 'The sixteenth-century grain trade' in N.J.G. Pounds, *An Historical Geography of Europe 1500–1840* (Cambridge, 1979) p. 246.

the "Great lady of the greatest isle"'.[3] In fact the island Ptolemy called
Albion had to be shared with Wales, formally incorporated by the English
crown in 1536, and Scotland, 'a country', opined Marchamont Nedham
in 1650, 'which sticks like a scab upon the fair body of this unfortunate
island'.[4] Not before the eighteenth century was Wales substantially incorporated and the cultural bifurcation of Scotland decisively reduced by
the highland clearances. As late as 1774 a Virginian could denounce the
word 'Britain' as an unfortunate 'Scotticism'. 'What chance can England
or America have for a continuance of their liberty or independence when
not only the principles, but phraseology of that accursed country is
prevalent everywhere?'[5]

Meanwhile, the political geography of England had been various and
complicated. In ancient times those territories had become part of a
Mediterranean empire. In modern times the country governed a global
one. Within the early modern period English writers imagined multi-
farious nations, and empires. Until 1557, from 1657 to 1662, and again
from 1714, England's rulers governed territories on both sides of the
English channel, as well as of the Irish Sea and of the Atlantic Ocean.
Between 1651 and 1653, having conquered Ireland and Scotland, and
sent rabble-rousing envoys to Bordeaux, England attempted to impose a
political union upon the United Provinces.[6] Throughout the seventeenth
century a struggle continued to subjugate Ireland, parts of America and
some outposts in Africa. Simms has described Hanoverian Britain as a
German power at the heart of Europe, with a Baltic as well as Atlantic
coast and strategic interests stretching to the Mediterranean.[7] Thus the
evolution of the early modern English state, to say nothing of the United
Kingdom, was a geographically complicated story involving parts of at
least three continents and many islands.

What its channel lacked in age (6,000 years) and breadth (twenty-one
miles from Dover to Calais), Albion made up in size, being Europe's
largest island. In regional terms Britain was the most recent of Europe's
peninsulas – comparable to Scandinavia, Iberia or Italy – to become
entirely surrounded by sea. A comparable example in another region
is Trinidad, which is seven miles from Venezuela. Whether the channel

---

[3] Canny, *Making Ireland British* p. 24.
[4] Quoted in Colin Burrow, 'New Model Criticism', *London Review of Books*, 19 June
2008.
[5] William Lee quoted by P.J. Marshall, 'A Nation Defined by Empire, 1755–1776',
reprinted in P.J. Marshall, *'A Free though Conquering People'* p. 222.
[6] Scott, *Commonwealth Principles* pp. 102–5, 266–70; Kerrigan, *Archipelagic English*
pp. 200–27.
[7] Simms, *Three Victories* chs. 3–4.

made any difference to the history of human settlement is unclear. In pre- and early modern Europe, when transport was efficient only upon water, seas did not divide; they connected (an opportunity better exploited, however, by Vikings than by Mongols, who twice failed to invade Japan). 'Landmasses contain the most formidable barriers to trade and social intercourse, mountains above all. Water transportation has long been much cheaper ... yet water geography remains an under-appreciated facet of history.'[8]

The precise role played by ocean depended on relative regional military mastery of that medium. From ancient times Britain was no less affected than Italy or Iberia by conquests and migrations. Indeed, without a comparable mountain barrier it was more exposed. However, further from Mediterranean and Near Eastern centres of power, it was also less so. The historical impact of geography, like geographic thought itself, is culturally relative.[9]

One recent history ended by wondering about 'Britain's persistent incapacity to resolve its relationship with Continental Europe'.[10] Another writer has taken 'The English Channel/La Manche to be a frontier, or liminal space, between England/Britain and France (and, more generally, the Continent).'[11] It is not that these suggestions about struggle and indeterminacy are anything other than sound. Yet, as a distinct geographic, cultural or political entity, 'continental Europe' does not exist.

Europe is not a, let alone the, continent.[12] Nor is all of Europe outside Britain continental. Most early modern European states included components of continent and island (in a contemporary Europe of more compact nation-states there are more exceptions to this rule). Under these circumstances all that can be 'resolved', certainly by a historian, is the reason for the (apparently British) invention of this concept. It has now gained wide European currency comparable to the French construction 'Anglo-Saxon', shorthand for an annoying combination of the United Kingdom and the United States. In an article in the *New York*

[8] Dennis O. Flynn and Arturo Giraldez, 'General Editors' Preface', in Tony Ballantyne (ed.), *The Pacific World: Lands, Peoples and History of the Pacific, 1500–1900, volume VI: Science, Empire and the European Exploration of the Pacific* (Aldershot, 2004) p. xiii.

[9] K. R. Howe, *Nature, Culture, and History: the 'Knowing' of Oceania* (Honolulu, 2000). For the cultural construction of geographic terms see Martin W. Lewis and Karen Wigen, *The Myth of Continents: a Critique of Metageography* (Los Angeles, 1997); John R. Gillis, *Islands of the Mind: How the Human Imagination Created the Atlantic World* (Houndmills, 2004).

[10] Peter Clarke, *Hope and Glory: Britain 1900–2000* (London, 2004) p. 443.

[11] Dominic Rainsford, *Literature, Identity and the English Channel: Narrow Seas Expanded* (Houndmills, 2002) p. 8.

[12] Cf. *The Economist*, 10–17 December 2009.

Times of 31 March 2009 Angela Merkel of Germany (including Saxony) and Nicholas Sarkozy of France agreed in rejecting an 'Anglo-Saxon' model of fiscal stimulus promoted by a Kenyan-American (Barack Obama) and a Scot (Gordon Brown).

While oceans are real – which is to say that they are wet – perceptions of oceanic distance are relative. Experiences of travel, and of distance, within Polynesian migrations across the Pacific, and during European circumnavigations, were not the same. Neither were they for European settlers arriving in the southern ocean before and after the advent of steamships. Sighting New Zealand after a three and a half week journey from Tahiti in 1835 Charles Darwin brought to bear a European perspective:

We may now consider that we have nearly crossed the Pacific. It is necessary to sail over this great ocean to comprehend its immensity. Moving quickly onwards for weeks together, we meet with nothing but the same blue, profoundly deep, ocean. Even within the archipelagoes, the islands are mere specks, and far distant one from the other. Accustomed to look at maps drawn on a small scale, where dots, shading, and names are crowded together, we do not rightly judge how infinitely small the proportion of dry land is to water of this vast expanse.[13]

Some scholars have claimed that in perceiving oceans as distances (or even wastelands) to be traversed, early modern Europeans displayed a 'continental' mentality. Francis Bacon commented: 'It is a strange thing that, in sea-voyages, where there is nothing to be seen but sky and sea, men should make diaries; but in land-travel, wherein so much is to be observed, for the most part they omit it.'[14] This last suggestion was not entirely correct. The compilations of both Hakluyt and Purchas included perilous and action-packed land journeys, as well as sea voyages and amphibious operations like the trek of Anthony Jenkinson via Moscow to 'Boghar in Bactria' on the Silk Road between 1557 and 1558.[15] A notable travel journal of 1580–1, that of Michel de Montaigne, traced the author's journey between Bordeaux and Rome, 'overland' though almost entirely along river valleys.[16] Purchas' work contained '*a History of the World in Sea Voyages and Lande Travells*'.

[13] Charles Darwin, *The Voyage of the Beagle*, (ed.) James H. Brix (New York, 2000) p. 440.
[14] Francis Bacon, 'Of Travel', in *Bacon's Essays*, (ed.) Edwin Abbot (2 vols., London, 1889) vol. I, p. 61.
[15] Richard Hakluyt, *The Principall Navigations, Voiages and Discoveries of the English Nation* (2 vols., London, 1589; facsimile edition, Cambridge, 1965) vol. I, pp. 333–74.
[16] Jonathan Sawday, *Engines of the Imagination: Renaissance Culture and the Rise of the Machine* (New York, 2007) p. 40.

As we will see, Bacon was not a conspicuously 'continental' thinker. There were many reasons other than available time for highly developed empirical maritime record-keeping.[17] It was precisely because it could be flat and featureless (or agitated and furious) that ocean had to be mapped. A more dessicated position on the wet/dry spectrum was taken up by the Chinese emperor Quianlong when he told a British emissary in Beijing in 1793 that China had no interest in a small country 'cut off from the world by intervening wastes of seas'.[18] Philip Steinberg has found a comparable mentality among medieval Arab voyagers across the Indian Ocean, and distinguished it from that of Caroline Islanders, whose conception of territory included sea as well as land.[19] Similar perceptions (of a sea of islands, rather than of islands separated by sea) have been described in Polynesia and the Caribbean.[20] Islands are relational entities and they may be understood, as in Europe, in their relationship to a continent or, as in the Pacific, in relation to oceanic space and to one another.

There is something to be said about European (and therefore English) perceptions of the ocean as wilderness. These changed over time, between the time when the oceans were barely crossable and that when they were regularly crossed (and militarily controlled). For an agricultural society the ocean was a wilderness not only in that it was largely uncultivated. In 1671 John Ogilby exulted that 'This watry part of the World, that almost through all Ages lay Fallow, hath in these later times been Furrow'd by several Expert and Stout Captains, who now by their Art and Industry, have given a good Account of, and made clear Discoveries from East to West, where-ever the Sun rises or sets.'[21] In addition the sea was made wild by weather, and this protean potential for danger remained central to all early modern writing on the subject.

---

[17] E. G. R. Taylor, *The Haven-Finding Art: a History of Navigation from Odysseus to Captain Cook* (New York, 1957). For the difference between marine and land surveying in the nineteenth century see D. Graham Burnett, *Masters of All They Surveyed: Exploration, Geography, and a British El Dorado* (Chicago, 2000) pp. 99–117.

[18] Quoted by McNeill and McNeill, *Human Web* p. 167.

[19] Philip Steinberg, *The Social Construction of the Ocean* (Cambridge, 2001) pp. 49–60.

[20] Rod Edmond and Vanessa Smith (eds.), *Islands in History and Representation* (London, 2003) pp. 1–3; Greg Dening, 'Deep Times, Deep Spaces: Civilizing the Sea', in Bernhard Klein and Geesa Mackentun (eds.), *Sea Changes: Historicising the Ocean* (New York, 2004). Compare the views of Samoans and Tongans in Donald Denoon with Stewart Firth, Jocelyn Linnekin, Malama Meleisa and Karen Neno (eds.), *The Cambridge History of the Pacific Islanders* (Cambridge, 1997) p. 119 with that of an Easter Islander in 'An Artist Sets Sail, but South Pacific Pulls Him Home', *New York Times*, 22 April 2006 p. A4.

[21] John Ogilby, *America: Being the Latest, and Most Accurate Description of the New World* (London, 1671) p. 1.

One source for this, as for other wilderness images, was the Bible. Daniel Defoe juxtaposed wilderness to Paradise (saying Scotland was neither).[22] The Bible described wilderness on sea and land, in the context of the smallness of man's efforts overwhelmed by a power beyond his control and understanding. Dedicating his *Navigations, Voiages and Discoveries* (1589) to Sir Francis Walsingham, Richard Hakluyt recalled how he had been inspired by 'the 107 Psalme … where I read, that they which go downe to the sea in ships, and occupy by the great waters, they see the works of the Lord, and his wonders in the deepe, &c'.[23] This passage is sometimes cited as a patriotic celebration of English maritime life. Yet what the Psalm described were not natural wonders, but the divine mercy of fearful prayers answered.

For he commandeth, and raiseth the stormy winde: which lifteth up the waves thereof. They mount up to the heaven: they goe downe againe to the depthes: their soul is melted because of trouble. They reele to and fro, and stagger like a drunken man; and are at their wits end. Then they cry unto the Lord in their trouble: and hee bringeth them out of their distresses. He maketh the storme a calme: so that the waves thereof are still. Then they are glad, because they be quiet: so he bringeth them unto their desired haven.[24]

In general, 'the view of the sea in the Bible is overwhelmingly negative'.[25] On land, wilderness existed in biblical Egypt: 'For the LORD shall comfort Zion: he wil comfort all her waste places, and he wil make her wilderness like Eden, and her desert like the garden of the LORD' (Isaiah 51.3). As Eden had been a garden, so early modern English devotional literature of many doctrinal hues spoke of the moral wilderness of man's unregenerate condition, and of the cultivation of faith.[26] More specifically, wilderness was what, in Ireland and America, lay outside the pale enclosing civility, and Protestantism. This included uncultivated landscape: bog, mountains and forests; and the wild Irish and Americans those places contained.[27] Uncultivated territory in England could also be wilderness as terrifying as the desert. Wrote Spenser (a resident of Ireland) of Britain's past:

> The Land which warlike Britains now possesse,
> And therein have their mightie Empire raised,

[22] Defoe, *A Tour* vol. II p. 691.
[23] Hakluyt, *The Principall Navigations* vol. I, Epistle Dedicatorie p. 1.
[24] *The Holy Bible, King James Version: a reprint of the edition of 1611* (Peabody, Mass., 2003) Psalm 107. 25–30.
[25] Sebastian I. Sobecki, *The Sea and Medieval English Literature* (Cambridge, 2008) p. 35.
[26] Christopher Hill, *The English Bible and the Seventeenth-Century Revolution* (London, 1993) ch. 5.
[27] Smyth, *Map-making* p. 45.

> In ancient times were salvage Wilderness,
> Unpeopled, unmanur'd, unprov'd, unpraisde.[28]

In 1725 Defoe wrote of Exmoor in Devon: 'Cambden calls it a filthy, barren Ground, and, indeed, so it is.'[29] Concerning the setting of Chatsworth in the Derbyshire Peak District, he exclaimed:

Upon the top of that Mountain begins a vast extended Moor or Waste ... and houling Wilderness, over which when Strangers travel, they are obliged to take Guides ... [thus] if there is any Wonder in *Chatsworth*, it is, that any Man who had a genius suitable to so magnificent a Design, who could lay out the Plan for such a House, and had a Fund to support the Charge, would build it in such a Place where the Mountains insult the Clouds, intercept the Sun, and would threaten, *were Earthquakes frequent here*, to bury the very Towns, much more the House, in their Ruins.[30]

As in descriptions of storms at sea (for not a few of which Defoe was also responsible), forbidding space invited devastating interaction with earth, clouds and sky. Later he described Drumlanrig as the Chatsworth of Scotland: 'the finest Palace in all that Part of *Britain* ... environ'd with Mountains, and that of the wildest and most hideous Aspect ... where nothing, but what was desolate and dismal, could be expected'.[31] In early eighteenth-century Germany, similarly, on water or land wilderness was what was not being used and had not been brought under control.[32] By contrast to the subsequent romantic celebration of just such spaces, for most early modern Europeans wild was dangerous and unknown. When technology permitted, the imperative was to master and domesticate.

A 'continental' ideology has also been discerned in the absence from European culture of 'the constraints [Pacific] island societies had devised against resource depletion ... Christianity lacks taboos on resource use, though it has strong taboos on abortion and infanticide.'[33] We will see extreme examples of European resource use in the Pacific from the penguin-bashing of Narborough (1669) to the sea-lion abuse of Shelvocke and his crew (1724). Certainly, although both Europe and Oceania contained many islands, the fact that the former were not separated by comparable oceanic distances had cultural consequences drawn

[28] *Faerie Queene* Book 2 Canto 10 stanza 5, quoted by John Speed, *The Theatre of the Empire of Great Britaine* (London, 1650), 'The British Ilands Proposed In One View' p. 1.
[29] Defoe, *Tour Thro' the Whole Island of Great Britain* vol. I pp. 263–4.
[30] Defoe, *A Tour* vol. II p. 583.
[31] Ibid. p. 727. For Defoe's non-romanticism see Esther Moir, *The Discovery of Britain: the English Tourists 1540–1840* (London, n.d.) p. 37.
[32] Blackbourn, *The Conquest of Nature* Introduction and ch. 1.
[33] J.R. McNeill, 'Of Rats and Men: the Environmental History of the Island Pacific', in J. R. McNeill (ed.), *Environmental History in the Pacific World* (Aldershot, 2001) p. 94.

out by William Camden among others.[34] Although within this context it may make sense to call Judeo-Christian belief a 'continental' system, European geography itself transcended such categories.

Europe incorporated parts of a continent, both inland and surrounding seas, peninsulas and many islands. In his first work (*Microcosmus*), Peter Heylyn explained: 'Europe is divided into Continent and Islands; the Continent is subdivided into *1. Spaine, 2. France, 3. Italie, 4. Belgia, 5. Germanie, 6. Denmarke, 7. Norway, 8. Sweden, 9. Muscovia, 10. Poland, 11. Hungarie, 12. Dacia, 13. Sclavonia, and 14. Greece.* The Islands are ... dispersed in the *1. Aegean Sea, 2.* the *Ionian Sea, 3.* the *Adriatique, 4.* the *Mediterranean, 5.* the *Brittish, 6.* the *Northerne* Seas.' In *Cosmography* this basic subdivision persisted, but the *'Continent'* lay 'all together' and the *'Islands'* were still 'dispersed' into their various seas.[35] This terminology, though not this division, had been conveyed to early modern discourse by Ptolemy, writing in first-century AD Alexandria, himself recording the analyses of 'earlier [writers]'.

According to Ptolemy there were three known continents, in order of size: Asia, Libye (Africa) and Europe. He was not concerned that they were all connected. The three most important seas were the Mediterranean and connected waterways (including the Black Sea), the Caspian Sea and the Indian Ocean. Ptolemy also knew of the unexplored Western Ocean (Atlantic) and Duecalidonian and Sarmatian Ocean (North Sea). Thereafter he listed 'islands and peninsulas' together in order of their noteworthiness: Taprobane (Sri Lanka), 'Albion, one of the islands of Britain', the Golden Peninsula (peninsular Malaysia), 'Hibernia, one of the islands of Britain', the Peloponnese, Sicily, Sardinia, Corsica, Crete, Cyprus.[36]

Later Bacon also classed isthmuses, islands and promontories together as sharing a relationship of land to sea. He projected a 'History of Land and Sea; of their Shape and Extent and their Structure in relation to each other, and of their Extent in breadth or narrowness; of Land Islands in the Sea, of Gulfs of the Sea, and of salt Lakes on Land, of Isthmuses, Promontories'.[37] Throughout the early modern period

---

[34] See below. An evocation of those consequences in the Pacific is Greg Dening, *Islands and Beaches. Discourse on a Silent Land: Marquesas, 1774–1880* (Honolulu, 1980).

[35] Peter Heylyn, *Microcosmus, Or, A Little Description of the Great World* (Oxford, 1621) p. 22, reproduced in Robert Mayhew, 'Geography, Print Culture and the Renaissance: "The Road Less Travelled By"', *History of European Ideas* 27 (2001) p. 360; Heylyn, *Cosmography In Four Books* p. 28.

[36] *Ptolemy's Geography* text pp. 109–10; plates 1–7; maps 1–8b. John Speed (*The Theatre of the Empire of Great Britaine* p. 1) took Taprobane to be Sumatra.

[37] Francis Bacon, *The New Organon*, (eds.) Lisa Jardine and Michael Silverthorne (Cambridge, 2000) p. 233.

Ptolemy's categories remained relevant, as did his geographical knowledge until well into the sixteenth century, and his cartography until the work of Mercator (1538) and Ortelius (1570).[38] This was true despite Europe's increasing conciousness of its modern navigational achievements. By 1671 Ogilby could write, 'The antient *Greeks, Phenicians*, and *Romans*, or whosoever that were Renown'd by Antiquity, and Listed in the number of their famous Navigators, were no less Timerous than Ignorant concerning Maritim Affairs, and are not fit to stand in the least degree of competition with our later Voyagers.'[39] Not everybody agreed.[40] But twenty years before Ogilby Heylyn had written: 'So that we of these Ages have very good cause (to use the words of the late L. Verulam [Bacon]) to congratulate the present times, in that the World in these our days, have *through-lights* made in it, after a wonderful manner; whereby we clearly see those things, which either were unknown, or blindly guessed at by the Ancients.' This was true of discoveries, and so new, or newly accurate, geographical knowledge. However, for his geographical categories and terminology Heylyn continued to rely upon Ptolemy.[41]

Comprising the north-western edge of Eurasia and its surrounding islands, Europe is bounded by oceans, ice, mountains and desert. Directionally the northern islands of Albion and Hibernia are like a continuation, or mirror image, of the southern peninsula and island of Italy and Sicily. Heylyn observed: 'They which have entertained a fancy of resembling every Country to things more obvious to the sight and understanding, have likened *Europe* to a *Dragon*; the head of which they make to be *Spain*; the two wings *Italy* and *Denmark*.'[42] Within their region, far from being exceptions to it, the British isles exemplified European geography more broadly.

In the analysis of Robert Thorne, the position of England and Ireland 'over against Flaunders' was one of several such European relationships of 'mayne land' to 'Iland[s]', such as 'Turcia [to] ... the Ila[n]des of Rhodes, Candie [Crete], and Cyprus; And over against Italie are the Ilandes of Sicilia + Sardinia. And over against Spaine is Majorca and minorca.' Thorne went on to explain that Europe was one of several world regions sharing such geography, as also in south Asia, south-east

---

[38] Anthony Grafton, *New Worlds, Ancient Texts: the Power of Tradition and the Shock of Discovery* (Cambridge, Mass., 1992) pp. 103–16 (Sebastian Munster's edition of Ptolemy's *Geography* was published in 1542), pp. 124–7.

[39] Ogilby, *America* p. 1.

[40] [Daniel Defoe], *A General History of Discoveries and Improvements* (London, 1725–6).

[41] Heylyn, *Cosmography* p. 20 and 'General Praecognitia of Geography'.

[42] Heylyn, *Cosmography* p. 28.

Asia and the Caribbean.[43] In all of these places components of continents and islands composed a system – an archipelago. In the early modern period, when these regions themselves became linked by shipping, they have been described as a meta-archipelago or even global 'machine'.[44] For Bacon, this made Europe privileged, 'both because most of the kingdoms of Europe are girt with the sea ... and because the wealth of both Indies seems ... but an accessary to the command of the seas'.[45]

In pursuit of the universal ambitions appropriate to a clergyman, Heylyn applied Ptolemy's categories not only to Europe, but to the world. In this he was following in the footsteps, vocational, political and intellectual, of Samuel Purchas.[46] The '*Terrestrial Globe*' was divided into '*Earth*' and '*Water*'. 'The ... Earth ... [is] divided commonly into *Continents, Islands*.'[47] The fact that Europe, Africa and Asia were not separated by water made it possible to consider them a single continent (an idea later revived by Howard Mackinder to speak of a 'World-Island').[48] 'A *Continent* is a great quantity of Land, not separated by any Sea from the rest of the World, as the whole Continent of *Europe, Asia, Africk*.' Alternatively the world's continents could be arranged not by space but by epistemological time: '*Known*, either Anciently, as *Europe. Asia. Africa.* [or] Lately, as *America*.'[49] In his 'On the Ebb and Flow of the Sea', Bacon divided the world into 'the two great islands of the Old and New World', both broad in the north and narrower in the south, and surrounded by the Indian and Atlantic oceans respectively.[50]

'An *Island* is a part of Earth invironed round about with some Sea or other; as the Isle of *Britain*, with the Ocean, the Isle of *Sicily*, with the Mediterranean.' In Heylyn's opinion islands had four types of origin. The first was '*Earthquake*', either breaking them from an adjacent continent ('and so *Euboea* was divided from the rest of *Attica*') or raising

[43] *The booke made by the right worshipfull Master Robert Thorne in the yeere 1527*, in R[ichard] H[akluyt] the Younger, *Divers Voyages Touching the Discoverie of America, and the Ilands adjacent unto the same* (London, 1582; facsimile, Ann Arbor, 1966) pp. C2–C3.

[44] Antonio Benitez-Rojo, 'The Repeating Island', in Julie Rivkin and Michael Ryan (eds.), *Literary Theory: an Anthology* (Oxford, 1998).

[45] Francis Bacon, 'Of the True Greatness of Kingdoms and Estates', in *Bacon's Essays*, (ed.) Abbott vol. I pp. 110–11.

[46] On this transition of scope between Hakluyt and Purchas see Andrew Hadfield, *Literature, Travel, and Colonial Writing in the English Renaissance 1545–1625* (Oxford, 1998) pp. 131–3.

[47] Heylyn, *Cosmography* pp. 18, 20.

[48] Peter Coclanis, '*Drang Nach Osten*: Bernard Bailyn, the World-Island, and the Idea of Atlantic History', *Journal of World History* 13, 1 (2002) pp. 169–82.

[49] Heylyn, *Cosmography* pp. 18, 28.

[50] Francis Bacon, 'On the Ebb and Flow of the Sea', in James Spedding, Robert Leslie Ellis and Douglas Denon Heath (eds.), *The Works of Francis Bacon, volume V. Translations of the Philosophical Works, Vol. II* (London, 1877) pp. 453, 456.

them from the deep ocean. Secondly they were created by silt carried by 'Great Rivers at their entry into the Sea'. A third origin was 'The Sea violently beating on some small Isthmus, wearing it through, and turneth the *Peninsula* into a compleat *Isle*. Thus was *Scicily* [*sic*] divided from *Italy*, *Cyprus* from *Syria*, *England* from *France*, and *Wight* from the rest of *England*.'[51] The final mode of island creation was retreat of the ocean, or reclamation of land ('So it is thought the Isles of Zealand have been once part of the main Sea'). Heylyn went on to delineate bodies of water – Ocean, Sea, Strait, Bay, Lake and River – discussing their properties of size, shape, relationship, direction and navigability. Of the global ocean he observed that it was 'higher' than the earth, known both because 'it is a body not so heavy; Secondly, it is observed by Saylors that their Ships move faster to the shore than from it; whereof no reason can be given than the height of the water above the land'. Despite giving a detailed account of the relationship between phases of the moon and tides, Heylyn left the 'other affections and properties of the Sea, as motion, saltness, and the like … to Philosophers'.[52]

The discipline pertaining to subsections of continents or islands, whether regional, national or provincial, was chorography.[53] By far the most influential such early modern English analysis was by William Camden. Camden is sometimes understood as having, in pursuit of a 'patriotic' project, presented Britain as cut off from the rest of the world ('this Isle … Nature … seemeth to have made it as a second world, sequestered from the other, to delight mankinde withal'). However, as Robert Mayhew notes, in this part of his text Camden is quoting Virgil.[54] The purpose of his own work was to 'restore Britain to her [European] antiquity, and her antiquity to Britain'. Published in Latin, in response to

---

[51] Heylyn, *Cosmography* p. 18.
[52] Ibid. pp. 20, 23. This motion, especially tides, was the subject of Bacon's 'On the Ebb and Flow'. For the separation of descriptive geography from theoretical sciences, including natural philosophy, in early modern France see Anne Marie Claire Godlewska, *Geography Unbound: French Geographic Science from Cassini to Humboldt* (Chicago, 1999) ch. 1.
[53] On the relationship between cosmography, geography and chorography see Mayhew, *Enlightenment Geography* pp. 25–32. Richard Helgerson distinguishes between the genres of chorography and voyage, the subject of one being internal to the nation, the other external (Helgerson, *Forms of Nationhood* chs. 3–4). The present analysis stresses the overlap between such writings (chorography, geography, cosmography, voyage) in terms of objectives and content. Later Defoe's *Tour* is an internal voyage which looks back repeatedly to Camden.
[54] Mayhew, *Enlightenment Geography* p. 50 (quoting a different translation) and note 3. Lesley Cormack sees this as a period when 'the English were increasingly defining themselves and their country as separate from the Continent … as self-contained and separate'. '"Good Fences Make Good Neighbours": Geography as Self-Definition in Early Modern England', *Isis* 82 (1991) pp. 640, 656.

a request by the Flemish geographer and cartographer Abraham Ortelius
'to display Britain to the scholars of ... Europe', this project (like that
of More, to be discussed) seems more properly described as humanist
and European. Camden's specific ambition, as his title indicated, was
to 'describe Britain as a province of the Roman Empire'.[55] This description had temporal and spatial components. The interdependence of
geography and history was exemplified by the maxim of Ortelius that a
map was 'the eye of history'.[56] For Heylyn, as geography borrowed from
hydrography, topography and chorography, so cosmology was composed
of '*History* and *Geography* ... intermixt'.[57]

For Camden, the history of Britain to which geography furnished
the key was migration. In this context, he boldly refuted myths (shortly
to be revitalized by Spenser) concerning the autochthonous or Brutan
(Trojan) peopling of the isle.

For the world was not all together and at once inhabited; but ... the countries
nearer adjoining unto the mountains of Armenia, (where the Arke rested after
the flood ...) were peopled before others; and namely Asia the lesse, and Greece
before Italy, Italy before Gaule, and Gaule before Britaine. The consideration
whereof is most delectable, in that the highest Creator, hath joined regions, and
withal dispersed the Ilands so, as there is no such great distance betweene any
of them, but that even those which lie farthest off, may from some one neere
adjoining, be seene & plainly as it were discerned by the eie.[58]

Europe's islands were divinely wrought stepping stones. Thus 'Gaule
lying so neere, and by a verie small streit of sea severed from it', Britons
ought

to be perswaded, that the ancient Gomerians of Gaule (now France) ... crossed
the sea and came over first into this Ile, which from the continent they were able

---

[55] Graham Parry, *The Trophies of Time: English Antiquarians of the Seventeenth Century* (Oxford, 2007) p. 22.
[56] Quoted in Smyth, *Map-making* pp. 24–5.
[57] Heylyn, *Cosmography* p. 24. For Heylyn geography required time in more ways than one. 'It is a great complaint with many, That they want time, either to undertake great matters, or to accomplish those they have undertaken: Wheras it is more truly affirmed by *Seneca*, that we do not so much want, as waste it ... We trifle out too much of our pre-cious time ... either in doing ill, or nothing, or else things impertinent' ('To the Reader' pp. 1–2). The background to this work was its author's involuntary retirement.
[58] William Camden, *Britain, Or A Chorographicall Description of the Most flourishing Kingdomes, England, Scotland, and Ireland, and the Ilands adjoining, out of the depth of Antiquitie ...* Written first in Latine by *William Camden ...* Translated newly into English by *Philemon Holland* (London, 1610) p. 11. Compare Robert Hughes on the migration of Australian aborigines: 'By trial and error ... it would then have been possible to get from Southeast Asia into Australia (via the Celebes and Borneo) across islands sprinkled in the sea like stepping-stones. Much of this voyage would have been done by eyeball navigation to coasts that the immigrants could have seen from their starting point.' *The Fatal Shore: the Epic of Australia's Founding* (New York, 1986) p. 8.

to kenne. And it stands to verie good reason ... that everie countrie received the first inhabitants from places neere bordering, rather than from such as were most disjoind. For, who would not thinke, that Cyprus had the first inhabitors out of Asia next unto it, Crete and Sicilie out of Greece neereby ... Corsica out of Italy a neighbour countrie: and ... Zeland out of Germanie the nearest unto it, as also Island [Iceland] out of Norway ... In like maner, why should not we thinke that our Britaine was inhabited first by the Gaules their neighbours, rather than either by the Trojans or Italians, the Albans and Brutians, so farre distant and remoove?[59]

This was confirmed by the fact that 'the ancient Gauls and our Britans used ... the self same language'.[60] That the next invaders were the Romans was a logical military outgrowth of their conquest of Gaul.[61] Following the collapse of 'the Romane Empire ... the Saxons, whom Vortigern had called foorth of Germany to aid him, made bloody and deadly war against those friends that invited ... them; insomuch as ... they wholly disseised the poore wretched Britans of the more fruit-ful part of the Iland'.[62] That 'we Englishmen are sprung from the[se] Germanes', who came from the Low Countries, is shown by the fact that 'the later and more moderne names of our townes end in *Burrow*, *Berry*, *Ham*, *Steed*, *Ford*, *Thorp*, and *Wich*, which carry a just and equall correspondence unto the terminations of the Dutch townes; *Burg*, *Berg*, *Heim*, *Stadt*, *Furdt*, *Dorp*, and *Wic*'.[63] Thus in his work of 1622, written to urge imitation of the 'freedome' and industry of the Dutch, Thomas Scott insisted: 'looke in to Master *Camden* in his *Britania* ... and also into Master *Speed*'s Chronicle ... and see what they say, both for the just praise of that people ... [and] for our and their consanguinity'.[64]

This military traffic was not one way: England governed territory in France until 1558 and again between 1658 and 1662. It was also com-mitted to the brutal and never entirely successful subjugation of Ireland. It is quite anachronistic to see this as laying the foundation for a future, and self-contained, archipelagic British state. It is not only that, even after the creation of the United Kingdom of Great Britain and Ireland (1801), the two remained formally distinct.[65] Before the Elizabethan period the only accurate maps of Ireland, and its west coast in particular, were Spanish and Portuguese.[66] Early modern Ireland was a complex

---

[59] Camden, *Britain* pp. 11–12.   [60] Ibid. p. 16.
[61] Ibid. p. 88.   [62] Ibid. p. 107.   [63] Ibid. p. 20.
[64] Thomas Scott, *The Belgicke Pismire* (London, 1622) p. 95.
[65] Jason McElligott, 'Introduction: Stabilizing and Destabilizing Britain in the 1680s', in Jason McElligott (ed.), *Fear, Exclusion and Revolution: Roger Morrice and Britain in the 1680s* (Aldershot, 2006) p. 12; C.A. Bayly, *The Birth of the Modern World 1780–1914* (Oxford, 2004) p. 113.
[66] Smyth, *Map-making* pp. 23, 28.

cultural entity with strong links to Roman Catholic as well as Protestant Europe. Its repeated wars in this period must be seen in three supra-national and supra-insular contexts.

The first was struggle between reformation and counter-reformation, which was not only European but global. Both the Anglo-Norman occupation of the Pale and the formal Henrician assumption of kingship over the whole island preceded this bifurcation, which was energized by the Council of Trent (ended 1558). But it was the Elizabethan generation that lived to see Alva's 'Council of Blood' in the Netherlands (1568) and the Massacre of St Bartholomew's Eve in France (1572) who came to regard the conquest of Ireland as essential to the survival of English and European Protestantism. Some of these individuals (Henry and Philip Sidney, the Earl of Leicester, Francis Walsingham and Edmund Spenser) articulated a 'plat' for this purpose which was applied most powerfully almost a century later.[67] A leading member of the English republic's Committee for Irish Affairs which passed legislation governing the planting of Ireland in 1653 was Sidney's grand-nephew Algernon.

Until his execution for treason in 1683 Algernon Sidney insisted, in the family tradition, upon the necessity of armed force, for the defence of both Protestantism and virtue.[68] Because this struggle knew no geo-political boundaries, it powerfully coloured English writing about the world between 1550 and 1650.[69] As Sir Philip had died fighting Spain in the Netherlands, so in 1638 members of Scotland's covenanting army returned from Swedish service to defend Protestantism at home. As Irish priests and laity relied upon educational and cultural ties with counter-reformation Spain, Austria and Flanders, so again in 1642 Irish troops in Spanish service returned to fight at home.[70]

The second context was an identifiably European process of English (rather than British) state formation.[71] This was driven by religious and humanist ideologies fusing the distinctions between reformation and counter-reformation, civility and barbarism. This too had global parameters. The Elizabethan Nine Years War in Ireland and the Dutch war of independence competed for resources during an epic struggle against

[67] Canny, *Making Ireland British* esp. chs. 1–2, 8–9; Hadfield, *Literature, Travel* p. 100.
[68] Jonathan Scott, *Algernon Sidney and the English Republic 1623–1677* (Cambridge, 1988) pp. 99–102; Scott, *Algernon Sidney and the Restoration Crisis 1677–1683* (Cambridge, 1991) chs. 11–14 and pp. 357–9.
[69] Hadfield, *Literature, Travel* pp. 91–133.
[70] Scott, *England's Troubles* pp. 136–42; Smyth, *Map-making* chs. 1–2; Canny, *Making Ireland* ch. 8.
[71] Braddick, *State Formation*; Brewer, *Sinews of Power*; Scott, *England's Troubles* Pt 3. For the distinction between state-building and state formation see Scott, *Commonwealth Principles* pp. 63–75.

Spain. The later Williamite conquest of Ireland occurred during a no less epic Anglo-Dutch contest against France. Throughout the period English military involvement in Ireland was one aspect of a wider struggle for confessional and military security, decreasingly bound by traditional categories of geography, culture, and indeed humanity. Humphrey Gilbert, the West Country hero who drowned returning from Newfoundland in 1583, was also the Elizabethan conquistador who paved his military progress in Ireland with parallel rows of severed heads.[72] By 1652, after a little more than a decade of conflict which did not spare men, women or children on any side, an Irish population of two million had been reduced by perhaps seven hundred thousand.[73] In addition to the liquidation of entire garrisons and armies, Nicholas Canny concludes,

The number of civilian casualties, according to the calculations of Sir William Petty, may have reached 400,000 deaths from slaughter, starvation, and disease. Here it is also important to recall that the decisive military victories of the entire eleven years of conflict were all commanded by officers who had been born in Ireland and who had been engaged in warfare there from the outset of the conflict.[74]

The third supra-national context was imperial. It has been suggested that Ireland was unusual within Europe in itself becoming a site for imperial expropriation and plantation. This experiment, in which both Scots and English participated without notable harmony, and which was resisted by Gaelic Irish, Gaelic Scots and Anglo-Irish, became a laboratory for the plantation of North America. However, within a comparative imperial context John Elliott has described Ireland as England's Granada. There were important differences. During the *reconquista*, as during the subsequent conquests in Mexico and Peru, the Spanish at least recognized that what they had overthrown were highly sophisticated, if alien, societies.[75]

In *Cosmography* (first published in 1652) Peter Heylyn had fused the categories of migration and plantation, so that there was no formal difference between movements of population within Europe and into the New World. 'It being in Plantations of Men, as in that of Bees, amongst whom one *Swarm* sends out another, that begets a *Castling*, till the whole ground or Garden grow too small to hold them. For thus (to seek no further an instance of it) the *Gauls* first planted *Britain*, the *Britains Ireland*,

[72] Smyth, *Map-making* p. 161. In 1569 – during Alva's crackdown in the Netherlands – Gilbert took twenty-three Irish castles in six weeks 'and slaughtered all occupants, men, women and children'.
[73] Ibid. p. 75.   [74] Canny, *Making Ireland British* p. 571.
[75] Elliott, *Empires of the Atlantic World* pp. 17, 59.

the *Irish Scotland*, and the Isles.'[76] As Camden had emphasized, some internal migrations had also been characterized by exceptional levels of violence and the establishment of empire (the Roman). Writing two years after Heylyn, John Streater also referred to the imperial behaviour of bees:

Many prudent States and Commonwealths have made great account of the solemnizing of Matrimony, accounted it a sacred thing ... thereby to increase their number, and inlarge their Territories; the Romans did often by sending their Colonies abroad, as the Bee doth their young swarms; out of one stock many are raised, so out of one Commonwealth many may be erected.[77]

Thus the fate of Ireland became bound up in a competitive process of confessional state-building intertwined with empire-building. A biographical encapsulation of its early stages was Sir George Downing (1623–81), born in Dublin, educated in Massachusetts, Scoutmaster General of the New Model Army in Scotland, ambassador to the United Provinces, and principal architect of the restoration administrative management of trade and plantations.[78] Whether the English and then British states built the empire, or the empire those states, is a question to which we will return.

Heylyn presented his cosmography in four books: Europe, Africa, Asia and finally America. This was also a historical presentation, beginning with the ancient world and moving to the modern. This helped to determine the order of presentation within Europe, beginning with Italy, 'once the Empress of the greatest part of the (then known) World'. Heylyn then proceeded over the Alps, as the Romans had done, to France, Germany and Britain. Surrounded by the islands of Corsica, Sardinia and Sicily, Italy was itself 'compassed with the *Adriatick*, *Ionian*, and *Tyrrhenian* Seas, [a] *Peninsula* or *Demi-Island*'.[79]

A generation later John Ogilby's title *America* (1671) recalled the multi-volume (and multi-language) work by Hakluyt's friend Theodor De Bry, with important English content, published in Frankfurt in 1594.[80] In his discussion of the origins of native American peoples Ogilby rejected the view that they constituted one of the lost ten tribes of Israel, and the arguments of Grotius that North Americans came by sea from Norway, and Peruvians by the same means from China. Only this, Grotius had contended, could explain the absence of horses from pre-Columbian

---

[76] Heylyn, *Cosmography* p. 7.
[77] John Streater, *Observations Historical, Political and Philosophical, Upon Aristotle's first Book of Political Government* (London, 1654) p. 18.
[78] Jonathan Scott, '"Good Night Amsterdam": Sir George Downing and Anglo-Dutch Statebuilding', *English Historical Review* 118, 176 (April 2003) pp. 334–56.
[79] Heylyn, *Cosmography*, Title Page and p. 30.
[80] Hadfield, *Literature, Travel* pp. 113–23.

America. Refuting these views, Ogilby pronounced himself certain, on grounds of language, customs and physiognomy, that the Americans had come by land from Tartary (central Asia, including Siberia). Across this they had proceeded from Armenia following Noah's Flood. Their horses had not made it because 'there is no Countrey a continu'd Pasture, but luxurious Vales separated with inaccessible Mountains, Lakes, and vast Wildernesses'.[81]

By the eighteenth century cosmography and geography had changed. In his *A New Royal Authentic and Complete System of Universal Geography Antient and Modern* (?1790), Thomas Bankes claimed that geography was now

a Science ... studied by the polite of all Nations ... and is useful, in an eminent Degree, to all Ranks of People. In particular, to Men of Letters, because no History can be properly understood without it, To Politicians, as being necessary to understand the true Interests of states and Kingdomes ... To military and naval Officers ... To naturalists ... To the Antiquarian ... To Merchants and Traders ... And to the curious Enquirer.[82]

Internally, Bankes' text reversed Heylyn's order of time (without rejecting Ptolemy's categorizations of space). Thus the *Universal Geography* began with a Pacific-centred map depicting New Holland (Australia), New Zealand, New Guinea, eastern China, Japan and north-western America. The first of five books looked at the islands of the Pacific, including Australia, New Zealand, New Guinea, Tahiti, the Marquesas, Easter Island and Hawaii. Until James Cook's first expedition in 1770, said Bankes (in fact, 1768–71), it had not been clear whether either New Holland or New Zealand were 'Island or Continent', but this had now been determined. Book 2 of the *Universal Geography* focused upon Asia, 'Continent and Islands'; Book 3 on Africa, 'Continent and Islands'; Book 4 on America; Book 5 on Europe. The treatment of Europe began with Greenland and Scandinavia and ended with Britain (south and north) and Ireland.

Thus the English channel and Irish Sea were parts of a wider maritime system which connected the Baltic, the North Sea and Mediterranean, the Atlantic and then the Pacific. Also informing this system were rivers, and sometimes canals. The first requirement for 'the Magnificence and Splendor of Cities', noted Heylyn, was 'a Navigable River, or some such easie passage by Sea, which will bring thither a continual concourse and

[81] Ogilby, *America* p. 43 (and pp. 27–43). It seems Ogilby was developing the arguments of Acosta, which Grotius had attempted to refute. Kidd, *British Identities* pp. 14–16.
[82] Bankes, *A New Royal Authentic and Complete System of Universal Geography Antient and Modern* (London, ?1790), Preface, p. 1.

trade of Merchants; as at *Venice, London, Amsterdam*'.[83] Rivers were much more than transport. They were 'a source of drinking water, and of water for washing and bathing. They irrigate crops and provide calorific energy directly in the form of fish. They flush away waste ... provide water for cooling ... drive waterwheels and complex turbines.'[84] Moreover,

Water was the single most reliable source of power known to early modern communities, providing the foundations upon which so much social, communal, and urban life depended ... so the sound of running water can be understood as one of the 'keynote sounds' of the early modern world, gushing through the innumerable pipes, conduits, and streams constructed to channel it to where it was needed not only for domestic and animal use, but, more importantly, to meet the community's demand for power.[85]

Supplies of fresh water were equally important to agrarian societies and urban ones. At the well-watered western edge of Europe, English people were conscious of relative agricultural abundance.[86]

Thus, in this part of the world islands and continents related to one another within a system connected by water, salt and fresh. This was the perspective through which early modern Europeans located themselves within their region and in relation to the rest of the world. As in the ancient world maritime access made islands militarily vulnerable, within a regional geography in which only mountains offered some refuge.[87]

As the Athenians found by their Attempts upon sever[a]ll Islands of the Arches, and Scicilia ... and the Carthaginians upon their attempt of the same island[,] Sardinia, Corsica, Majorca, Minorca +c. And the Romans after they were Masters by Sea Conquerd all those places with Candia, Cyprus and Rhodes.[88]

Thus Camden noted, amid invasions by Romans, Germans, Danes and then Normans, the survival in Albion only of that battered remnant of Britons who had made it to Wales. The narrow sea which, for

[83] Heylyn, *Cosmography* p. 4.   [84] Blackbourn, *The Conquest of Nature* p. 7.
[85] Sawday, *Engines of the Imagination* p. 34.
[86] For such 'wet-country people' colonization of Australia would be a challenge. Cathcart, *The Water Dreamers* pp. 8, 32–3.
[87] Fernand Braudel, *The Mediterranean and the Mediterranean World in the Age of Philip II* (Berkeley and Los Angeles, 1995) vol. I.
[88] [Richard Gibson], 'Observations Upon Islands in Generall and England in particular relating to safety and strength at Sea', NMM, REC/6 Item 17, f. 275. Another version, 'Enquirys touching Islands in General + England in perticuler, relating to Safety + Strength at Sea', BL Add MS 11684 ff. 22–9, was published by S.R. Gardiner and C.T. Atkinson (eds.), *Letters and Papers Relating to the First Dutch War, 1652–4* (2 vols., London, 1899) vol. I, pp. 33–47. Cf. Jeremy Black, *The British Seaborne Empire* (New Haven, 2004) pp. 8–9.

Shakespeare's Richard II, served 'in the office of a wall / Or as a moat defensive to a house', was rather for Samuel Purchas a bridge.

> [T]he Sea ... Uniter by Traffique of al Nations ... yields ... the World to the World ... And as he hath written this Equity in man's heart by Nature, so hath he therefore encompassed the Earth with the Sea, adding so many inlets, bayes, havens and other naturall unducements and opportunities to invite men to this mutual commerce. Therefore hath he also diversified the Windes, which in their shifting quarrels conspire to humaine trafficke. Therefore hath hee divided the Earth with so many Rivers, and made the shoares conspicuous by Capes and promontories ... wherein Nature ... by everlasting Canons hath decreed Communitie of Trade the world thorow.[89]

In the later sixteenth century Giovanni Botero had agreed that God created water as 'a most ready means to conduct and bring goods from one country to another ... [that] there might grow a community'.[90] In 1674, John Evelyn mused similarly:

> when we ... behold in what ample Baies, Creeks, trending-Shores, inviting Harbours and Stations ... The Earth ... appears spreading her Arms upon the Bordures of the Ocean; whiles [sic] the Rivers, who re-pay their Tributes to it, glide not in direct, and praecipitate Courses from their Conceil'd, and distant Heads, but in various flextures and Meanders (as well to temper the rapidity of their Streams, as to Water and refresh the fruitful Plains) methinks she seems, from the very Beginning, to have been dispos'd for Trafick and Commerce.[91]

English writers did not distinguish themselves from these perspectives, but contributed to them. We now turn to a sixteenth-century kingdom possessing only one considerable city, with its river passage to the sea. How were these understandings deployed, and in response to what challenges? What came over the sea, or could be seen over it, and how did English writers, politicians and counsellors respond?

[89] Samuel Purchas, *Hakluytus Posthumus or Purchas His Pilgrimes. Contayning a History of the World, in Sea voyages & lande-Travells, by Englishmen & others* (4 vols., London, 1625) vol. I p. 5.
[90] Giovanni Botero, *Greatness of Cities* (1588), quoted by Clarence J. Glacken, *Traces on the Rhodian Shore: Nature and Culture in Western Thought from Ancient Times to the End of the Eighteenth Century* (Berkeley, Calif., 1967) p. 371.
[91] John Evelyn, *Navigation and Commerce, Their Original and Progress* (London, 1674) p. 2.

2   Queen of Sparta

> Ne was it Iland then, ne was it paisde
> Amid the Ocean waves, ne was it sought
> Of Merchants far, for profits therein praised,
> But was all desolate, & of some thought ... brought
> By Sea to have bin from the Celtick Mainland.
>
> Edmund Spenser, *The Faerie Queene*[1]

If nations are culture, then the inhabitants of an island, particularly one with a significant land area within sight of a continent, may still constitute a nation of landlubbers by whom the sea has barely been noticed. This would help to explain the embarrassment recorded by Richard Hakluyt in 1589, reading a French 'commendation of the Rhodians, who being (as we are) Islanders, were excellent in navigation ... woondereth much that the English should not surpasse in that qualitie'.[2]

How maritime was a sixteenth-century England with an agricultural economy, a rural society, a crown which still claimed to be the legitimate governor of France, outnavigated by the Portuguese and Spaniards, outfished and outtraded by the Dutch? In the mid-seventeenth century the last drew the following taunt from Andrew Marvell:

> *Holland*, that scarce deserves the name of Land,
> As but th'off-scowring of the *British* sand;
> And so much Earth as was contributed
> By *English* Pilots; when they heav'd the Lead;
> Or what by th'Oceans slow alluvion fell,
> Of Shipwrackt-Cockle and the Muscle-Shell;
> This indigested Vomit of the Sea,
> Fell to the *Dutch* by just propriety.[3]

---

[1] *The Faerie Queene* Book 2, Canto 10, stanza 5, quoted in Speed, *The Theatre of the Empire of Great Britaine* (1650), 'The British Ilands Proposed In One View' p. 1.

[2] Hakluyt, *The Principall Navigations* Epistle Dedicatorie p. 3. For the little and late character of sixteenth-century English travel and travel writing see William Sherman, 'Stirrings and Searchings (1500–1720)', in Peter Hulme and Tim Youngs (eds.), *The Cambridge Companion to Travel Writing* (Cambridge, 2002) pp. 18–23.

[3] Andrew Marvell, *The Character of Holland* (London, 1672) p. 1.

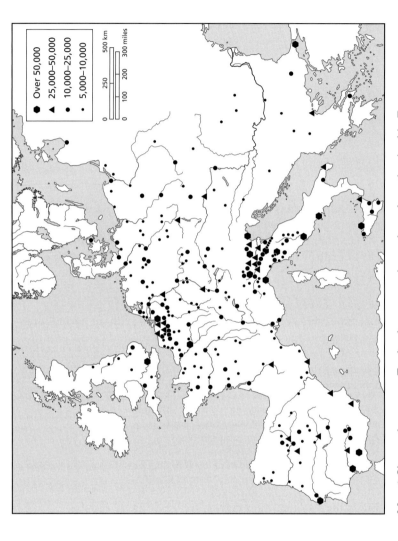

Map 2 Sixteenth-century England was conspicuously under-urbanized in European terms. Map based on the chief cities of Europe in the first half of the sixteenth century, from Pounds, *Historical Geography of Europe* p. 222.

Legend:

● Over 50,000
▲ 25,000–50,000
● 10,000–25,000
· 5,000–10,000

0 250 500 km
0 100 200 300 miles

Scholars of English literature have found in the Norman conquest, and the arrival of the Anglo-Norman system of land-holding, a turn away from the sea. Before then a greater literary and spiritual 'connectivity' had existed around the Irish and North seas.[4] 'Medieval England', Brendan Simms writes, 'was never an island: Normandy and Gascony were far closer to London than Wales or Scotland.'[5] By the sixteenth century English sailors did ply their coasts and, in limited numbers, further afield. The Newcastle colliery was the largest source of English coastal trade, and so of maritime expertise (even in 1772 James Cook's *Resolution* was a converted collier). In the export of woollen textiles to Flanders, the Baltic and elsewhere most ships were operated by foreigners, Hanse, Flemish and Dutch (the later observation by Samuel Pepys that 'The trade of England till Henry 8th was drove by the Easterlings and strangers; consequently our coasts [were] known to them at that time better than by ourselves' in fact applied well into the seventeenth century).[6] By the Elizabethan period fishermen from the West Country worked the Newfoundland Banks alongside French, Spanish and Portuguese, attempting with difficulty to create a settlement on the island during the reign of James VI and I.[7]

There were semi-regular if hazardous expeditions to the Mediterranean, Baltic and Barents seas, the Caribbean, and central and North America. A flurry of privateering operations preceding and accompanying war with Spain (1585–1604) accidentally produced the first English circumnavigation (1577–80). John Evelyn noted that although the first voyage of circumnavigation had been led by Ferdinand Magellan in 1519, 'our Drake' was 'the First of any Mortal, to whom God vouchsafed the stupendous Atchievement of Encompassing, not this *New*-World alone, but *New* and *Old* together', because Magellan had been killed in the Philippines. This was to say that Drake was the first captain to achieve this feat. Later English writers looked back with pride to the 'Names of *Drake, Hawkins, Cavendish, Furbisher* [sic], *Davis, Hudson, Raleigh,* and others of no less merit'.[8]

However, in the words of Kenneth Andrews: 'Behind … Elizabethan legend and nationalist propaganda lay a long and painful series of failures and disasters, only occasionally relieved by some brilliant feat such

[4] Sobecki, *The Sea*, Introduction.   [5] Simms, *Three Victories* p. 10.
[6] Kenneth R. Andrews, *Trade, Plunder and Settlement: Maritime Enterprise and the Genesis of the British Empire, 1480–1630* (Cambridge, 1984) p. 7; Samuel Pepys, *Samuel Pepys' Naval Minutes*, (ed.) J. R. Tanner (London, 1926) p. 343.
[7] [John Oldmixon], *The British Empire in America, Containing the History of the Discovery …* (London, 1741) pp. 1–27; Andrews, *Trade* pp. 49, 334–9.
[8] Evelyn, *Navigation and Commerce* p. 57.

as Drake's voyage.'[9] By European standards the English merchant and
fishing fleets were small and the Royal Navy (founded by Henry VIII)
smaller. Attempts to maintain all three in the first half of the seventeenth century faced extreme difficulties and ferocious competition.
Elizabethan sailors and other voyagers failed to find a north-west passage to Cathay; failed to establish a prosperous Muscovy trade; failed to
prevent Dutch domination of the East Indies, and Spanish of the West;
and failed to establish a large-scale fishery even in Scotland.

Although the foundation of the English East India Company in
1599 preceded that of the Dutch (VOC) by three years, it was by comparison woefully under-capitalized and sent out in its first nine years
twelve ships, compared with fifty-five sent by the Dutch company in
its first seven years.[10] Of the first eighty-one ships sent, only thirty-five
returned.[11] Other trading associations (the Muscovy Company in 1555;
the Levant Company in 1592) were dependent upon royal patents but
private capital. Much the same approach was taken to naval administration. Although the long Elizabethan war with Spain furnished a for-
mative context for the acquisition of maritime military experience, this
was dominated by privateering. Despite its scale, this deployed privately
owned (merchant and gentry) ships and lacked the cumulative impact of
a centralized effort. Even when faced by invasion, English naval power
depended overwhelmingly upon private shipping. Vessels of the Royal
Navy over one hundred tons numbered twenty-eight in 1548, twenty-five
in 1558 and thirty-one in 1603. This was during a period when the scale
of European warfare on land and sea was being transformed. The belated
military actions of the state during the Spanish war were dominated by
land campaigns in the Low Countries and Ireland.[12]

In addition to being royal and aristocratic, sixteenth-century England
was rural and agrarian. It was far less urbanized than the neighbouring Netherlands in particular, but also France, the Holy Roman Empire
and Mediterranean Europe. This was partly a function of relatively low
population density (by comparison with the Netherlands, France and
Italy). However, rurality was not only demographic, but cultural. It is
partly because, for their elites, Spain was a culture of cities (that was

---

[9] Andrews, *Trade* p. 1.
[10] K.H.D. Haley, *The British and the Dutch: Political and Cultural Relations through the Ages* (London, 1988) p. 58.
[11] Andrews, *Trade* p. 23.
[12] John C. Appleby, 'War, Politics and Colonization 1558–1625', in Nicholas Canny (ed.), *The Oxford History of the British Empire, volume I: The Origins of Empire* (Oxford, 1998) pp. 55–6, 65–7; Kenneth Andrews (ed.), *English Privateering Voyages to the West Indies 1588–1595* (Cambridge, 1959); Andrews, *Trade* p. 25.

the meaning of *civitas*) while England was one of rural great houses and villages that these were the patterns of settlement reproduced in their respective American colonies.[13] As Peter Heylyn observed, essential to a city was

continual confluence of Nobles, Gentry, Merchants, and all sorts of Trades: And by this means, *Madrid*, not long since a poor beggarly Village, is grown the most populous City in all *Spain* ... [moreover] the Residence of the Nobility, beautifieth a City with stately and magnificent Buildings; which makes the Cities of *Italy* so much excel ours in *England*; their Nobles dwelling in the Cities, and ours for the most part in their Country houses.[14]

This was true despite a doubling of the English and Welsh population between 1520 and 1640 which also made towns bigger. Between 1500 and 1650 it is estimated that the number of English people living in towns of more than 10,000 inhabitants increased from 80,000 (3.1 per cent) to 495,000 (8.8 per cent).[15] Yet these figures are dominated by the phenomenal growth of one city. London had 50,000 inhabitants in 1550, 120,000 in 1620, 400,000 in 1665, 550,000 in 1700. Before the late eighteenth century, when British urbanization became national, this was the most remarkable product of a European regional development. Rather than being, like Paris, the creation of a court and state, early modern London was the outgrowth of a North Atlantic economy and culture which eventually wrought its own political institutions.[16]

It was, as a result, a regional, and eventually imperial, rather than simply national, city. It was a Protestant metropolis where stranger churches enjoyed freedoms to worship unavailable to locals until they were secured by a Dutch invasion. It became a mercantile as well as aristocratic capital uniquely combining the institutions of court, parliament, national bank and stock exchange. It is because so many of Britain's nineteenth-century cities were new that, as Boyd Hilton has observed, 'unusually in Europe, Britain's major cities contain so little medieval or early modern

---

[13] Elliott, *Empires of the Atlantic World* ch. 2. That 'British America remained in comparison with Spanish America an overwhelmingly rural society' (p. 43) also reflected the differing settlement patterns and population densities of indigenous peoples. In *Map-making* p. 13, by contrast, Smyth notes 'striking similarities between Latin America and Irish colonial societies, particularly in the centrality of the "colonial city and town" and "the great estate" in both cultures'.

[14] Heylyn, *Cosmography* p. 4.

[15] Phil Withington, *The Politics of Commonwealth: Citizens and Freemen in Early Modern England* (Cambridge, 2005) pp. 5–6.

[16] Compare the maps of European urbanization in the sixteenth and nineteenth centuries in N.J.G. Pounds, *An Historical Geography of Europe 1500–1840* (Cambridge, 1979) pp. 222, 325.

architecture, and conversely ... Britain's medieval and early modern towns have remained relatively small'.[17]

What long-distance English maritime activity occurred during the sixteenth century was dominated by the West Country (Plymouth, Falmouth, Bristol). The scale of the country's overall investment in maritime culture was not transformed until that process was led by London. Meanwhile, the dominant themes of English rural life were to be glimpsed in its nucleated villages and woodlands, its vernacular and Latin literature, its most controversial economic issue (enclosure of arable land for pasture) and its most pressing social problem: a growth of population which stimulated the poor laws of 1572 and after, and a widespread perception of growing poverty, crime and vagrancy.

We see many of these themes in Thomas More's *Utopia* (1516) in which, founding a society where agricultural work was equally shared, the lawgiver Utopus also 'changed its geography ... cut[ting] a channel fifteen miles wide where their land joined the continent, and thus caused the sea to flow around the country'.[18] This image of England was a mirror image located in the temperate southern hemisphere. Utopia was discovered by a Portuguese national accompanying a Florentine explorer whose maritime wandering was described as Greek: 'his sailing has ... been like ... that of Ulysses, or ... of Plato'.[19] More's text, published in Latin, was set in Antwerp. The ways of the island's people were 'outlandish' for 'that new world ... [is] distanced from ours not so much by geography as by customs and manners'.[20] *Utopia* was translated into German, Italian and French before the first English edition appeared in 1551, and the first Latin edition in England was not published until 1663.[21]

In another Greek echo, More's island commonwealth was also a ship. It had been Plato's argument in *The Republic* that there could be no safe passage for the ship of state without an adequately trained crew. This entailed many years 'studying the seasons of the year, sky, stars, and winds, and all that belongs to ... the science of navigation'.[22] In *Utopia*,

---

[17] Boyd Hilton, *A Mad, Bad, and Dangerous People? England 1783–1846* (Oxford, 2006) p. 6.

[18] Thomas More, *Utopia*, (eds.) George Logan and Robert Adams (Cambridge, 2000) p. 43.

[19] Ibid. p. 10. This does not support the claim by John Gillis that early modern utopias were 'detached from all historical as well as geographical connections' (Gillis, *Islands* p. 78).

[20] For a broader analysis of *Utopia* as a work of cultural inversion see Carlo Ginzburg, *No Island is an Island: Four Glances at English Literature in World Perspective* (New York, 2000) ch. 1. For More's European geographical circle see E. G. R. Taylor, *Tudor Geography, 1485–1583* (London, 1932) pp. 7–8.

[21] J. C. Davis, '"Concerning the Best State of a Commonwealth": Thomas More's *Utopia*: Sources, Legacy and Interpretation', draft essay pp. 3–4.

[22] Plato, *The Republic*, (ed.) F. M. Cornford (Oxford, 1941) p. 191.

the character Thomas More appealed to Raphael: 'Don't give up the ship in a storm because you cannot direct the winds.'[23] In fact Raphael, 'who studied Greek more than Latin because his main interest is philosophy', knew his Plato. When More first saw him in Antwerp, he 'had a sun-burned face ... I took him to be a ship's captain.'[24] Unlike More, Raphael had been outside the cave.[25] He had not given up the ship, but chosen it wisely.

Half a century later, as we have seen, Camden's *Britannia* was another Latin product of Flemish inspiration. Camden's work had a European Protestant reception as well as genesis.[26] Echoing More, Camden discussed the belief of Virgil and Claudian that '*Britaine ... was in times past joined to the maine.*'[27] Hence 'between the said Fore-land of Kent and Calais in France ... the sea, is so streited, that some thinke the land there was pierced thorow, and received the seas into it, which before-time had been excluded'.[28] According to Camden, after becoming an island, and becoming known to the seafaring Greeks ('And ... better knowen ... than either to Plinie or to any Romane'), Albion was successively inhabited by Gauls, Romans, Germans, Danes and Normans.[29]

Publishing two years before the descent of the Spanish armada, Camden worried about England's continued vulnerability to inva-sion: 'For, an usuall maner it ever was of this nation (like as it is at this day also) to shew themselves feeble in repressing the enemies forces, but strong enough to civill wars, and to undergoe the burdens of sinne.'[30] For another contemporary,

A kingdome cannot bee to well garded, especially such a one as [has] bene so often conquered ... And it is not impossible for this kingdome to be conqured as well nowe as ever ... yet never for *want of men nor money* but for want of souldiers ... I cannot see why this kingdome may not bee in as great danger now as ever yt hath beene; for *war is growne fuller of Arte*, and yet wholly forgott in this kingdome, And this kingdome had never *so greate and powerfull ennimyes* against yt, as att this day, Therefore I could wish ... [that] although yor Maties *subjects be carelesse*; yet god does looke that yor Matie should be so much the *more carefull.*[31]

[23] More, *Utopia* p. 36.   [24] Ibid. pp. 9–10.
[25] Eric Nelson, 'Greek Nonsense in More's *Utopia*', *Historical Journal* 44, 4 (2001) p. 892.
[26] Kevin Sharpe, *Sir Robert Cotton 1586–1631: History and Politics in Early Modern England* (Oxford, 1979) pp. 9–11, 84–6; see chapter 1 above.
[27] Camden, *Britain* p. 4. On the 'quite widely held belief' in England's recent island status see E. G. R. Taylor, *Late Tudor and Early Stuart Geography, 1583–1650* (London, 1934) pp. 91–2.
[28] Camden, *Britain* p. 1.   [29] Ibid. pp. 27, 28.   [30] Ibid. pp. 108, 110.
[31] BL Harleian MS 6843 f. 226: 'How the Coast of yor Ma[je]sties Kingdome may be defended against any enemie'.

During the same reign John Speed drew up a map of 'The Invasions of England and Ireland with al their Civill wars since the Conquest'. His accompanying text, 'A brief Description of the Civill Warres, and Battailes fought', listed seventy-four such clashes from 1066 to the 1572 revolt of the Northern Earls. His point (though circulated privately, and not published until after the Queen's death) was that England had a special problem in these areas.

> Cease civill broyles, O England's subject cease,
> With streames of blood staine this faire soyle no more:
> As God, so Kings must be obey'd with peace.[32]

In 1558, following its loss of Calais, wrote Fernand Braudel, 'England, without realizing it at the time, became ... an island, in other words, an autonomous unit, distinct from continental Europe. Until this turning-point, despite the Channel, the North Sea and the Straits of Dover, England had been bodily linked with France, the Netherlands and the rest of Europe.'[33] Yet, as elsewhere Braudel emphasized, islands were not autonomous.[34] Moreover, England's links to the rest of Europe did not end in 1558. It assisted the revolt in the Netherlands from 1572, was inundated with French and Dutch Protestant refugees, and entered the war against Spain in 1585. 'In 1572 the Spanish ambassador guessed that there were 20,000 of his master's subjects who had found shelter in England and who looked for Alva's overthrow by ... William the Silent.'[35] England entered the Thirty Years War (in 1624–9), attempted to federate with the United Provinces (1651–4), captured Dunkirk (1658), became a satellite of Louis XIV's France (1670–85), was invaded by the United Provinces (1688), and under a Hanoverian dynasty remained heavily militarily involved in Europe throughout the eighteenth century.[36]

Braudel is certainly correct, as we have seen, that the English did not realize that they were autonomous 'at the time'. Again the monarch was a woman, 'matter of encouragement to Enemies both abroad and at home to designe upon *England*'.[37] This time, however, she was Protestant, excommunicated, unmarried and childless. The survival of the church, dynasty and realm were all uncertain. Military engagement in both Scotland and the Low Countries followed.

---

[32] Speed, *The Theatre of the Empire* pp. 5–8.
[33] Fernand Braudel, *Civilization and Capitalism, 15th–18th Century, volume III: The Perspective of the World*, trans. Sian Reynolds (London, 1984) p. 353.
[34] Braudel, *The Mediterranean and the Mediterranean World*.
[35] Haley, *The British and the Dutch* p. 32.
[36] Scott, *England's Troubles*; Simms, *Three Victories*.
[37] [Marchamont Nedham], *The Case Stated Between England and the United Provinces* (London, 1652) p. 2.

The latter constituted the first of three early modern periods of unusual Anglo-Dutch political proximity. Registering the dire military circumstances faced by the rebels following the assassination of William the Silent in 1584, Elizabeth was offered sovereignty over the United Provinces. Although she did not accept this offer, the Treaty of Nonsuch drew the two countries closer together politically as well as militarily. For confessional nationalists like Richard Hakluyt, military engagement against Spain in the Low Countries, Ireland and the New World was not simply a religious duty. It was a defensive necessity, and the *Short Account of the Destruction of the Indies* by Bartolomé de Las Casas, first translated into English as *The Spanish colonie* in 1583, showed what Protestants everywhere could expect if this effort failed.[38]

Opined Elizabeth, improbably, to the Dutch ambassador: 'your state is not a monarchy and we must take everything together and weigh its faults against its many perfections ... we kings require, all of us, to go to school to the States-General'.[39] The most dramatic consequence for England of its entry into the European war was the attempted Spanish invasion of 1588. The failure of the Spanish plan to land 44,000 troops from Spain and Flanders owed little to English military prowess, and nothing to government competence.

Elizabeth's vacillation and indecision before the Armada was launched left her country unprepared and stopped her navy from averting the looming catastrophe, and her parsimony even while the Spaniards were at her door so hamstrung her fleet that it was deprived of the chance to complete the Armada's destruction; but her actions in the aftermath of the battle were the most despicable of all. While her favourites and courtiers fawned upon her, lauding her courage and martial prowess, the naval commanders and officials who had done most to secure her throne were shunned and criticized, and the seamen who risked their lives on her behalf were abandoned to their fate ... That the English losses of personnel from ships that came through the battles virtually unscathed were every bit as heavy as those of the battered and shipwrecked Armada tells its own terrible story.[40]

This lucky escape was put in perspective by subsequent successful invasions by Scotland (1640) and the United Provinces. In addition, between 1616 and 1642 Barbary corsairs captured four hundred English ships and almost seven thousand men, many from English waters. In September

---

[38] Hadfield, *Literature, Travel* pp. 91–104.
[39] Quoted in Haley, *The British and the Dutch* p. 45.
[40] Neil Hanson, *The Confident Hope of a Miracle: the True History of the Spanish Armada* (London, 2003) p. 471; James McDermott, *England and the Spanish Armada: the Necessary Quarrel* (New Haven, 2005).

1639 the English fleet helplessly watched the Dutch destroy the Spanish fleet in the Downs.[41] As Robert Burton had put it in 1624: 'Who is not sicke, or ill disposed ... in whom doth not passion, anger, envy, discontent, fear and sorrow raigne?'[42] That the country's military vulnerability became a huge issue in English writing during the next century and a half is hardly surprising.

It was in this context that English writers picked up the Homeric trope of floating islands. This would be given Elizabethan, early and later Stuart, and eighteenth-century incarnations.[43] In addition to their setting, such lands themselves exhibited the properties of water. More than a destination, they were travelling. This might reflect the character of their inhabitants, or the impact of tides, wind or weather. It was on Aiolia, the floating island, that Odysseus was given a bag of winds by Aiolos, 'for the son of Kronos had set him in charge of the winds, to hold them still or start them up at his pleasure'. From the ox-skin bag 'tied fast with silver string' only the west wind was released to take Odysseus' vessel home. But as he slept the bag was opened by his crew, resulting in a storm which 'swept them over the water weeping, away from their own country'.[44] In *Gulliver's Travels* Jonathan Swift depicted the floating island of Laputa as populated by hopelessly distracted, and abstracted, Pythagorians.[45]

Thus floating islands were unstable, in danger and/or dangerous. Edmund Spenser's *The Faerie Queene* was written during the Elizabethan crisis of Protestantism, and published during the war with Spain. In a letter to Walter Ralegh the author explained that he had (as John Dee would also) made use of the history of King Arthur '*for the excellency of his person ... and also furthest from the daunger of envy, and suspition of present time*'.[46] However, to any who might have trouble grasping the reality of the Kingdom of Faery, he reminded his readers, and his Queen, that until recently

---

[41] N.A.M. Rodger, *The Safeguard of the Sea: a Naval History of Britain 660–1649* (New York, 1998), pp. 384, 413.

[42] [Robert Burton] Democritus Junior, *The Anatomy of Melancholy: What it is* (Oxford, 1624) p. 14. Publishing two years earlier, Thomas Scott also noted the national condition of 'Melancholy' (*Belgicke Pismire* Preface p. 1).

[43] For a modern example see 'And Sometimes, the Island is Marooned on You', *New York Times Sunday*, 6 November 2005 pp. 1, 27.

[44] *The Odyssey of Homer* Book 10 lines 20–49.

[45] Jonathan Swift, *Gulliver's Travels: a Facsimile Reproduction ...* (ed.) Colin McKelvie (New York, 1976) pp. 5, 147; Part 3. Having begun by describing Laputa as 'floating or flying', Swift eventually settled for the latter. Thus it was in this text that islands stopped floating on water and started to do so in air.

[46] Edmund Spenser, *The Faerie Queene*, (ed.) A.C. Hamilton (2nd edn, Harlow, 2001), 'A Letter of the Authors' p. 715.

Who ever heard of th' Indian *Peru*?
Or who in venturous vessel measured
The *Amazons* huge river now found trew?
Or fruitfullest *Virginia* who did ever vew?
Yet all these were when no man did them know,
Yet have from wisest ages hidden beene
And later times thinges more unknowne shall show.
Why then should witlesse man so much misweene
That nothing is but that which he hath seene?[47]

In Book 2 Canto 12, having survived the '*Gulfe of Greedinesse*' and the '*Rocke of Reproch*', Sir Guyon the knight of temperance encounters float-ing islands.

At last farre off they many Islands spy,
On every side floting the floods emong:
Then said the knight, Loe I the land descry,
Therefore old Syre thy course do thereunto apply.
That may not be, said then the *Ferryman*
Least we unweeting hap to be fordonne:
For those same Islands, seeming now and than,
Are not firme lande, nor any certein wonne,
But straggling plots, which to and fro do ronne
In the wide waters: therefore are they hight
The *wandring Islands*. Therefore doe them shone;
For they have oft drawne many a wandring wight
Into most deadly daunger and distressed plight.

Guyon is pursued by a siren ('the wanton *Phaedria*'), imperilled by quicksands, whirlpools and sea-monsters, and tempted by mermaids and a weeping maiden.[48] His objective, which he must destroy, is the lair of

Acrasia a false enchaunteresse,
That many errant knights hath foul fordonne:
Within a wandring Island, that doth ronne
And stray in perilous gulfe, her dwelling is;
Faire Sir, if ever there ye travel, shone
The cursed land where many wend amis,
And know it by the name; it hight the *Bowre of blis*.[49]

As, in the words of his friend Ludowick Bryskett, 'perfect in the Greek tongue', Spenser followed in the Platonic moral tradition of More and

---

[47] Ibid., Book 2, Proem, stanzas 2–3.
[48] Ibid., Book 2, Canto 12, stanzas 10–11 (quotation); stanzas 3–28.
[49] Ibid., Canto 1, stanza 51.

Philip Sidney.[50] What had arrived between the two was the struggle of Protestantism. The violent opposition counselled by Spenser, and offered by Sidney, to the 'deadly danger' of popery, has reasonably been seen as a change of emphasis from Erasmian Christian humanism. It was the view of Erasmus that 'a prince will never be more hesitant or more circumspect than in starting a war; other actions have their different advantages, but war always brings about the wreck of everything that is good'.[51]

We need not see Spenser's stance as a fundamental break from this tradition, not only because it remained in line with its Greek sources, but because in Spenser, as in Milton, it was precisely the Christian content of this humanism (now Protestant) which called for military action, where in Erasmus it had called for peace. It is the Elizabethan and early Stuart struggle against counter-reformation which helps to explain the peculiar combination within later English republicanism of Platonic Christian humanism and Machiavellian militarism. This was exemplified across the spectrum from the Erasmian Milton to the Machiavellian Algernon Sidney.[52]

One necessity for defence of the Elizabethan commonwealth lay, it was agreed, in the creation of English naval power. However, dauntingly, what this required was mastery of a new element. For although it is correct to describe water as the only efficient transport surface, this does not begin to engage with its complex and challenging physical properties. It was, opined John Evelyn, not only the most fruitful but also the 'most impetuous, and unconstant element'.[53] Lack of constancy, or continuity, meant change. Change was dynamite in the early modern period – arguably the modern in early modern – and water its embodiment. It had internal qualities of movement driven by currents, flood and tide. It could be harnessed by machines and whipped into mountains by wind. One Elizabethan scholar remarks, 'Safe arrival somewhere meant a briny hell had been successfully negotiated; it unfortunately also meant that hell had to be traversed again on the homeward journey.'[54]

[50] Quoted in Canny, *Making Ireland British* p. 8; Eric Nelson, *The Greek Tradition in Republican Thought* (Cambridge, 2004) pp. 100–2; Sidney, *The Defence of Poesy*, in Sir Philip Sidney, *Selected Writings*, (ed.) Richard Dutton (Manchester, 1987) p. 134; Scott, *Commonwealth Principles* pp. 45–8.
[51] Erasmus, *The Education of a Christian Prince*, (ed.) Lisa Jardine (Cambridge, 1997).
[52] Canny, *Making Ireland British* pp. 37–8; Scott, *Commonwealth Principles* chs. 2, 5, 8, 10.
[53] Evelyn, *Navigation and Commerce* p. 17.
[54] Jonathan P.A. Sell, *Rhetoric and Wonder in English Travel Writing, 1560–1613* (Aldershot, 2006) p. vii.

In 1832 Charles Darwin wrote: 'I hate every wave of the ocean with a fervour … I loathe, I abhor the sea and all ships which are on it.'[55] Yet there is plenty to suggest that enduring a medium in constant motion over a period of years helped to insinuate into the seasick scientist a perspective on nature preoccupied with change and process.[56] Storms were a staple of maritime voyage narratives, including that which 'devoured and swallowed uppe' Sir Humphrey Gilbert on the return journey from America, though not before he had echoed Raphael Hythloday by quoting Cicero: 'Wee are as neere to heaven by Sea, as by lande.'[57] The 'terrible seas' fatal to Gilbert had 'broken short and high Pyramid wise. The reason whereof seemed to proceede either of hilly grounds high and lowe within that sea, (as we see hils and dales upon the land) … or else the cause proceedeth of diversitie of windes.'[58] Perhaps the most famous contemporary account of a 'dreadfull Tempest' was that by which a shipload of pilgrims to Virginia were wrecked on Bermuda in 1609, and which may have helped to inspire Shakespeare's play of the same name.

[A] dreadfull storm and hideous began to blow … [and] beate all light from heaven; which like an hell of darknesse turned blacke upon us … our clamours dround in the windes, and the windes in thunder … For surely … as death comes not so sodaine nor apparent, so he comes not so elvish and painfull … as at Sea … It could not be said to raine, the waters like whole Rivers did flood in the ayre … What shall I say? Windes and Seas were as mad, as fury and rage could make them … there was not a moment in which the sodaine splitting, or instant over-setting of the Shippe was not expected.[59]

Shakespeare's dramatic creation made sense, since in addition to being terrifying, such storms were theatrical. *The Tempest* took the elemental potential of water to a new level. Its characters were wrecked on an island which was, if not floating, then enchanted. 'What a strange drowsiness possesses them! / It is the quality o' th' climate.' This magic affected the water (raising the tempest), land and air. Like the rigging of a ship, Caliban's island was never silent. 'Where should this music be? I'th'air

[55] Quoted in Iain McCalman, *Darwin's Armada* (Melbourne, 2009) p. 40.
[56] Thus he speculated concerning the formation of coral reefs: 'the ocean throwing its water over the broad reef appears an invincible enemy, yet we see it resisted and even conquered by means which would have been judged most weak and inefficient'. Ibid. p. 79.
[57] David Armitage, 'Literature and Empire', in Canny (ed.), *The Origins of Empire* pp. 107–8.
[58] Hakluyt, *The Principall Navigations* vol. II p. 695.
[59] Sir Thomas Gates, *A true repertory of the wracke, and redemption of Sir Thomas Gates Knight; upon, and from the Ilands of the Bermudas*, published in Purchas, *Purchas His Pilgrimes* vol. IV Book 9 pp. 6–8. The connection to Shakespeare is vigorously debated. See Sobecki, *The Sea* p. 163.

or th'earth?' According to Michael Witmore, this music made the water and air a 'single vibrating membrane'.[60] Nor was it only the island which became alike with them in terms of sound and movement. As the ocean enveloped the island and its characters, taking them to it at the beginning, and away from it at the end, so it enveloped the audience also. From arrival to departure, the play was a ship aboard which, in their tiered timber seats, those watching found they were travelling.

Such tropes of oceanic voyage narrative were so securely established by the later seventeenth century that they were included even in works of fiction like Defoe's *Robinson Crusoe*, or else ostentatiously omitted.

This volume would have been ... twice as large, if I had not made bold to strike out innumerable Passages relating to the Winds and Tides, as well as to the Variations and Bearings in the several Voyages; together with the minute Descriptions of the Management of the Ship in Storms, in the Style of Sailors: Likewise the Account of the Longitudes and Latitudes; wherein I have Reason to apprehend that Mr *Gulliver* may be a little dissatisfied.[61]

Meanwhile, to grapple with these elements successfully was the haven-finder's art. In the words of John Dee, as 'this *Art of* Navigation, requireth a great skill and industry', so it called for 'many Thousands of Soldyers ... not only hardned, well to broke all rage and disturbance of Sea, and endure healthfully all hardnes of lodging and dyet there, but also ... well practiced, and easily trained up, to great perfection of understanding all maner of fight ... at Sea'.[62]

Dee's master text for this purpose was not the Bible, as it had been for Hakluyt, but Thucydides' *History of the Peloponnesian War*. It was in particular 'the Incomparable ... Greke Captain *Pericles*, in his Oration ... to the Parlement Senators of *Athens* ... Comparing their State, to the State of the Lacedemonians'. Describing the Spartans as 'farmers, not sailors', Pericles had advised: 'Suppose we were an island, would we not be absolutely secure from attack? As it is we must try to think of ourselves as islanders; we must abandon our land and our houses, and safeguard the sea and the city.'[63]

[60] William Shakespeare, *The Tempest*, (eds.) Alden T. Vaughan and Virginia Masan Vaughan, *The Arden Shakespeare*, series 3 (New York, 2005) 2.1.199–200; 1.2.388; Michael Witmore, 'An Island of One: Spinoza and Shakespeare's *Tempest*', talk given at Duquesne University, Pittsburgh, 2007.

[61] Richard Sympson, 'The Publisher to The Reader', in Lemuel Gulliver, *Travels into Several Remote Nations of the World* (London, 1726) in Swift, *Gulliver's Travels* p. viii.

[62] John Dee, *General and Rare Memorials pertaining to the Perfecte Arte of Navigation* (London, 1577) pp. 4–5.

[63] Thucydides, *History of the Peloponnesian War*, trans. Rex Warner (Harmondsworth, 1972) pp. 121–2.

To win its war with Sparta, this was to say, Athens must draw upon the experience which had enabled it to defeat Persia at Salamis in 480 BC. The architect of that victory had been Themistocles, a name also in the mind of Walter Ralegh: 'This was Themistocles opinion long since, and it is true, That hee that commaunds the sea, commaunds the trade, and hee that is Lord of the Trade of the world is lord of the wealth of the worlde.'[64] Ralegh was thinking not only of the Mediterranean, of course, but of the Atlantic. In Athens the advice that the city prefer sea power and trade to 'our land and our houses' was controversial. It was one thing to resort to this in an emergency, as in 480, but another to advocate it, as Pericles did, as ongoing state policy. How could Athens, a continental city, turn itself into an island?

The answer to this question had two components, both initiated by Themistocles and maintained by Pericles. One was the sea power which Athens had been accumulating 'ever since the end of the Persian wars'. The other was the long wall defending Athens, especially its port of Piraeus, from land-based attack (and built, in its first incarnation, to link Athens and Megara).[65] The resulting Athenian empire, linking the island-city with other islands and cities across the Aegean, was maritime. It took the form, that is, of an archipelago rather than a continental confederacy like Sparta's Delian League. This was Dee's model for an Elizabethan 'islandish monarchy', which he described oddly (everything about Dee was odd) as including England, Ireland, the Netherlands and the Orkneys.[66] In a subsequent work addressed to Elizabeth, and not published in his lifetime, his model was not Aegean but Arthurian, and these borders were extended to include North America, Greenland, Iceland, Scandinavia, Denmark, western Muscovy and Castile (Spain).[67]

It is important to pay attention to the geographic, rather than simply the political, basis of this Greek model. Despite Dee's depiction of Pericles as a member of parliament, Athenian democracy did not greatly assist his attempt to put the case for its contemporary relevance (a point later forcefully made by Hobbes). What made the Athenian case indispensable for Dee, Hakluyt and others was not simply that city's choice

---

[64] Quoted in Andrews, *Trade* p. 9.

[65] Frisch (ed.), *The Constitution of the Athenians* pp. 63–87.

[66] For the political context see Glyn Parry, 'John Dee and the Elizabethan British Empire in its European Context', *Historical Journal* 49, 3 (2006) pp. 656–60.

[67] John Dee, *The Limits of the British Empire*, (ed.) Ken MacMillan with Jennifer Abeles (Westport, Conn., 2004) pp. 43–97. Thus Anthony Grafton's comment that 'Dee and other Elizabethan intellectuals went not to ancient but to medieval sources for their justifications of English empire' (Grafton, *New Worlds, Ancient Texts* p. 147) is true of *The Limits* but not of the *Perfecte Arte*.

of sea over land power. It was the broader cultural politics within which this had become embedded in Greek texts. This laid the basis for what Edward Said would later famously call orientalism. In addition to informing these Elizabethan discussions, this would be greatly developed by English and Scottish writings of the eighteenth century.

Said noticed 'orientalism' in some of the earliest surviving Athenian texts. One was Aeschylus' *The Persians* because, for Athens, Persia was the 'oriental' power. Ostensibly luxurious, slavish and despotical, this culture became the antitype against which Athenians defined and projected the manners and institutions of their city. At the heart of that projection, in Pericles' Funeral Oration as rendered by Thucydides, or the work of early modern European humanists and republicans who drew inspiration from it, was liberty.[68] Yet, despite devoting a section of his book to the 'imaginative geography' of orientalism, Said paid little attention to the specific geographical content of this argument. It was, he concluded, 'A line ... drawn between two continents. Europe is powerful and articulate; Asia is defeated and distant.'[69] But what if it was, instead, a line drawn between a continent and islands; or between land and water?

This possibility is clear enough even in the Aeschylian chorus from which Said quotes.

> Now all Asia's land
> Moans in emptiness.
> Xerxes led forth, oh oh!
> Xerxes destroyed, woe woe!
> Xerxes' plans have all miscarried
> In ships of the sea.

It was in the fact that Xerxes was stopped by ships of the sea, and in its own role in that achievement, that Athens' claim to Greek leadership resided. As Athenian envoys put it to Sparta: 'Out of the 400 ships, nearly two-thirds were ours ... And the courage, the daring that we showed were without parallel. With no help coming to us by land ... we chose to abandon our city and sacrifice our property ... we took to our ships and chose the path of danger.'[70] Herodotus documented Xerxes' struggles with water: when his bridge was destroyed by a storm, he 'gave orders that the Hellespont should receive three hundred lashes and have a pair of fetters thrown into it'.[71] Subsequently, according to Thucydides, Pericles

---

[68] Scott, *Commonwealth Principles* pp. 27–8.
[69] Edward W. Said, *Orientalism* (New York, 1979) pp. 56, 57.
[70] Thucydides, *Peloponnesian War* p. 79.
[71] Quoted by John Burrow, *A History of Histories: Epics, Chronicles, Romances and Inquiries from Herodotus and Thucydides to the Twentieth Century* (New York, 2008) p. 18.

divided 'The whole world before our eyes ... into two parts, the land and the sea ... Of the whole of one of those parts you are in control – not only of the area at present in your power, but elsewhere too, if you want to go further.' He associated the land with unnecessary luxury (gardens and other elegances that went with wealth) and the sea with what was necessary for the defence of 'our freedom' and 'our empire' from 'slavery'.[72]

In this Athenian text, this is to say, Sparta was orientalized. It was not only that Athens, a maritime city, was free, while the agrarian Spartans lived under an aristocracy/oligarchy. On the eve of the war the Corinthians agitatedly juxtaposed the characters of the two protagonists.

An Athenian is always an innovator, quick to form a resolution and quick at carrying it out. You, on the other hand ... never originate an idea, and your action tends to stop short of its aim ... they ... in the midst of danger, remain confident. But your nature is always to do less than you could have done, to mistrust your own judgement ... while you are hanging back, they never hesitate; while you stay at home, they are always abroad ... If they win a victory, they follow it up at once, and if they suffer a defeat, they scarcely fall back at all ... In a word, they are by nature incapable of either living a quiet life themselves or of allowing anyone else to do so ... But ... your whole way of life is out of date compared to theirs ... Your inactivity has done harm enough.[73]

The essence of an Athenian was motion (*kinesis*). Sparta was a case study in 'oriental' lethargy. Historians have asked whether Thucydides attributed the former to the energizing (and ultimately destabilizing) effect of democracy. But motion and change, energy and danger, were also properties of water, by contrast to relatively immobile land. During the seventeenth century, as we will see, several English writers attributed the striking capacity of the Dutch for innovation to their dynamic relationship to water.

What is clear about Thucydides' text is that the speeches of the Corinthians and of Pericles are part of a larger orientalization. The name Peloponnesian War, like Persian War, is an orientalizing construct. These are maritime defensive struggles against continental invasion. In the end the Athenians are defeated only by another maritime democracy (Syracuse) and the Spartans prevail only by turning to Persia itself for military assistance.

Thus this orientalism was a cultural rather than geographic construct. In Athenian texts, what may have originated as, or later become, 'a line drawn between Europe and Asia' was redrawn within Europe, and within Hellas. Since it was drawn with water and stone it even cut across Attica.

---

[72] Thucydides, *Peloponnesian War* pp. 160–1.   [73] Ibid. pp. 76–7.

Because of its sea power and walls, Athens, though not an island, could behave as though it were one. Because they were on an island, the only wall that England and Scotland needed (if they could agree) was sea power itself.

Like the Corinthians, Elizabethan maritime boosters (Dee, Hakluyt, Ralegh) were trying to mobilize a conservative society. In the face of the military threat from Spain, Elizabethan inactivity had done harm enough. It was the mission of these writers to persuade the English, although they were, like the Spartans, farmers not sailors, to begin to '*think* of ourselves as islanders'. Until this challenge was met England's situation, where 'to our great Shame, and Reproche … many hundreds of forrein Fisherboats … doo come, (in [a] maner) home to our doores: and … deprive us, yerely, of many hundred thousand pownds',[74] was precisely opposite to that of the Athenians.

Dee devoted himself to the theoretical foundations of navigation and its mechanical instruments. He was influenced by his knowledge of Portuguese developments in particular, and by his experience at the University of Louvain.[75] Written less for scholars than for sailors, William Bourne's *A Regiment for the Sea* (1574) described its subject as 'how to direct one's course upon or thorow the sea, where he findeth no path … how to attayne the port … appointed in the shortest time, how to preserve the shippe … in al common disturbances, as stormes … &c.'. That no knowledge was more important, claimed Bourne, was a function both of the country's 'situation … invironed rounde aboute with the Sea' and of 'this time'.[76]

Hakluyt's work too was 'the advancing of navigation, the very walles of this our Island, as the oracle is reported to have spoken of the sea forces of Athens'.[77] He called for establishment of a 'lecture' in 'the art of navigation, + breading of skilfulnesse in the seamen'. In a book dedicated to Sir Philip Sidney he repeated that the English must learn from 'the examples of the Grecians and Carthaginians'.[78] Like Dee's, Bourne's and Ralegh's, Hakluyt's geographical ambitions also lay further afield.[79]

---

[74] Dee, *Rare Memorials* pp. 6–7.   [75] Taylor, *The Haven-Finding Art* pp. 192–208.

[76] William Bourne, *A Regiment for the Sea: Conteyning most profitable Rules, Mathematical experiences, and perfect knowledge of Navigation*, in Bourne, *A Regiment for the Sea and Other Writings on Navigation*, (ed.) E.G.R. Taylor (Cambridge, 1963) Preface to the Reader p. 139.

[77] Hakluyt, *The Principall Navigations* p. 3. The oracle advised Athens to trust to its wooden walls, a trope to resurface later in the work of Richard Gibson.

[78] R[ichard] H[akluyt] the Younger, *Divers Voyages* p. 2.

[79] The second edition of Bourne's *Regiment* (1680) contained a 'Hydrographicall discourse to shew the passage unto Cattay five manner of waies, two of them knowen and the other three supposed'. Bourne, *Regiment* p. 301.

THE PRINCIPALL
NAVIGATIONS,VOIA-
GES AND DISCOVERIES OF THE
Englifh nation,made by Sea or ouer Land,
to the moſt remote and fartheſt diſtant Quarters of
the earth at any time within the compaſſe
of theſe 1500.yeeres: Deuided into three
ſeuerall parts,according to the po-
ſitions of the Regions wherun-
to they were directed.

The firſt,conteining the perſonall trauels of the Englifh vnto *Iudæa,Syria,A-*
*rabia,*the riuer *Euphrates,Babylon,Balſara,* the *Perſian* Gulfe, *Ormuz, Chaul,*
*Goa,India,*and many Iſlands adioyning to the South parts of *Aſia :* together with the like vnto *Egypt,* the chiefeſt ports and places of *Africa* within and without the Streight of *Gibraltar,* and about the famous Promon-
torie of *Buona Eſperanza.*

The ſecond,comprehending the worthy diſcoueries of the Englifh towards
the North and Northeaſt by Sea,as of *Lapland, Scrikfinia, Corelia,* the Baie
of *S.Nicholas,* the Iſles of *Colgoieue, Vaigats,* and *Noua Zembla* toward the
great riuer *Ob,*with the mightie Empire of *Ruſſia,* the *Caſpian* Sea,*Georgia,*
Armenia,Media,Perſia,Boghar in *Bactria,*& diuers kingdoms of *Tartaria.*

The third and laſt,including the Englifh valiant attempts in ſearching al-
moſt all the corners of the vaſte and new world of *America,* from 73.de-
grees of Northerly latitude Southward,to *Meta Incognita,Newfoundland,*
the maine of *Virginia,* the point of *Florida,*the Baie of *Mexico,* all the Inland of *Noua Hiſpania,*the coaſt of *Terra firma, Braſill,* the riuer of *Plate,*to
the Streight of *Magellan:* and through it,and from it in the South Sea to
Chili,Peru,Xaliſco, the Gulfe of *California, Noua Albion* vpon the backfide
of *Canada,* further then euer any Chriſtian hitherto hath pierced.

Whereunto is added the laſt moſt renowmed Englifh Nauigation,
round about the whole Globe of the Earth.

By *Richard Hakluyt Maſter of Artes, and Student ſometime*
of Chriſt-church in Oxford.

Imprinted at London by GEORGE BISHOP
and RALPH NEWBERIE, Deputies to
CHRISTOPHER BARKER, Printer to the
Queenes moſt excellent Maieſtie,
1589.

Figure 1 Cover page of volume I of Richard Hakluyt, *The Principall
Navigations, Voiages and Discoveries of the English Nation* (2 vols.,
London, 1589; facsimile edition, Cambridge, 1965). Hakluyt
ordered his compilation by voyage direction (south-east, north-east,
west) and chronologically within each of these subsections. This
format was widely imitated.

Concerning the possibility of a north-west passage – 'a straight and short way open into the West even unto Cathay' and so the riches of the East – he reported the belief of Sebastian Cabot 'that all the North part of America is divided into Islandes'.[80] That in North America a dream of islands would gradually give way to the fact of a continent was the reverse of the later experience in the South Pacific (see chapter 9). In a manuscript written for the Queen of Sparta herself (Parsimonia), Hakluyt's focus became the many advantages which would accrue to England from a plantation of North America.

These were religious, following establishment of a Protestant counterweight and boundary to the Spanish empire. This was also a duty to the natives, who stood otherwise between the Scylla of pagan and Charybdis of popish idolatry. 'Nowe the Kinges and Queenes of England have the name of Defenders of the Faithe: By which title I thinke they are not onely chardged to mayneteyne and patronize the faithe of Christe, but also to inlarge and advaunce the same: Neither oughte this to be their laste worke but rather the principall and chefe of all others.'[81] These advantages were also social, given the opportunity furnished by such a colony to 'deliver our common wealthe from multitudes of loyterers and idle vagabondes' who 'be either mutinous and seeke alteration in the state, or at leaste very burdensome … [and] pitifully pine awaye, or els at lengthe are miserably hanged'.[82]

One of the most important benefits would be the 'increase, mayneteynaunce and safetie of our Navye, and especially of greate shipping wch is the strengthe of our Realme'. But Hakluyt also projected North America's natural resources as replacing all trade commodities acquired elsewhere. From Florida, 'beinge aunswerable in climate to Barbary, Egyipte … Persia, Turky, Greece, all the Ilandes of the Levant sea', there would come dates, cypresses, spices, 'great aboundaunce of perles' and gold.[83] In the middle latitudes 'of the temperature of the coaste of Gascoigne and Guyann', there was venison, fruit, nuts, corn, 'greate store of vynes' and olive oil. From the north, as far as 67 degrees northern latitude, could be harvested fish, whales, timber and furs. Thus in North America, with its great climatic range, lay an alternative to 'all our olde decayed and daungerous trades in all Europe, Africa, and Asia'.[84]

[80] Hakluyt, *Divers Voyages* pp. 3, 4.
[81] Richard Hakluyt, 'Discourse of Western Planting, 1584', in E. G. R. Taylor (ed.), *The Original Writings and Correspondence of the Two Richard Hakluyts* (2 vols., London, 1935) vol. II p. 215.
[82] Ibid. pp. 211–12, 234.   [83] Ibid. pp. 222–3.   [84] Ibid. pp. 213, 222–33.

Hakluyt attributed to letters patent granted to Sebastian Cabot, a Venetian, by the English crown 'the title which we have to that part of America which is from Florida to 67 degrees northward' (the arctic circle). The whole of this territory, Hakluyt explained, was 'nearer unto her Maiesties Dominions, then to any other part of Europe'. England had the same geographic advantages in relation to North America that the 'Portingales' had regarding Brazil: 'truly the danger and way is shorter to us then to Spaine or Portugall'.

Notwithstanding 'this Realme of England ... is compassed with the sea', its princes had 'traveled and passed the Seas making warre ... and conquered many rich and faire Dominions ... to enlarge your kingdome and demaund ... tribute of the French king'. It was said that the North Atlantic could be navigated only with 'great danger, difficultie and peril'. However, this problem was partly compensated for by the fact that in summer it enjoyed 'perpetuall cleerenesse of the day without any darknesse of the night'.[85] Finally time was short. 'I can assure you that Abraham Ortelius the great Geographer told me at his last being in England in 1577 that if the warres of fflaunders had not bene, they of the Lowe Contries had meant to have discovered those partes of America, and the northwest straite before this tyme.'[86]

Hardly less important than what lay over the water was what was under it. Dee's interest in the fishery related mainly to its potential as a training ground for sailors. But his interest also included, as more capaciously did that of William Monson, veteran of the Elizabethan struggle against Spain, resources of food and for trade.[87] According to Monson, one pillar of an English maritime culture and economy was the coal trade to London from Newcastle ('our north Indies, by the commoditie and strength that ariseth to the Kingdome by it').[88] The other should be imitation of the Dutch fishery conducted off British coasts. 'What better light can we have for this work, then from our nearest and intimatest ffreinds the Hollanders, who by their long travels, their excessive paines [and] their ingenious inventions ... exceed all other nations ... out of their labours and our ffish only.'[89] Monson explained the mechanics of this Dutch 'Golden mine' from its invention 'since ye year 1307 to

[85] Hakluyt, *Divers Voyages* pp. 2–6, B, B2.
[86] Hakluyt, 'Discourse of Western Planting' p. 279.
[87] G.R. Elton, 'Piscatorial Politics in the Early Parliaments of Elizabeth I', in N. McKendrick and R.B. Outhwaite (eds.), *Business Life and Public Policy: Essays in Honour of D.C. Coleman* (Cambridge, 1986); see the digression on overfishing, the taking of fry and the 'Stinching, Soyling ... [and] Beslovening ... of the Thames' in Dee, *Rare Memorials* pp. 41–50.
[88] 'How to imploy our ffleet against Spain' NMM REC/4 Item 12 ff. 7–8.
[89] Ibid. f. 4.

their un measurable wealth + our shame, and for ye Honor of him that first found out the secret of Pickleing of Herrings, wch was one Wm Backalew'.[90] He analysed the annual pursuit by 'well nigh 20000 [*sic*] ffishing vessels' of 'ye scull of the Herrings like a Hound that pursues the Head of a Dear in hunting', to their sale 'esteemed as a precious food, in all parts of Europe and that the return thereof giveth them means ... in maintaining their inestimate war against so great and potent an Enemie as the King of Spaine'.[91]

Unfortunately, Monson continued, English and Scottish imitation of this achievement faced several obstacles. One was that the English did not like eating fish. Monson's was one of several proposals aiming to address this problem by a seasoning of compulsion. To those who worried that enactment of a second weekly 'fish day' would be 'an Innovation', one writer responded that, on the contrary, it would restore the situation pertaining before the Dissolution of the Monasteries when the self-flagellating inhabitants of '500 howses of religion' frequently ate fish.[92]

More problematically, fishing was 'out of the Element and breeding of Gentl[men] and others that applies themselves to ye profit of the lands + not the sea'.[93] For it to succeed 'all men in this worke must become M[e]rchants not only for themselves but for their prince and Country'. In such a case some were 'afraid' that merchants and mariners might 'overgrow other states of men, and be dangerous'. To the objection that the necessary investment capital could not be found, Monson replied that this 'would seeme ridiculous to strangers' given English luxury, ostentation and 'needless expences'. Finally, however, compared with agriculture fishing was cold, wet and dangerous. Whereas this was cheerfully borne by 'all manner of people of wt degree soever in Holland', in England it faced 'the sluggishness + evill disposition of our people'.[94]

During the late Elizabethan and early Stuart periods there were a series of English missions to learn about the construction, administration, provisioning and sailing of Dutch and Baltic shipping.[95] With the

[90] NMM REC/4 Item 14: 'On the fishery' p. 1.   [91] Ibid. ff. 10, 13.

[92] NMM REC/3, 'Arguments to prove that it is necessary for the restoring of the Navie of England to have more ffish eaten and therefore one day more in the weeke ordained to be a ffish day' ff. 116, 117.

[93] Sir William Monson, 'Relating to ye Fishery' NMM REC/4 Item 13 f.3.

[94] Ibid. ff. 14–15. Monson was a patron of Tobias Gentleman, 'Fisherman and Mariner', author of *The Best Way to Make England the Richest and Wealthiest Kingdome in Europe, By Advancing the Fishing Trade ... [and] Building ... Busses and Pinks after the Holland Manner* (London, 1660).

[95] NMM REC/3 ff. 119–22: 'The Order and Manner of ye Ships of Warre with their provisions in the United Provinces'; ibid. ff. 123–7: 'Answers to the demands concerning the Navie of the United Provinces ... R. Rodenberg 22 April. 1600'; ibid. ff. 129–32: 'Instructions for the Voyage into Holland and Zeland'; ibid.

accession of the Stuarts there was, dynastically at least, a British archipelago. Within this context the fishery might furnish the basis of an archipelagic economy, the migration routes of herring surrounding the 'many hundred Island[s] belonging to this Kingdome of Scotland + Ireland – Shetland, Orkney and Hybrades'.[96] For Monson the result was to be not only a means of employment and prosperity but, thereby, religious and moral reform of Scottish Highlanders and Islanders – particularly those on the perfectly placed Lewis – as barbarous and bloody as the Irish. In practice, however, the three kingdoms were not united, religiously or politically. Nor were they insulated from the violent religious politics of Europe.[97]

The writers here discussed (with the exception of Monson) published for domestic and/or broader European readerships. In addition Dee, Hakluyt, Spenser and Monson composed works of political counsel. All sought to influence public opinion and policy, partly by addressing the Queen herself. All were preoccupied, in the absence of mastery of the ocean, by the problem of English military vulnerability. Most sought to drive the nation into a dynamic relationship with the sea and its mobility. By the successful establishment of such a relationship, and implantation of such a culture, danger might give way to opportunity. By the events of the following century the salience of these concerns would be dramatically illustrated.

ff. 133–8: 'Concerneinge the Navie of Denmarke to inform himselfe'; 'The like Inquiry to be made of the state of the Navie of Swede and a[t] Lubeck, Dantiske and att other ... townes'.

[96] Monson, 'Relating to ye Fishery' ff. 27–30.
[97] Scott, *England's Troubles* chs. 1–6.

3   The discipline of the sea

> Yet thy brave beames excluded from their right
> Maintaine there Lustre still, & shining cleere
> Turne watrish Holland to a crystalline sphere.
> Mee thinkes, in that Dutch optick I doe see
> Thy curious vertues much more visibly:
> There is thy best Throne. For afflictions are
> A foile to sett of worth, & make it rare.
>
> George Herbert, *To the Queene of Bohemia*[1]

A Scottish king, coming also to wear the English crown, established claim to a British dynasty, if not a single island kingdom. The first and most important ambition of King James VI and I was to turn this dynastic into a political (and religious) union: a melding of nations which would be not only insular but archipelagic, the Anglo-Scottish planting of Ireland one of its instruments. Writing later, Thomas Hobbes credited that 'most wise King' with pursuing a Roman strategy of incorporation 'Which if he could have obtained, had in all likelihood prevented the Civill warres, which make both those Kingdomes, at this present, miserable'.[2]

That neither James nor his son Charles obtained this end resulted not only from the great cultural, religious and political differences to be overcome, but from the growing discrepancy between the ambitions and jurisdictions, and the actual military and political power, of the crown. Both of these problems were to be dramatically exacerbated by the European military conflict of 1618–48, of which the wars of the three Stuart kingdoms became one theatre.[3] When Charles I spoke in 1625 of his intention that there be 'one uniforme course of Government, in, and through, our whole Monarchie ... Our Royall Empire, descended upon Us and undoubtedly belonging and pertaining unto us', he was referring not only to England, Scotland and Ireland, but also to Virginia and New

---

[1] George Herbert, *The Poems of George Herbert* (2nd edn, Oxford, 1961) p. 202.
[2] Thomas Hobbes, *Leviathan*, (ed.) Richard Tuck (Cambridge, 1996) p. 138.
[3] Scott, *England's Troubles* chs. 2–6.

54

England. Here as elsewhere Charles (who had visited Madrid in 1623) might have taken Castile as a model but entirely lacked the resources to give effect to this vision.[4]

During James' reign John Speed articulated the new dynastic geography. With a notable change of emphasis from Camden, describing 'the outward body and Lineaments of the now flourishing *British Monarchy*', Speed focused upon 'the Ilands ... in actuall possession, (for with others, no less justly claimed in the Continent, we meddle not)'.[5] These islands comprised England, Scotland, Wales, Ireland and Man. Noticing of 'the Iland of Great Britaine' that Ptolemy had listed it second in size after Taprobane, and Lipsius second after Cuba, Speed made an inadvertent concession to European context by settling for the 'honour ... that it was (without question) the greatest Iland of the *Romane World*'.[6] Noting the view 'divers have stiffly held, that once it was joined by an arme of land to the continent of *Gallia*', and quoting '*Spencer*' to this effect, Speed resisted such backsliding as 'a matter merely conjecturall'.[7] His was the first English geography within which insularity, distinguished and defended from a continent, was the central organizing principle.

As an instrument of dynastic policy this island idea became politicized, deployed by the crown in support of Anglo-Scottish political union, and resisted by English parliamentarians claiming liberties either native to part of the island ('those laws in the government of the Saxons ... of that vigour and force as to overlive the Conquest')[8] or inherited from a larger European cultural area, whether classical republican or 'gothic'.[9] Cutting across these political-dynastic lines were competing confessional geographies. That of a Calvinist like George Abbott emphasized the commonalities and interdependence of England, Scotland, the United Provinces and parts of Germany. The 'Arminianism' of Peter Heylyn or of Charles

---

[4] Elliott, *Empires of the Atlantic World* p. 117 and ch. 5 in general.

[5] Speed, *The Theatre of the Empire*, 'The British Ilands Proposed In One View' p. 1.

[6] Ibid.   [7] Ibid.

[8] 'Pym's speech at Manwaring's impeachment, 4 June 1628', in J.P. Kenyon, *The Stuart Constitution 1603–1688: Documents and Commentary* (2nd edn, Cambridge, 1993) p. 15. This reference was to the 'ancient and fundamental law ... the first frame and constitution of the kingdom' (ibid.). In the Petition of Right this was supplemented by 'other the good laws and statutes of this realm [by which] your subjects have inherited this freedom' (ibid. p. 68).

[9] Kenneth R. Olwig, *Landscape, Nature and the Body Politic: From Britain's Renaissance to America's New World* (Madison, Wisc., 2002) chs. 2–3; Kidd, *British Identities* p. 291; Scott, *Commonwealth Principles*. Classical republican liberties originated in Greece and Rome; gothic ones among the 'northern nations' by which the Roman empire had been overrun.

I identified an ancient and unique English constitution in church and state capable of uniting the archipelago.[10]

The related Jacobean development with a powerful Caroline consequence was military, including naval, decay and (mis)management. It was related not only because dynastic policies and claims presumed at least a theoretical capacity for military enforcement, but because the rationale for monarchy and aristocracy was military. The result was more than a 'divergence' between early Stuart rhetoric and power. When the relevant cultural fissures became militarized, and when Jacobean military inaction was succeeded by Caroline failure, the eventual result within the British archipelago was the abolition of monarchy and the House of Lords.

These calamities succeeded a period of peace (1604–24) and of the policies of a king committed to peace. One way of attempting to secure peace within the increasingly polarized and fraught European theatre might have been carrying a big stick. But James lacked the inclination as well as resources. In the absence of a standing army his gentry acquired what military experience was available in the Low Countries. The naval records of the reign 'are but a sorry collection of relations of frauds, embezzlements, commissions of inquiry, and feeble palliatives'. James personally 'knew at least as early as 1608 of the iniquities daily occurring in every branch of the service, but he contented himself with making an "oration"'. Nor do we have any 'reason to suppose that James I would have seen any cause for interference merely on behalf of seamen who were starved and robbed, or of the English people whose chief defence was being destroyed, and whose money went to enrich a ring of thieves. So far had the traditions of Plantagenet and Tudor kingliness degenerated into Stewart "kingcraft".'[11]

In fact Elizabeth's naval management, as we have seen, had not been conspicuously kingly. Although she came to use naval power and to give adventurers and privateers their openings, she did so inconsistently, hesitantly and meanly: these expeditions were expected to turn the crown a profit. After the armada, 'Whether the cause was incompetence or a criminal parsimony ... [the sailors'] fate, after having saved their country, was to perish in misery, unheeded and unhelped except by the officers who had fought with them. In the conceit of Elizabeth and her like they were only "the common sort".'[12]

[10] Robert Mayhew, 'Geography's English Revolutions: Oxford Geography and the War of Ideas', in D. Livingstone and C. Withers (eds.), *Geography and Revolution* (Chicago, 2005) pp. 260–3.

[11] H. Oppenheim, *A History of the Administration of the Royal Navy and of Merchant Shipping in Relation to the Navy* (repr., London, 1961) pp. 185, 215.

[12] Oppenheim, *Administration* p. 143. Oppenheim's verdict is discussed in Andrews, *Trade* pp. 235–6. These charges are amplified by Hanson, *Confident Hope of a Miracle* pp. 455–71.

James also expected a return on naval investment. What this meant in peacetime was that naval office constituted a leading source of patronage. In the award of senior office emphasis was placed upon the social quality appropriate to support monarchy, rather than the experience required to win a war. Lesser offices were sold, corners were cut, ships disintegrated, everybody bribed and was bribed, and as usual sailors (devoid now even of the 'officers who had fought with them') died in droves from bad food, disease and terrible conditions. During the reign Oppenheim describes a system riddled with abuses evolving into an organized program of plunder within which 'the chief Officers bear themselves insolently, depending on powerful friends at court'.[13] In 1681 Samuel Pepys made the same complaint in language so identical as to make one wonder whether Oppenheim was reading it back into the earlier period. Even in peacetime this situation was dangerous, as demonstrated by the state's inability to defend its merchants from piracy so that 'the merchantmen dare hardly sail'.[14] With the outbreak of European war, and England's belated entry into it (1624), the consequences became far-reaching.

An undated paper written in peacetime addressed a complex of issues which would come to dominate early Stuart analysis and complaint.

[I]t were to bee wished that the Cheife officers under the Lord Admirall, Tre[asure]r, Controuler, Surveyor ... should be men of the best experience in Sea Service as well as of Judgemt and practise in the utensils ... belonging to Shipping. Instead sometimes men are preferred by the special favour of Princes and many times by the Mediation of greate men for the prefermt of their Servants ... some people very raw and ignorant ... to the greate hinderance of his Maties Service ... in matters soe nearly concerninge the Service and Safetie of the Kingdome Wherein all private respects should bee layde aparte, and virtue truly regarded for itself.[15]

It was participation in the European war which exposed the English government to invidious comparisons with the United Provinces. As Hobbes wrote later: 'I doubt not, but many men, have been contented to see the late troubles in *England*, out of an imitation of the Low Countries; supposing there needed no more to grow rich, than to change, as they had done, the forme of their Government.'[16] One who advocated such imitation was the preacher Thomas Scott. What impressed Scott about the Dutch was not their material but their moral wealth, as well as their Protestantism and military prowess. He published in London, a year after the fall of Bohemia, a book to 'shew the necessarie dependancie betwixt

---

[13] Oppenheim, *Administration* p. 193.   [14] Ibid. p. 199.
[15] NMM CAD/D/19 Item 2: 'Observacons touchinge the Royal Navy and Sea Service' pp. 1–2, 20.
[16] Hobbes, *Leviathan* p. 225.

our Kingdome of *Great Brittaine* and the *united Provinces*'. He hoped that James would not 'so much seeme to neglect his owne honour and safety, or our lives and liberties, as to leave us in the hands of our enemies ... or suffer us to bee led into temporall or spiritual captivity'.[17]

For Scott, the Dutch struggle with water had equipped the country to withstand the subsequent inundation of the Inquisition.[18] From idleness it had extracted diligence; from the vice of 'privacie', interdependence and community.

The Sea lyes continually raging upon their Coasts in such a manner, as if it would hourly eate them up ... It over-lookes them, and they seeme to lye under it: yet they keepe out this strong enemie at the armes end by art and industrie ... it is incredible what paines they take, setting a kind of long grasse upon the ... barren sands, as curiously and carefully, as wee set flowers and hearbes in our gardens: which grasse once getting root, bindes the earth together, that the winde cannot readily come to blow it away, and teacheth them by the like combination to turne their weaknesse into the like strength.[19]

No less challenging than this ocean were the '*fresh*-waters ... within' the country.

But see what profit they make of this Adversarie, whilst cutting large passages from place to place with incredible cost, these waters worke for them continually as faithfull servants, conveying their carriages by this meanes, to and fro, in a cheape, easie, and safe manner ... Nay not only the water, but the winde also is their journeyman, and labours continually for them by Mils and other Engines; some pumping and forcing the waters out of their surrounded pastures; some pressing oyles, others bearing flaxe, hempe, copper; some grinding corn, others spice; some making paper, others sawing timber; and briefly, neither man, woman, nor child, neither sea nor land, neither water nor winde suffered to be idle, but whatever it blowes, it blowes good to some of them.[20]

Thus for Scott, in the United Provinces the mobility of water and wind had been harvested physically and morally. Like the Athenians, this 'diligent and happie people' were never at rest. When they had enough they laid up more. Rejecting sloth, they had rather chosen 'a safe Warre ... then an unsafe peace'.[21] As in Athens, the reward of this industry was liberty. In addition to liberty of conscience, 'I observe a generall freedome permitted and used, where generall actions which concerne all, and are maintained by all, are generally debated, argued, sifted and censured by all men without contradiction.'[22] By contrast (in an echo of More, to

[17] Scott, *Belgicke Pismire* Preface pp. A2, A4.
[18] Ibid. pp. 50–75. 'Thus wee see how this people maintaine their owne, both against the King of *Spaine* and the Ocean' (p. 69).
[19] Ibid. pp. 67–8.   [20] Ibid. pp. 69–70.
[21] Ibid. pp. 51, and 59–90 in general.   [22] Ibid. pp. 89–90.

whom Scott referred), a corrupt Jacobean state run by an 'effeminate ... Nobilitie ... educated in an idle course of life .... onely to hunt, to hawke, or daunce, or drinke, or court' subjected the people to 'slaverie'.[23] 'To fill the veines of a decayed estate, to inrich a Commonwealth, to restore libertie, and to rule by vertuous Lawes: this requires wisdome.'[24]

Scott's moral meditation on water would later be echoed and developed by Sir William Temple. Seeking to explain the most remarkable feature of Dutch society – its capacity for innovation – Temple discerned in the relationship of land, wind and water a force for change. 'No man can tell the strange and mighty Changes that may have been made in the face and bounds of Maritime Countreys, at one time or other, by furious Inundations, upon the unusual concurrence of Land-Floods, Winds and Tides.'[25] The issues of water which constantly moved and shaped the land included not only waves and tides but 'the rolling of Sands upon the mouths of three great Rivers, which disembogued into the Sea through the Coasts of these Provinces'. One result was a physical landscape unrecognizable alongside the 'Isle of *Batavia*' described by Tacitus.[26] Another, 'after a long contention between Land and Water, which it should belong to', was a country

divided between them: For to consider the great Rivers, and the strange number of Canals that are found in this Province. And do not only lead to every great Town, but almost to every Village, and every Farm-House in the Countrey; And the infinity of Sails that are seen every where coursing up and down upon them; One would imagine the Water to have shar'd with the Land; and the people that live in Boats, to hold some proportion with those that live in Houses.[27]

Not only the landscape, but also the air, was filled with water. This, too, resulted in diligence.

The extream moisture of the Air, I take to be the occasion of the great neatness of their Houses, and cleanliness in their Towns. For without the help of those Customs, their Countrey would not be habitable by such Crowds of people, but the Air would corrupt upon every hot season, and expose the Inhabitants to general and infectious Diseases ... The same moisture of Air makes all Metals apt to rust, and Wood to mould; which forces them by continual pains of rubbing and scouring, to seek a prevention or cure: This makes the brightness and cleanness that seems affected in their Houses, and is call'd natural to them, by people who think no further ... As indeed most National Customs are the Effect of some unseen or unobserved natural Causes or Necessities.[28]

---

[23] Ibid. pp. 27, 30–2.   [24] Ibid. p. 37.
[25] Temple, *Observations Upon the United Provinces* p. 121.
[26] Ibid. pp. 122–3.   [27] Ibid. pp. 126–7.   [28] Ibid. pp. 132–3.

The Dutch scrubbed and swabbed their country as seamen scoured a ship. Finally, if motion was one product of this elemental indeterminacy, this ceaseless 'contention between Land and Water', another was the need to mark the constantly changing boundaries between the two. It was this which made so striking Temple's image of sails coursing up and down the land. It also accounted for several other famous features of the Dutch landscape. 'Thus, in the paintings of ... Jacob van Ruisdael (1628/9–82), watermills and mill machinery are shown as monumental, heroic, presences ... calming and taming the elemental ferocity of water ... Mills and canals, along with distant church steeples, were marks on the land, helping to fix one's bearings in an otherwise featureless terrain of sky, water, and fenland.'[29]

Scott's praise of the Dutch commonwealth did not go uncontested. His earlier work having been banned, he had fled to Utrecht where he was stabbed to death in 1625. While Dee had recommended to Elizabeth the example of Periclean Athens, in 1629 Thomas Hobbes published the first complete English translation of Thucydides' *History* as an anti-democratic cautionary tale.[30] According to Hobbes, what Thucydides said of Athens, and Scott of the United Provinces, far from being the solution to any English problem, was itself the problem. It was not simply that both were popular states, and maritime states. If the Athenians were (like water) constantly in motion, incapable of living a quiet life or of allowing anyone else to do so, then they were, as their own history showed, exemplary causes of war. Of the Peloponnesian War Thucydides explained, in Hobbes' translation: 'the truest quarrel, though least in speech, I conceive to be the growth of Athenian power; which putting the Lacedaemonians into fear necessitated the war'.[31] Athenian motion, vanquishing Spartan immobility, brought about 'the greatest motion [*kinesis*] in Greek history'.

From Thucydides' account of this tragedy, Hobbes eventually derived his mature political philosophy: that the world was material in perpetual motion; that a thing 'will eternally be in motion, unless somewhat else stay it'; that a human state of such motion without such stay was one of 'war of all against all'; that the most important informant of such a state

---

[29] Sawday, *Engines of the Imagination* p. 11.
[30] Thomas Hobbes, 'On the Life and History of Thucydides' and 'To the Reader', in R. B. Schlatter (ed.), *Hobbes' Thucydides* (New Brunswick, N.J., 1975); Jonathan Scott, 'The Peace of Silence: Thucydides and the English Civil War', in Jeffrey Rusten (ed.), *Oxford Readings in Classical Studies: Thucydides* (Oxford, 2009).
[31] Quoted in Jonathan Scott, 'The Peace of Silence: Thucydides and the English Civil War', amended version in G. A. J. Rogers and Tom Sorell (eds.), *Hobbes and History* (London, 2000) p. 122.

was that species of 'Interiour ... Voluntary Motions; commonly called the Passions'; that from an analysis of the way these passions worked a power could be created capable of bringing peace.[32]

While William Monson had praised Dutch industry and ingenuity, in a separate manuscript written in about 1624 he mounted an extraordinary attack. This identified the 'cunning courses' of the Dutch as 'the immediate causes of the poverty that daily assails our glorious kingdom'. It accused Dutch immigrants to England of engrossing manufactures, financial transactions and trade. 'What maritime town, or other of account within twenty miles of sea, opposite to Holland, that is not stuffed and filled with their people, to the impoverishing of the inhabitants and dwellers'?[33]

Scott claimed the opposite: that within his home 'City of Norwiche' its 'wealth, people, beauty, order, and ... quicke trading ... The ... good government of the Magistrates, the diligence of the Citizens', the thriving agriculture and industry were all 'principally occasioned by the example of ... Dutch' settlers.[34] Monson's account reeked of envy, but levelled the accusation of ingratitude. Like other early Stuart commentators he spoke of the United Provinces as an English creation.

Was it security, honour or profit to us ... to have maintained their principality, making mechanic persons equal to princes, raised an oligarch commonwealth against a monarchy ...? Was it security ... to suffer our prime soldiers ... to be under their subjection, the most part of our wealth exhausted thither, and by consequence to be in their power to dispose of this kingdom as pleased most voices of their select council, which is ... opposite to monarchy? For wheras monarchy propounds honour as the first thing, the second the public good, and the third interest, a popular State prefers private profit, makes the common good the second, and honour the last.[35]

In 1624–5 following the failure of the first military campaign to recover the Palatinate, the honour of the British monarchy was at neap tide.[36] It was in this context that one English manuscript advised the wholesale adoption of Dutch policy and manners.

---

[32] Hobbes, *Leviathan* pp. 37–46, 91, 149; Scott, 'Peace of Silence' (2000) pp. 122–5.

[33] Sir William Monson, *An Addition to the Sixth and last Book of Fishing, and the reasons why it was divided from the other former Discourse*, in Monson, *The Naval Tracts of Sir William Monson*, ed. M. Oppenheim (5 vols., London, 1902–14) vol. V pp. 303–4.

[34] Scott, *Belgicke Pismire* pp. 95–6. For the actual situation see Murray, 'The Cultural Impact of the Flemish Low Countries'.

[35] Monson, *An Addition* pp. 307–8. See Purchas, *Purchas His Pilgrimes* vol. I, 'A Note touching the Dutch' following 'To The Reader', for the delicacy of English discussions of the Dutch in this period.

[36] Scott, *England's Troubles* pp. 103–6.

The best waie a State can ... provide for a Warr is by Imitations of Those that have had the longest experience both of the provision + expense; and are nearest our owne times, if the Land bee capable of the same meanes. The united Provinces, through their Policy of Govnm.t have subsisted long against One of the most potent Kings of the World ... notwithstanding they are but a small people.[37]

The recipe for this Dutch success had three ingredients. The first was 'Frugality ... the Foundation of a wise state ... [and] Mother of all other Industries of Profitt'. In the contrary presence of 'Prodigality ... [parliamentary] Subsidies make a great Noise but little Warr; the subject thinking they will doe miracles (how insufficient soever) by cause they are exhausted by sumes which they Feele; and for which they did not provide'. Second was 'Traffique ... As Frugality is a Wealth raised att home, soe Traffique is a Wealth brought home.' Again, by contrast, English economic arrangements were painfully inadequate: 'The Revenue of a Kings Land, is but as the Domaines of a Lordship, not to bee trusted unto but for a Mans private [income] Wheras a war being a publique worke must have a publique meanes ... which nothing can better performe then Traffique: The meanes to inrich both king and Subject.' Observation of 'the Lowe Countries' showed that 'Traffique' was 'restrained by Impositions; and exceedingly hindred', but promoted by inviting 'all Strangers and Strangers of all Religions by Freedome and Good Usage'. The final Dutch master-stroke was

Excise; a Revenewe drawne from Things belonging to Victuall and Cloaths, and to bee imposed generally upon the Subject; When the Prince is to make a greate and necessary Warre by the Act of a Parliament ... This may bee spoken in the Approbation of Excise: 1: That itt is no fantastique Invention, but brings Example for Authority; as wee may have observed in the long Warres of our Neighbours the States. 2: That itt is more generall and continuall: and in the Collection of Subsidies many of the people are of necessitie ommitted ... 3: That itt is a more easy way of Imposition to the Subject to pay by little and little in such a manner as if itt were in use hee would hardly ... feele ... itt.[38]

To the objection that excise would fall too heavily on the poor, this writer insisted 'Lett us observe the Lowe Countries in that Respect also ... who out of the same Revenewe doe soe help to provide not only for their owne poore, but for the poor of all Nations borne there; as a Man shall very seldome meet a beggar among them.'[39] 'These Reasons for this way of

---

[37] NMM REC/3, p. 240: 'How a State may the best provide itself for a Warr'.
[38] Ibid. p. 241; see also Francis Bacon, 'Of the True Greatness of Kingdoms and Estates', in *Bacon's Essays*, vol. I, p. 105.
[39] NMM REC/3, p. 242.

Excise; noe true Comon=Wealths Man will quarrel with being grounded both upon long Example, and prosperous Experience. They must be men either of Faction, Opinion Jealousy or Ignorance that oppose itt.'

Strikingly this advocate of wartime economic and fiscal reform addressed 'those afraid of entertaining a Course for which wee have noe Precedent of our owne'. In fact, 'wee have a Guide; which wee account safe even in a strange Country'. Moreover, 'to thinke that all times either have or ought to have followed Presidents only, is an Errour; for then nothing had beene either helped or amended, and then had beene noe President at all'.[40] This was a bold anticipation of John Milton's later defence of regicide 'without precedent', as arguing 'the more wisdom, virtue, and magnanimity, that they know themselves able to be a precedent to others'.[41]

In fact, Charles I's wartime innovations in taxation went in the opposite direction, associated by contemporaries not with the United Provinces but with France.[42] For this the King's hostility to Dutch republicanism, and what he described as 'enemies to monarchy' in his own House of Commons, were certainly reasons.[43] It was the subsequent naval disaster at Cadiz (1626) which introduced into English maritime discourse its most potent theme of the succeeding century: the land- versus sea-based command of ships. The fraught relationship on shipboard of gentlemen and mariners had played some role in the execution by Francis Drake of gentleman volunteer Thomas Doughty in Patagonia in 1578. Drake blamed Doughty for 'these mutinies and discords that are growne amongst us ... Gentelemen are verye necesarye for governments sake in the voyadge ... [but] I must have the gentleman to hayle and draw with the mariner, and the mariner with the gentleman.'[44] But it was apparently Cadiz which prompted the first treatise on the subject.

Perhaps this Cadiz expedition indicates the low water mark of English seamanship. There have been many previous and subsequent occasions when fleets were sent to sea equally ill found and ill provided, but never, before or since, have we such accounts of utter incapacity in the mere every-day work of a sailor's duties. The shameful picture of that confused mass of ships crowded together helplessly, without order or plan ... is the indictment against the

---

[40] Ibid. p. 242.
[41] John Milton, *The Tenure of Kings and Magistrates* (1649), in *Complete Prose Works*, (ed.) D.M. Wolfe *et al.* (8 vols., New Haven, 1953–82) vol. III p. 237.
[42] *To all English Freeholders*, 24 January 1627, quoted in Richard Cust, *The Forced Loan and English Politics 1626–28* (Oxford, 1987) pp. 172–3.
[43] John Reeve, *Charles I and the Road to Personal Rule* (Cambridge, 1989) p. 132.
[44] Quoted in Glyndwr Williams, *The Great South Sea: English Voyages and Encounters 1570–1750* (New Haven, 1997) p. 23.

government of James I which had allowed the seamanship of Elizabeth to die out in this generation.[45]

Contemporaries had firm opinions about who or what was to blame. Another anonymous advocate of reform, 'fearing to be censured as over-bould + by speaking the trueth to drawe Envye upon my selfe ... [had] forborne theise two yeares + more to give mine opinion herein (Although entreated by some honorable personages thereunto)'. Now, however, he was driven to explain that the backbone of England's military security had been, not its navy, but the merchant marine.

Theis kingdoms of England, Scotland and Ireland, By the divine providence ... bounded ... round with the Ocean ... neede not feare the power of any forraine adversary being never so Potent by land except hee can bee also M[aster] of the seas. In Regard hereof the native shipping of this kingdome hath ever beene ... esteemed as Walls of Brasse to secure it from forraine invations or Incursions so long as we remaine Masters of ye seas.[46]

By native shipping was meant 'the Number + strenght [*sic*] of ye shipps of ye subjects which are built and maintained without ye charge of ye state, by private men ... + not onely ye powr of his Maties Royall Shipping'. The importance of private ships lay in the training they furnished to seamen. Without experienced sailors ships of war 'of themselves are but as engines or Weapons wch ... Valiant sea souldiers or Marriners (who knoweth how to Manage them) can onely use'. Without such mariners, even valiant soldiers on ships 'neede no enemy to destroye them, for they will soone destroye themselves ... the Boysterous stormy sea, will make them sicke + bereave them of Legges, stomack and couradge'.[47]

In 1588 the 'armado of Spaine' had been defeated 'through the power of God' and 'the experience and courage of ye seamen, being bredd up and inured to ye war [rather] then in ye strenght [*sic*] of ye shipping itselfe'. Whereas in the whole Elizabethan fleet had been no more than five ships 'above 200 Tunnes', now, in part to provide protection against 'ye Piratts + Turks of Algeeire', ships of '300–500 Tuns' were built routinely. Yet in the absence of appropriate expertise these were worse than useless.

---

[45] Oppenheim, *Administration* p. 221. For a more recent autopsy see Rodger, *The Safeguard of the Sea* pp. 357–63, 401–3.

[46] NMM REC/1, Naval Miscellanies, Item 56: 'A Discourse on the Necessity of Maintaining Freedom of the Seas by Keeping Shipping in an efficient state' ff. 1, 15–16. This thirty-five page tract is neither signed nor titled: the title given here is an (inaccurate) archival description, along with the date '*c*.1620'. Internal evidence dates the tract to the reign of 'king Charles' (p. 5) at a time when 'nowe wee have warres with Spain + france' (p. 30), namely 1627–8.

[47] NMM REC/1 Item 56: 'A Discourse on the Necessity of ... Shipping' ff. 6–7.

The first reason for this dearth was the serious decline of English trade during the first quarter of the seventeenth century. One cause of this was the inability of English merchants to compete with low-margin Dutch carrying. It is not clear whether such complaints, which were numerous, correctly described an absolute decline or rather simply the contrast with domination of English trade by the United Provinces.[48] A related problem was the failure of the Stuart government to imitate the Dutch and 'Venician State's Care for their Navigation' by forbidding the 'transportacon of English goods, in forraine Bottomes'. The United Provinces and Venice, of course, were mercantile republics. When England became a republic the accusation was repeated that

through the negligence of former Kings, and the corruption of their Ministers of State … these [Dutch] people … had not only got a Staple of Trade … but had almost ingrost all our Trade, and thereby spoyled us of our Navigation and Maritin Defence. Our long voyages about the world, which carried the reputation of *England* through all the parts thereof, being curted to their borders, and mostly in their own ships, to fetch from their stores at the second hand, and to retail it to *England*.[49]

Among the republic's answers to this problem was the Navigation Act of 1651 which forbade the import of English goods in foreign ships.

The other reason for 'ye danger of ye ruine of ye Navigation of this kingdome; + the discipline + honor thereof w.ch is almost lost', was social and political.[50] Most mariners were 'borne of poore or meane parentage'. Relatedly, 'none but hard Bodies + bould spirits will endure it … being enured to eminent daungers, + escaping many tymes the peril of ye sea (beyond hope)'. Any experienced mariner 'after they betake themselves to ye sea Is hardy daungerous and painefull, They must undergoe hunger, thirste, heate, could, wett, watching, and much paines'. 'It is the stormes + Tempest that doth discover ye able seaman from ye Idler and ignorant.'[51] This was not an argument for aristocratic naval command. Just as 'there is no comparison betwixt ye sea service + ye land service It being more facile to attaine the experience wch is done on ye land then on ye sea', so on board ship land-based social rank was irrelevant. '[I]t is absurd to think that a gentleman That hath been a voyage or two at sea (who in foule weather is sicke, or if not sicke, cannot stand …) should be an Able Seaman or comander.'[52]

---

[48] Taylor, *Late Tudor and Early Stuart Geography* pp. 100–3.
[49] [Nedham], *The Case Stated Between England and the United Provinces* p. 13.
[50] NMM REC/1 Item 56: 'A Discourse' f. 16.
[51] Ibid. ff. 9, 11.   [52] Ibid. f. 11.

Sailors had their own language. 'For the sea gibberish (as I may terme it) ... is proper only to them-selves, + none others.' 'The seamans desire is to be Comanded by ... one of their owne breeding ... as understandeth their lawes + customes, + can speake to them in their own language.'[53] A commander who had not learned this 'wilbe like Babells confounded builders' who will hear 'a barbarous language wch hee understands not'. This was not a matter of 'learning of words as a parrot (wch can speake words but understands them not) But by laborious + hazardous experience'. Seamen were 'ready to runn unto any desperate or evill action ... if they love and feare' their captain, and would be correspondingly 'stubborn and perverse, where they perceive that their commander is ignorant of the discipline of the sea'.

This discipline of the sea was inseparable from moral discipline more generally. Vigilant commanders took as much care to 'encourage and cherish the best deserving as to reprove + punish ... sloth and base cowardice'. Captains 'have the care of their Christian instruction, As well as of their civill governmts: That are under his charge ... for if the seamen be left without discipline at sea, there can be nothing but Confusion, through Blasphemyng drunkennesse ... Thefts ... Quarrells, Murthers and Contempt of all commanders'.[54] Officers had at their disposal punishments 'sufficient to tame ye rudest and savagest people in the world'. However, these should be reserved for only the most serious offences and never applied 'in fury or passion'. And alongside punishment and personal example there were many other instruments for improving an 'able and honest crew' including 'wholesome + good foode'.

In Scott's *Belgicke Pismire* the model for the Dutch (or English) commonwealth was that of the ant, whose diligence, foresight and colony-mindedness made 'her Nest a perfect plat-forme of a Commonwealth, as knowing herselfe by this confederacie, to be safer from forraine invasion, and that to dwell together in community'.[55] For the anonymous author of the unpublished 'Discourse', the model commonwealth was a ship, likened in fleet formation to a hive of bees. A ship was a commonwealth because it was a social community grounded in language and experience. It was a commonwealth, or republic, because it was a school of virtue. Finally, during a voyage, a ship's crew were interdependent and self-governing.

[T]his little common wealth consisting of 100/200/or 500 such men hardy and desperate ... being innured within ye wooden walls or little floating Island of a shipps corps or hull, where weale or no is to be endured + cannot always be

[53] Ibid. f. 10.   [54] Ibid. f. 13.   [55] Scott, *Belgicke Pismire* p. 25.

avoided or fled from having no supreame to appeale to (whilst they are at sea) but their own captaine – which in the affaires of Our Marchants … some tymes one shipps lading is worth 50,000 [pounds] some tymes 100,000 yea 200000 in one bottome being ye value of ye best shipps of warr.[56]

Having thus shown 'the nature, breeding and condition of our sea-men … + shutt them upp in their little common wealth + shewed you how they should be provided for, And how best govern'd, + by what lawes + rules', the tract went on 'to shew you ye severall offices By whome … theise little severall common wealthes (like bees) being small + of little power (being single) doe ioinctly together become ye walls of brasse to this kingdome'.[57]

However, in Charles I's England, 'because he is a seaman … [a cap-tain] is refused, And another man who is no seaman is placed captaine over him, and yet in his own ship'.[58] This was to be contrasted with the practice of 'ye united provinces whose safetie depends chiefly upon their sea affaires and who for some yeares past have … cheifely pose[d] their brede + expert seamen to goe commanders + capt.nes'. In 'ye furnish-ing out of our late great fleete when wanting seamen to man them, they have beene forced to prest – Bargemen, watermen, Lightermen + land-men'. In England naval commands were sold, 'and … he that will give most money is preferred to them, without … regard of their honesty or sufficiency to perform the services wch they undertake'.[59] The reason mariners had been given 'corrupt + unwholesome victuals … that … kill them' is that 'ye office of ye victualler, + the Surveyor of those Victualls for their goodnesse, weight + measure is in one man's hands'.[60]

Of course this explanation of military failure, mercantile and anti-aris-tocratic, was contested. A precisely opposite argument was that the prob-lem lay in a failure 'to breed young gentlemen for the sea service'. What was necessary was to raise officers' pay so that 'gentlemen of worth and quality might be encouraged to go to sea'. Otherwise 'the state must have relied wholly on mechanick men that have been bred up from swabbers', which 'would cause sea service in time to be despised by gentlemen of worth, who will refuse to serve at sea under such captains'.[61]

To assess the significance of these arguments several factors need to be borne in mind. The first is that under Charles I the promotion of an aristocratic officer corps at sea was a political project designed

---

[56] NMM REC/1 Item 56: 'A Discourse' f. 11.
[57] Ibid. p. 15.   [58]   Ibid. f. 12.   [59]   Ibid. ff. 31–2.
[60] Ibid. ff. 15, 31. These charges are supported by Oppenheim, *Administration* ('Not even a nominal system of inspection existed in the victualling Department' p. 222) and Rodger, *Safeguard of the Sea* pp. 375, 395–403.
[61] British Library Egerton MSS 2541 f.13 quoted by Oppenheim, *Administration* p. 226.

to support the monarchy, just as reform of the church was political, with the same objective. Although it is hard to say which of the two did most damage, it was certainly the combination of Calvinist outrage provoked by one of these policies, accompanied by royal military incapacity exacerbated by the other, which led to the fall of the Stuart crown. The King's insistence on officers of social quality rather than occupational experience not only divided the navy, but divided its command structure from that of the private merchant vessels upon which the navy depended and which it was supposed to protect. During the Personal Rule this division acquired religious as well as political and social characteristics.[62] The same policy vividly explained 'the loathing, yearly growing in intensity, the seamen, or "mechanick men", had for their courtier captains'.[63]

The cause of this loathing was not that the officers were courtiers – though on the Rhé expedition (1628) Lord Admiral Buckingham's personal transport contained cards and dice (cost 2 pounds), wine (164), nine cattle (59), eighty sheep (60), fifteen goats (10), twelve pigs (8), 980 chickens (63), two thousand eggs, pickled oysters, lemons, tapestries and turkey carpets – but that they were incompetent.[64] After Cadiz England's military disasters continued, until Buckingham was himself murdered by a returned sailor. The King withdrew from the European conflict and inaugurated the experiment of rule without parliaments. This he accompanied with new modes of fiscal exaction and anti-Calvinist religious reform. Refugees from the latter found refuge in both the United Provinces and North America.

By the 1630s there were thirty English reformed churches in the United Provinces, with many members who were to become prominent during and after the English civil wars, including Philip Nye, John Goodwin, John Lilburne and Hugh Peter, whose Rotterdam congregation had one thousand members before his departure for New England in 1635. During the Personal Rule, representative assemblies established themselves elsewhere in Massachusetts Bay, Maryland, Connecticut, Plymouth, New Haven and Barbados.[65] During the civil wars two attempts were made to plant a colony on Madagascar. The first, outside the East India Company, aspired to compete with Batavia in the spice trade. The second, absorbed by the Company, envisaged itself as a new Barbados. Unlike England, Madagascar was to be 'a quiet peaceable

[62] Rodger, *Safeguard of the Sea* pp. 409–10.   [63] Oppenheim, *Administration* p. 226.
[64] *State Papers, Domestic* vol. CXIV p. 48 quoted by Oppenheim, *Administration* p. 234.
[65] Elliott, *Empires of the Atlantic World* p. 135.

secure and wealthy habitation, in so excellent, pleasant and fruitfull a Country, a little world in it self'.[66] In fact the natives were warlike, the island malarial, and these dreams evaporated.

In January 1642 two thousand officers – the entire fleet minus one vessel – offered their service and protection to parliament. In the words of Bernard Capp, 'Charles's concern for the navy had always focused on his ships, not on feeding, clothing or paying the men who sailed them, and resentments ran deep.'[67] Oppenheim opined that the basis of this decision was material rather than ideological. All the sailor 'could associate with the crown were memories of starvation and beggary, of putrid victuals fraught with disease, and wages delayed ... The parliament paid him liberally and punctually, and he, on his side, served it honestly and well.'[68] These administrative and material issues were very important. But that there was also a maritime occupational and social ideology would be demonstrated not only under the English republic, but during the earlier civil wars. As Mark Kishlansky demonstrated for the New Model Army, in times of military crisis professional grievances could become politicized.[69] Later Sir William Coventry would observe to Samuel Pepys that the cause of the defection of the fleet under Charles I had been 'a continual interposing of land commanders upon seamen, who as they can never do the King's work as seamen, so they shall never have the affection of them they command'.[70]

In 1642 those remaining gentleman officers within the parliament-controlled navy were replaced by tarpaulin commanders, often with mercantile experience, under Lord Admiral Robert Rich, Earl of Warwick. One was William Rainsborough, and after his death his son Thomas, defender of universal manhood suffrage at Putney.[71] The Rainsboroughs had close ties to New England (Thomas' sister was the second wife of Governor John Winthrop) and several New Englanders returned to England to defend Protestantism in the civil wars.[72] Among these, chaplain to the fleet in 1642–3 was Hugh Peter.

---

[66] Quoted in Games, *Web of Empire* p. 192.
[67] Bernard Capp, 'Naval Operations', in John Kenyon and Jane Ohlmeyer (eds.), *The Civil Wars: a Military History of England, Scotland and Ireland 1638–1660* (Oxford, 1998) p. 161.
[68] Oppenheim, *Administration* pp. 240–1, 243.
[69] Mark Kishlansky, 'The Army and the Levellers: the Roads to Putney', *Historical Journal* 22, 4 (1979).
[70] Pepys, *Samuel Pepys and the Second Dutch War: Pepys' Navy White Book and Brooke House Papers*, (ed.) Robert Latham (London, 1996) p. 226.
[71] Rodger, *Safeguard of the Sea* pp. 414, 415.
[72] Whitney R.D. Jones, *Thomas Rainborowe (c.1610–1648): Civil War Seaman, Siegemaster and Radical* (Woodbridge, 2005).

Thomas Rainsborough was listed by Richard Gibson (of whom more in the next chapter) with 'Francis Drake, Sr John Hawkins Generall Deane … Sr John Narborough Sr Wm Penn' among those who 'came to deserved Honour from having been Cabben Boyes'.[73] When, having served at sea, and then on land, the independent Rainsborough was imposed as Vice Admiral in 1648 on a predominantly Presbyterian navy this was resisted as evidence of a 'design of introducing land-soldiers into every ship, to master and overawe the seamen'.[74] By the following year Rainsborough was dead, but so was Charles I.

Thus, during the reign of Charles I, failure in war at sea had stimulated an explicitly anti-aristocratic maritime military ideology with vital practical consequences. So what if, in time of war, a country's geography itself had political implications? What if Sir Francis Bacon was correct – whatever he meant – that 'To be master of the sea is an abridgement of a monarchy'?[75] This is one perspective from which to revisit the famous line in Shakespeare's *The Tempest*: 'What cares these roarers for the name of king?' The roarers in question are waves agitated by a storm. The audience for the Boatswain's outburst (which continues 'To cabin. Silence!') are a group of useless aristocrats impeding management of a ship. When he is warned 'be patient', the Boatswain replies: 'When the sea is …!'[76] If the security of the state required mastery of the sea, if mastery of the sea required seamen, and if the making of seamen lay in the hands of the sea itself, what was to prevent the government – like those of Athens and the United Provinces – from being shaped by its winds, its currents and waves?

In Thomas Gates' narrative the storm preceding the 'wracke' on Bermuda lasted for three days and four nights. By this crisis even socially mandated (aristocratic) idleness was overridden.

[M]en might be seene to labour, I may well say, for life, and the better sort … not refusing their turne, and to spell each the other … And … such as in all their life times had never done [an] houres worke before (their mindes now helping their bodies) were able twice fortie eight houres together to toile with the best.[77]

The only remaining visible social distinction concerned clothing.

---

[73] BL Add MS 11602 f. 39.   [74] Quoted in Jones, *Rainsborowe* p. 107.
[75] Bacon, 'Of the True Greatness of Kingdoms and Estates', *Bacon's Essays* p. 110.
[76] William Shakespeare, *The Tempest*, (ed.) David Lindley (Cambridge, 2002) pp. 92–3. In the analysis of David Norbrook ('What Cares These Roarers for the Name of King? Language and Utopia in *The Tempest*', in R.S. White (ed.), *The Tempest* (Basingstoke, 1999)) these references are to the unruly forces of nature. I argue that water bore tide-, current- and weather-induced properties of unruliness peculiar to itself.
[77] Gates, *A true repertory* pp. 9, 11.

The common sort stripped naked, as men in Gallies, the easier both to hold out, and to shrinke from under salt water, which continually leapt in among them, kept their eyes waking, and their thoughts and hands working, with tyred bodies, and wasted spirits ... destitute of outward comfort, and desperate of any deliverance, testifying how mutually willing they were, yet by labour to keepe each other from drowning.[78]

As Scott and Temple recounted, the sea was a leveller, architect of the Low Countries, and also of community.

In 1636 William Strode's *The Floating Island: a Tragi-Comedy* was 'Acted before his Majesty at Oxford ... By the Students of Christ-Church'. 'After the Appearance of a FLOATING Island', a Prologue emerged from the sea, saying:

> Whatever Element we light upon,
> (Great Monarch & bright Queen) 'tis yours alone,
> Shook from my station on that giddy Shore,
> That flotes in Seas, in wretchednesse much more,
> I hardly scap'd to tell what stormes arise
> Through rage of the Inhabitants: mine eyes
> Behold a wonder; Blustring Tempests there,
> Yet Sun and Moon fair shining both so neer.
> Should your Land stagger thus, I wish the Age,
> Might end such acting sooner then the Stage:
> Yet in these Tumults you shall only see
> A tottring Throne held firme by Majestie.[79]

For this monarch – his *Sovereign of the Seas* an attempt to override rather than harness the ocean – fluidity remained uppity and staggering. A few years later Sun and Moon would presumably have been less entertained by this laboured fiction of a tottering throne. In Strode's account a rational and stoic ruler was temporarily deposed by disordered passions ('Which is more waving, yonder Sea, or Land, or Passions dwelling there, we doubt') including lust, malice, anger, cowardice and melancholy ('a Malecontent turn'd Puritan'). Before their rebellion, in the first of several references to Strode's Homeric source the passions complained that the monarch had locked up their 'winde like *Aeolous*; 'tis calm'd, And may not issue forth ... a whisper'.[80] Their bad intentions were tied inside a bag of ox-hide fastened by silver string. When this was untied, and following their confused and risible bid for liberty, lessons were learned. What had appeared to be chains were revealed as justice and

---

[78] Ibid. pp. 9–10.

[79] William Strode, *The Floating Island: a Tragi-Comedy, Acted before his Majesty at Oxford, Aug. 29. 1636* (London, 1655), Prologue.

[80] Ibid. Act I, Scene ii.

temperance. Under a 'King ... whose Rule is Reason ... The Isle is settled, rage of Passions laid'. Then 'each breast / Will cease its Floating, and as firmly rest'.[81] Two years later Scotland signed a National Covenant for armed defence of its reformation.

Given England's own religious and political divisions, excacerbated by the European conflict, the Scottish challenge of 1638–40 posed several questions to which no persuasive royal answer was forthcoming. How could this monarch recover the ability to wield military force? In the absence of force, how could the Stuart crown make good its claims to be not only British, but imperial? In the absence of such force, outside Scotland and Sweden how was Protestantism to be defended? If the island was not floating, the crown was tottering. Within its territories subjects had acquired the stormy properties of wind and water. After the storm (in England at least), 'The Scaffold play'd the Stage'.[82]

In their book *The Many-Headed Hydra* Peter Linebaugh and Marcus Rediker describe the discipline exercised aboard early modern ships – and on land – as 'terror'. Their discussion of *The Tempest* identifies Shakespeare as a capitalist investor in the Virginia Company and his unruly Boatswain as advertising his fitness for the gallows.[83] My interest in this chapter and beyond is in the discipline exerted by the sea itself and its economic, military and political implications. We have seen in both published and unpublished material that this issue animated contemporaries. We have seen that it had vital practical consequences. Within an aristocratic society and polity being powerfully underpinned as such by royal policy, one historian has discerned a 'noble revolt'.[84] But what of the revolt against militarily incompetent nobility? In a country at war, abroad and then within itself, what of the impact of the discipline of the sea?

We have considered this question within the context of the collapse of monarchy. Its importance is dramatically underlined by what followed. This was a republic and empire fully apprised of its mercantile and naval interests and potential.

---

[81] Ibid. Epilogue.   [82] Ibid. Author's Dedication.
[83] Peter Linebaugh and Marcus Rediker, *The Many-Headed Hydra: Sailors, Slaves, Commoners, and the Hidden History of the Revolutionary Atlantic* (Boston, 2000) ch. 1.
[84] John Adamson, *The Noble Revolt: the Overthrow of Charles I* (London, 2007).

4   Ark of war

> Is this, saith one, the Nation that we read
> Spent with both Wars, under a Captain dead?
> Yet rig a Navy while we dress us late;
> And ere we Dine, raise and rebuild their State.
> What Oaken Forrests, and what golden Mines!
> What Mints of Men, what Union of Designes!
> Unless their Ships, do, as their Fowle proceed
> Of shedding Leaves, that with their Ocean breed.
> Theirs are not Ships, but rather Arks of War,
> And beaked Promontories sail'd from far;
> Of floting Islands a new Hatched Nest;
> A Fleet of Worlds, of other Worlds in quest;
> An hideous shole of wood-Leviathans,
> Arm'd with three Tire of brazen Hurricans;
> That through the Center shoot their thundering side
> And sink the Earth that does at Anchor ride.
> Andrew Marvell, *The First Anniversary of the Government under O.C.*[1]

The revolution of 1649 entailed much more than 'the settling of the government ... in way of a Republic, without King or House of Lords'. During the civil wars parliament had abolished parliamentary subsidies and replaced them by monthly assessment and excise. The former paid the army and the latter funded the fleet. In addition, parliament and then the republican government funded their military ventures by the proceeds of delinquency compositions and the sale of royal and episcopal lands. Between 1642 and 1660, it has been estimated, government income from these and other sources totalled ninety-five million pounds ('what golden Mines!'), an annual income more than five times that available to Charles I in the heyday of Ship Money.[2]

---

[1] Andrew Marvell, *The First Anniversary of the Government under O.C.*, in *The Poems and Letters of Andrew Marvell*, (ed.) H.M. Margoliouth (2 vols., Oxford, 1927) vol. I pp. 111–12.
[2] Oppenheim, *Administration* pp. 303–4.

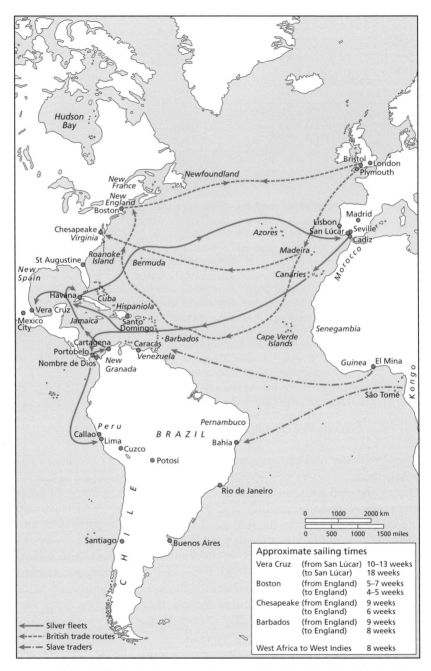

Approximate sailing times		
Vera Cruz	(from San Lúcar)	10–13 weeks
	(to San Lúcar)	18 weeks
Boston	(from England)	5–7 weeks
	(to England)	4–5 weeks
Chesapeake	(from England)	9 weeks
	(to England)	6 weeks
Barbados	(from England)	9 weeks
	(to England)	8 weeks
West Africa to West Indies		8 weeks

⟶ Silver fleets
⊷ British trade routes
⊷·⊷ Slave traders

Map 3 The Atlantic narrows between Newfoundland and Ireland and between north-west Africa and Brazil. Map based on 'The early modern Atlantic world', in J. H. Elliott, *Empires of the Atlantic World: Britain and Spain in America 1492–1830* (New Haven, 2006) p. 50.

Partly because the civil war had been fought in alliance with the City of London, the English republic prioritized 'traffique'. One sign of this was the more than doubling of the merchant as well as the naval fleet between 1649 and 1653. Another was the Plantation Act of 3 October 1650 to 'reduce all ... parts and places [in America] belonging to the Commonwealth of England' (Virginia, Maryland, Antigua, Barbados and Bermuda had declared for Charles II).[3] Most striking was the Navigation Act of 1651, demanded by English merchants since at least the 1620s, and described by John Streater as 'that Act for Trade, that never to be forgotten Act ... which occasioneth a Chargeable and Dangerous War with *Holland*'.[4]

These measures were accompanied by an extraordinary build-up and projection of naval power. In mid-1651 a Venetian observer reported:

Owing to the care of parliament they have 80 men of war, which are certainly the finest now afloat, whether for construction, armament, or crews. They can increase these numbers with incredible facility to 150, 200 or more sail ... [In addition] trade ... has made great strides for some time past, and is now improved by the protection it receives from parliament, the government of the commonwealth and that of its trade being exercised by the same individuals.[5]

Whereas during wartime Charles I had built one or two new ships a year, the English republic built tens and dozens – twenty-two in 1654. Whereas it had taken the early Stuart crown a year to plan 'a peaceful summer cruise in the narrow seas', the republic patrolled the channel, Mediterranean and Caribbean simultaneously.[6] This reflected the strategic challenges faced by the new regime, as well as the resources available to it. Naval administration was reformed under a new Admiralty Committee headed by Henry Vane. Officers' pay was substantially increased and shipboard discipline tightened. A century and a half later, during the British naval mutinies of 1797 at Spithead and the Nore, when 'An attempt was made to give to the ships in mutiny the name of "The Floating Republic"', petitions from the mutineers recalled the pay increases of January 1652 as having established the wage levels upon which sailors still attempted to live.[7]

Peter Linebaugh and Marcus Rediker have written in this context of 'the terrifying discovery by Cromwell and Parliament in 1649 that they

[3] Robert Bliss, *Revolution and Empire: English Politics and the American Colonies in the Seventeenth Century* (Manchester, 1990) pp. 45–61.
[4] Quoted in Steven Pincus, *Protestantism and Patriotism: Ideologies and the Making of English Foreign Policy, 1650–1668* (Cambridge, 1996) pp. 11–12.
[5] *Calendar of State Papers and Manuscripts relating to English Affairs ... in the archives ... of Venice* (London, 1927) vol. XXVIII pp. 187–8.
[6] Oppenheim, *Administration* p. 303.
[7] G.E. Manwaring and Bonamy Debree, *The Floating Republic: an Account of the Mutinies at Spithead and the Nore in 1797* (Edinburgh, 1935) Frontispiece and pp. 21, 23.

had only fifty naval vessels with which to defend their republic against the monarchs of Europe, who did not look happily upon the severed head of Charles I'.[8] The speed with which this situation was rectified, so that the number of naval vessels in 1688 was 173, makes it possible to say that 'Cromwell inaugurated the [English] maritime state and Charles II realized its promise.'[9] Such a formulation, however, entirely overlooks the extent to which this navy, these trading and colonial policies, and this state were republican in foundation. In 1649 Cromwell was not Lord Protector, but Lord General. The republican navy, and the Anglo-Dutch war which followed, were created by his rivals, and may have provoked his dissolution of the government in 1653. Certainly his anger on that occasion was directed against individuals whose successful management of a naval conflict was increasingly expensive, and creating a locus of military power alternative to that of the army ('Oh Henry Vane!').[10] Writing later in the Netherlands, Algernon Sidney, one of those individuals, said of the war: 'they [the Dutch] were endangered and we destroyed by it'.[11] Sidney's friend Slingsby Bethel lamented:

When this late Tyrant, or Protector (as some calls him) turned out the Long Parliament, the Kingdome was arrived at the highest pitch of Trade, Wealth, and Honour, that it, in any Age, ever yet knew ... Our Honour, was made known to all the world, by a Conquering Navie, which had brought the proud *Hollanders*, upon their knees, to begg peace of us, upon our own Conditions, keeping all other Nations in awe.[12]

As we will see, this naval prowess did not transfer to Charles II (or James II). Meanwhile, the republican achievement was not only a question of money. No less important were management and manners.[13] These included a new administrative efficiency and a recognizably non- or post-aristocratic frugality. In France Cardinal Mazarin was advised:

[8] Linebaugh and Rediker, *The Many-Headed Hydra* p. 145.   [9] Ibid. p. 146.
[10] Scott, *Commonwealth Principles* pp. 105, 260, 267–72.
[11] Algernon Sidney, *Court Maxims*, (eds.) Hans W. Blom, Eco Haitsma-Mulier and Ronald Janse (Cambridge, 1996) p. 171. Sidney's account of the dissolution quotes Cromwell as specifically blaming Vane. Scott, *Algernon Sidney and the English Republic* p. 102.
[12] Slingsby Bethel, *The World's Mistake in Oliver Cromwell ... shewing, That Cromwell's Mal-administration ... layed the Foundation of Our present ... Decay of Trade* (London, 1668) p. 3.
[13] For the argument that seventeenth-century republicanism was primarily a question of manners see Scott, *Commonwealth Principles*. On 17 June 1681 the merchant Samuel Atkins recorded: 'After Dinner wee ... came to Luca, a free state, under noe Subjection but its owne, being governed by ... Magistrates att ye Election of ye People ... small ... but very cleane, quiet and well govern'd, great restraints upon all vices ... the quietest place I ever saw, a Schene of great Malancholly.' NMM JOD/173 Journal of Samuel Atkins 1680–4 p. 39.

Not only are they powerful by sea and land, but they live without ostentation, without pomp, without emulation of one another. They are economical in their private expenses, and prodigal in their devotion to public affairs, for which each one toils as if for his private interests. They handle large sums of money, which they administer honestly, observing a severe discipline. They reward well, and punish severely.[14]

The following year (1651) the Brandenburg envoy Hermann Mylius recorded Master of Ceremonies Oliver Fleming claiming that under the republic 'no attention was paid to outward display; that men in Parliament with incomes of 60, 70 and more thousands of pounds sterling who maintain whole manors nowadays often go on foot, without servants, let themselves be served a wretched dinner (*those were his words*) and so go on'.[15] Oppenheim ascribed this to 'steel-edged' Puritanism, to be contrasted with 'sleek' Dutch prosperity.[16] But as we have seen, in English commendations of Dutch government and society sleekness did not arise. What was admired were excise, traffic, frugality, diligence and community. William Temple also remarked upon 'the simplicity and modesty of [Dutch] ... Magistrates in their way of living ... I never saw ... Vice-Admiral *De Ruiter* ... in Clothes better than the commonest Sea-Captain ... Pensioner *De Wit* ... was seen usually in the streets on foot and alone, like the commonest Burger of the Town.'[17]

If corruption had now been replaced by discipline, this was not simply the discipline of the sea. According to Mylius again: 'Never has there been seen an army more modest and ... scrupulously religious ... which submits so willingly and obediently to such strict discipline. Depravity, blasphemy, swearing, profanation of the Sabbath or any wantonness, in word or deed, are neither heard nor seen.'[18] In a reversal of Stuart fortunes, by 1651 the English republic had militarily united Britain and Ireland. This unprecedented achievement was accompanied by a proposal for Anglo-Dutch political union 'of the sort which Parliament had recently imposed, by force, on Scotland'.[19] The English republican project had developed from implementation of key Dutch policies to the attempted absorption of the United Provinces themselves.

---

[14] Quoted in Robert Brenner, *Merchants and Revolution: Commercial Change, Political Conflict, and London's Overseas Traders 1550–1653* (Princeton, 1993) p. 582.
[15] Quoted in Leo Miller, *John Milton and the Oldenburg Safeguard* (New York, 1985) p. 37. See also Milton's praise of republics in these terms: *The Readie and Easie Way to Establish a free Commonwealth* (2nd edn, 1660) in *Complete Prose Works* vol. VII pp. 424–5.
[16] Oppenheim, *Administration* p. 306.
[17] Temple, *Observations Upon the United Provinces* pp. 112–13.
[18] Miller, *Oldenburg Safeguard* p. 40.
[19] Israel, *The Dutch Republic* p. 714; Scott, *Commonwealth Principles* pp. 102–5.

The plan was, in the words of the commonwealth's newspaper *Mercurius Politicus*, that 'These two great republics ... equally hated by all monarchies in Europe ... [should] become as one entire body.' Between November 1651 and February 1652 John Milton made a series of entries from Machiavelli's *Discourses* in his manuscript Commonplace Book, including: 'That a federation or a league formed with a republic can be trusted more than one with a prince.' Needless to say this proposal was vigorously resisted by the Dutch. When military hostilities commenced in May 1652 negotiations in London were continuing for a 'nearer Union & Confoederacy then hath formerly beene', which would have allowed any Protestant citizen of either commonwealth to 'freely dwell and inhabite', own and inherit property, and enjoy full legal rights in the other.[20] The first Anglo-Dutch war was, among other things, the second Dutch war of independence.

In the policies of these years may be discerned the prehistory of the eighteenth-century British empire.[21] This intertwined land power, sea power, commercial, political and fiscal reform. The republican empire had British, American and European dimensions.[22] It is as occurring within this context that we must understand the second moment of early modern Anglo-Dutch proximity. This differed from the first in several ways. Now the initiative for union came from England. In addition it came from a government which had itself followed the United Provinces in becoming a religiously tolerant, maritime republic. Many historians (primarily those looking at it from a Dutch perspective) have seen the causes of the war which followed as primarily economic.[23] Using English sources a counter-analysis has been offered.[24] From this longer-term Anglo-Dutch perspective, however, the war can be seen as part of an English project with political, religious and economic dimensions.

The political ambition was to extend and defend European republicanism (or liberty) territorially by establishing it in a single state straddling the North Sea. English wartime propaganda made no attempt to deny that the United Provinces was a republic. 'Actions are the effects of Interests, from whom they proceed, and to whom they tend naturally as the stone doth downward ... For the Interests of Liberty, it is true,

---

[20] Leo Miller, *John Milton's Writings in the Anglo-Dutch Negotiations 1651–1654* (Pittsburgh, n.d.) p. 173.

[21] Jonathan Israel, 'The Emerging Empire: the Continental Perspective, 1650–1713', in Canny (ed.), *The Origins of Empire* p. 423; Armitage, *Ideological Origins* chs. 4–5.

[22] For republican ideologies of empire see Scott, *Commonwealth Principles* ch. 10.

[23] Charles Wilson, *Profit and Power: a Study of England and the Dutch Wars* (London, 1957); Jonathan Israel, 'England, the Dutch Republic and Europe in the Seventeenth Century', *Historical Journal* 40, 4 (1997) pp. 1117–21.

[24] Pincus, *Protestantism and Patriotism.*

they are in a condition of a Free State.'[25] It was because the United
Provinces had pursued the interests of a Free State while England lan-
guished under a monarchy governed by private favours and bribes that
the gap between their power and prosperity had become so great. The
problem with the Dutch republic was that it sought this liberty only self-
ishly. Indeed it was

so far from establishing others in the same condition, who have groaned under
the sad oppression of Tyrants; that it is known to *Europe*, how their great
designe hath been to be Free Men themselves, and to make the world ... their
slaves ... So far have they been from the true Principles of Freedom, which is
ready to make others as free as itself.[26]

The English republican understanding of liberty, by contrast, was imperial. Being God-given, liberty was compulsory ('till the whole *Creation*
that is now groaning under the exorbitant and wicked lusts of Kings and
great ones, whether in *Monarchies* or *States*, be delivered into freedom').[27]
This allows us to understand the religious content of England's Anglo-
Dutch imperial scheme. Concerning 'the Interest of the Protestant
Religion: True it is that it hath been there for many years professed, and
exercised ... and they have been a place of Refuge to many precious Saints,
from the bitter persecutions of the Enemies of God, and true Religion'.[28]
English republicans had reason to remember this, since so many of them
had previously been members of congregations in the United Provinces.
The problem with the United Provinces was, however, that 'all other
Religions, have had their professions there as well as the Protestant'. For
the safety not only of republicanism, but of Protestantism, liberty of conscience must be for Protestants only. During the interregnum, no less
than during the later Elizabethan period, English imperialism remained
confessional, making it, in this respect, more like its Spanish than its
Dutch counterpart.

   To say that the Anglo-Dutch union scheme was a political and religious project does not mean that it did not have an economic agenda.
On the contrary, its economic content was one of its most interesting
features. Within an economy and society which remained overwhelmingly agrarian the new policies were urban and mercantile. This reflected
the by now overwhelming fiscal and political dominance of London.
It equally reflected the Dutch economic and political model, with an
English Council of Trade, a lowering of customs duties, and simultaneous amplification of the country's navy and merchant marine. In the

[25] [Nedham], *The Case Stated Between England and the United Provinces* pp. 23, 29.
[26] Ibid. p. 29.   [27] Ibid. p. 53.   [28] Ibid. p. 23.

mercantilist mental world of finite resources, similitude of policy underlined the potential for conflict. Part of the interest of the union proposal
is that confederation was considered as an alternative. However, partly
because the English republic, itself a product of war, had its own cross-
channel security issues, if union could not be achieved by negotiation,
then it would be attempted by force.

One participant in the Anglo-Dutch naval war of 1652–4 was Richard
Gibson. Born in Great Yarmouth in 1635, son of a 'Master of a Shipp
of that Towne using the French trade', Gibson entered the navy at
age thirteen.[29] After service pursuing royalists off Portugal and in the
Mediterranean, he was appointed purser on the frigate *Assurance* on
6 January 1653. This was six weeks before Blake's crucial victory off
Portland on 20 February. Gibson left an account of this battle, during
which the *Assurance* had seventeen men killed and seventy-two wounded,
as well as of many other highlights of his thirty-six-year sea service.[30] This
was probably recorded at the behest of Samuel Pepys, to whom Gibson
became clerk and who recalled in 1667 Gibson at dinner 'telling me so
many good stories relating to the war [of 1652–4] and practices of commanders, which I will find a time to recollect: and he will be an admire-
able help to my writing a history of the Navy, if I ever do'.[31]

Pepys' *Diary* records a later conversation with Gibson as making 'me
understand so much of the victualling business and the pursers trade,
that I am shamed' at having previously known so little.[32] Gibson claimed
that during the period 1641–9 'the Bread and Beere for ye Fishery was
of the best ... And ... for Victualling the Navy'. He believed that commanders from 'the Newcastle Colliery ... knew best [how] to Ride the
Great Wooden Horses of the Navy ... For ... true Courage is presence of
minde in Danger; strengthened by Experience as every Collier Master
of a Ship in Winter ha[s].' Subsequently Gibson lamented the slaughter
of more than six hundred men aboard the *Royal James* in 1672 when

---

[29] Richard Gibson, 'Petition to the King concerning the mismanagement of the Navy', BL
Add MS 11602 f. 125. The date of Gibson's death is not known, but this document was
written after November 1714. See also Gibson, 'A Reformation in ye Royall Navy most
Humbly Proposed to His Majesty King George by Richard Gibsen Gent', BL Add MS
11602 f. 84.

[30] Richard Gibson, 'A few Instances of English Courage and Conduct at Sea within the
Memory of Richard Gibson', BL Add MS 11684 ff. 2–21. Published in S. R. Gardiner
and C. T. Atkinson (eds.), *Letters and Papers Relating to the First Dutch War, 1652–4*, vol. I
(London, 1899) pp. 2–30, see esp. pp. 13–17.

[31] Quoted in Richard Ollard, *Pepys: a Biography* (London, 1974) p. 194. Three years earlier
Sir William Coventry had suggested to Pepys that he write a history of the first Anglo-
Dutch war, 'which I am glad to hear, it being a thing I much desire, and sorts mightily
with my genius, and, if well done, may recommend me much' (ibid.).

[32] *The Diary of Samuel Pepys*, (eds.) R. C. Latham and W. Matthews (11 vols., London,
1971–83) vol. VI: 1665 pp. 315–16.

they could have been saved by one manoeuvre 'not known to any other
sort of Men than Seamen using the Newcastle Cole Trade for 70 yeares
past ... And such as at all times mann'd their Shipps without Pressing'.[33]
He recalled having been present when 'Hugh Peters in Harwich Church
in November 1653 told his Auditors that he had known severall English
Seamen Athiest [*sic*] but not one of them a Papist in all his life.'[34]

Gibson's strongest conviction was that 'no Nation or People of the
World ever put their Navy into the Hands of their Gentry but thereby
gave away the Command of the Sea'.[35] The reason 'why we arrived to
that high[t] of success by sea ... in the time of Rebellion' related both to
the manning of the navy and its administration. Under the republic the
Admiralty was 'managed by Comision, made up of meane industrious
and Experienced Men. And not by a Ld High Admll whose greatness or
Birth covers his inexperience partiality or sloth.' The Navy Committee
was 'made up of such as are more fitt for Accon then Council in a mixture of Seamen + Accomptants. And not Noblemen Worne out Seamen,
or Ignorant County Gentle[me]n.'[36]

Oppenheim agreed that, beginning with victualling arrangements,
naval administration was transformed under the republic. The 'most
striking point of difference' was that 'matters affecting the health and
comfort of seamen were not ignored as in previous periods'. This change
was 'even more clearly marked among captains, admirals and commissioners than among ... politicians, although members of the government
were doubtless not unaffected by the prevailing spirit'.[37] Specifically
Oppenheim supports Gibson's claim concerning the work of the

Navy Commissioners, who, so far as may be judged from the letters and papers
relating to them and their work, laboured with an attention to the minutest
details of their daily duties, a personal eagerness to ensure perfection, and a
broad sense of their ethical relation towards the seamen and workmen ... with
a success the Admiralty never attained before and has never equalled since.[38]

The implication of this judgement is that, if Britain ever came to rule the
waves, it was during and because of the republican interlude in English
(and then British) history, however short. In addition, Gibson continued,
'[O]ur floating Commonweales',[39] the ships themselves, were manned

[33] Gibson, 'Petition' pp. 126–7. On the Battle of Sole Bay and the fate of the *Royal James*
see John Spurr, *England in the 1670s: 'This Masquerading Age'* (Oxford, 2000) pp. 30–1.
[34] Gibson, 'A Reformation' f. 77.
[35] Ibid.   [36] Ibid. f. 86.   [37] Oppenheim, *Administration* p. 325.   [38] Ibid. p. 347.
[39] BL Add MS 22546 f.160, Sherwin to Major Burton, 27 January 1653[4?]. Bernard
Capp, *Cromwell's Navy*, agrees that 'The navy of the 1650s contained very few of the
gentleman-captains prominent in the 1630s and none of the aristocratic captains ... to
be found after the Restoration ... The interregnum navy probably came as near to providing a career open to talent as was possible in that age' (pp. 175, 185).

'By Seamen well chosen not only to Comand but to mennage every place of charge in a ship, and not Courtiers, Gentle[me]n, Decayed Cittizens or Pages'.[40] The qualifications of a seaman were industry, sobriety, valour, 'Experience, diligence + Honesty'. The first Anglo-Dutch war was won by 'Courage and Conduct', by putting merit in place of 'Bribery' and birth. It was won by these means against an adversary which had itself pioneered and perfected them.

[T]he then Long Parliamt by putting the Navy into ye Hands of ye Seamen … Secured London that depended soly on Trade; Recovered ye Revolted Shipps – And in a few yeares gave lawes to all Nations by sea. It was by Seamen under Count Van der Marke that ye Briell was taken from ye Spaniard. And afterwards the siege of Leiden raised by Prince Wm of Orange And by securing their Navigation the states of Holland got out of ye Spanish Tyrany and arrived at what they are.[41]

Gibson subsequently composed 'Heads of a Discourse between an English and Dutch Sea Captain how ye English came to Beate the Dutch at Sea in Anno 1652 + 1653'. Probably based on personal experience, this depicted a conversation in October 1653 between Captain Foster of the fourth rate frigate *Phoenix* and the Master of 'a Rich Dutch Shipp going to Stockholm' which he had taken as a prize.[42] Foster asked the Master why the Dutch had been tempted 'to make war on us' given England's strategic location in relation to Dutch trade:

the wind blowing westerly on our coast for more than three quarters of a year, did thereby make all our headlands and bays far better harbours than any they had? And that our country, like eagles' wings, lay extended over the body of theirs for 120 leagues from Scilly to the Maas in Holland one way, and thence to Orkney the other.

---

[40] Gibson, 'A Reformation' ff. 85–6 (and see ff. 57–61). This was an analysis initially prepared when 'The Late John Trenchard Secretary of State sent for me … to give him my opinion of the Errours of our Sea Conduct wch I gave him in my letter of 25 July 1693'. For correspondence of the republic's Navy Committee see Add MSS 18986, 22546.

[41] Gibson, 'A Reformation' f. 73.

[42] Richard Gibson, 'Heads of a Discourse between an English and Dutch Sea Captain how ye English came to Beate the Dutch at Sea in Anno 1652 + 1653', BL Add MS 11602 ff. 90–1. Another version, possibly in Gibson's hand, is: 'A Discourse then between an English Sea-Captaine and a Dutch-Skipper how the English came to Beate the Dutch at Sea', April 1654, BL Add MS 11684 ff. 30–2. The latter was published in Gardiner and Atkinson (eds.), *Letters and Papers Relating to the First Dutch War* pp. 31–3. Gibson gave a copy to Samuel Pepys, from whose papers it is reproduced in *Samuel Pepys' Naval Minutes*, (ed.) J. Tanner (London, 1926) Appendix II, pp. 447–9. There was a real *Phoenix*, which was taken as a Dutch prize on 7 September 1652 and taken back by English sailors led by Owen Cox in November. Cox remained captain until killed in action in July 1653. Oppenheim, *Administration* p. 345.

The 'ingenious Dutchman' replied that although this was true, following 'a successful war against the Spaniard … [they] were well skilled at sea' and England had 'but a small navy, like him that had one pair of breeches, which when torn, would oblige us to lay a bed till mended'. The Master went on to attribute Dutch defeat not to the unexpectedly capacious English naval wardrobe, but rather to political tampering with the Dutch sea command following a purge of Orangist officers in the aftermath of the death of William II in 1650. '[B]y this we came to fight you with gentlemen captains, and you us (by a like jealousy of turning out all the King's captains (that were gentlemen)) with seaman captains; by which you came to beat us.'

Gibson composed a history of the Elizabethan navy, finding

many Accidents to have happened for want of Tarrpawling Commanders, or Gentlemen thoroughly acquainted with Maritime Affaires, as may readily be seene by compareing the Conduct of Sr Francis Drake, Sr J Hawkins, Sr William Burroughs, Sr Martin Frobisher and Sr William Monson, wth that of my Lord Effingham, the Earles of Southhampton, + Cumberland, Lord Thomas Howard Sr Richard Lewsham Sr Richard Greenville, Capt Lister Sr Francis Veere, Sr William Brookes etc.[43]

He claimed that off the coast of Spain in 1590 the King of Spain had been too frightened to attack Drake and Frobisher's two ships with twenty of his own, when the former were 'knowne to be under the Command of Experienced and tryed Tarpawling Captaines … I further Observe that the Merchants were adventurous … with Sr Francis; as having full Assurance of his Courage and conduct.'

Yet, even if Gibson was correct that there was 'a naturall as well as accidentall Antipathy between ye Genius of a Seaman and their Gentlemen Commanders – As King Charles the first … found Experimentally true', how had the needs of the republic's navy been supplied in what remained an aristocratic and agrarian society?[44] Part of the answer lay, as it did in the United Provinces, in a close state-sponsored relationship between merchant and naval fleets. However, Gibson also emphasized the legislative creation of a military meritocracy which transcended the distinction between land and sea.

[43] Richard Gibson, 'Observations on Queen Elizabeth's gentlemen sea captains' ill-conduct', BL Add MS 11602, Item XVI, ff. 50–1.
[44] NMM REC/6, Item 16: [Richard Gibson], 'Discourse on our Naval Conduct' f. 268. Another two copies exist in BL Add MS 11602 ff. 37–41 and 43–9. The tract was published as *Reflections On Our Naval Strength*, in J. Knox Laughton (ed.), *The Naval Miscellany*, vol. II (London, 1912) pp. 149–68.

The ... Long Parliamt in King Charles ye 1st days, were brought so low as to bee forced to take the Covenant before the Scotts would assist them; And after that were not safe from the Treachery, Negligence Ignorance Cowardize + Covetousness of their Officers by Sea and Land until they came to ye Selfe denying Ordnance that no one Member of their Houses should hold any office in the Army, Navy, etc.[45]

The Self Denying Ordinance had forced the resignation of the Earl of Warwick as Lord Admiral as well as of the Earl of Essex as Lord General. The measure which created the New Model Army also facilitated a New Model Navy. Both administrative and fiscal-military modernization (along Dutch lines) had been crucial to the military achievements of the English republic. But for Gibson the transformation which this made possible was moral: the replacement of treachery, ignorance and covetousness with industry, experience and valour.

The same conclusion was reached by Algernon Sidney, a manager of the Anglo-Dutch war.

When Van Tromp set upon Blake in Foleston-Bay, the parliament had not above thirteen ships against threescore ... to oppose the best captain in the world ... Many other difficulties were observ'd in the unsettled state: Few ships, want of money, several factions ... But such was the power of wisdom and integrity in those that sat at the helm, and their diligence in chusing men only for their merit was blessed with such success, that in two years our fleets grew to be as famous as our land armies; the reputation and power of our nation rose to a greater height, than when we possessed the better half of France ... All the states, kings and potentates of Europe, most respectfully, not to say submissively, sought our friendship; and Rome was more afraid of Blake and his fleet, than they had been of the great king of Sweden, when he was ready to invade Italy with a hundred thousand men.[46]

Like Gibson, Sidney here set praise of this achievement within the context of credit due to the Dutch. Even mariners petitioning the Lord Protector against impressment in October 1654 complained not only, as the Levellers had in 1647, that the practice was 'inconsistent with the principles of Freedom and Liberty', the 'fruits of all their bloodshed and hardships', but begged that 'your petitioners may be as free as the Dutch seamen, against whom they have been such instruments in the Lord's hands'.[47]

---

[45] Gibson, 'A Reformation' f. 68.
[46] Algernon Sidney, *Discourses Concerning Government*, (ed.) Thomas West (Indianapolis, Ind., 1992) pp. 278–9; Scott, *Algernon Sidney and the English Republic* pp. 100–2.
[47] *An Agreement of the People for a firm and present peace* (1647), in Kenyon, *The Stuart Constitution* p. 275; *Resolutions at a Council of War* quoted by Oppenheim, *Administration* p. 318. This joins other evidence against the thesis that sailors' interests were purely material.

It has become a commonplace to say that in 1649 England experienced a political and religious, but not a social, revolution. However, it is the implication of the contemporary commentary quoted here that there was a social transformation of military government, and of government policy and culture. Alongside the dramatic improvement in competence, elimination of gentleman officers from the fleet certainly had a social impact.

It is ... from this period that dates that sense of solidarity among officers and men which is at once the sign and consequence of an organized and continuous service ... between 1642 and 1660 every available English sailor must have passed a large portion of those years on the state's ships; and the captains and officers were kept in nearly continuous employment, with the result of the formation of a class feeling, and the growth of especial manners and habits, characteristic of men working under conditions which removed them from frequent contact with their fellows. The numerous notices in Restoration literature of the particular appearance, modes of expression, and bearing, stamping the man of war officer – references never before made – show how rapidly the new circumstances had produced their effect.[48]

The frontispiece to Marchamont Nedham's English translation of Selden's *Dominion of the Sea* (1652) explained: '[Since before] the old *Roman* Invasion ... the Soveraigntie of the Seas flowing about this Island ... has ... been held ... as an inseperable appendant of the British Empire.' Following the republic's triumphs on land 'the eyes of all the world, are fixt upon the carriage and conduct of this noble enterprise by Sea'.[49]

We cannot tell what might have happened had this government not been driven out by an army coup before the war's end. What followed, in the Protectorate, was an attempt to reorient not only foreign, but social, economic, religious and political policy. Government strategy and structures became more monarchical and religiously traditional, and less anti-aristocratic. This was so both politically, with the eventual establishment of an Other House, and economically, with gradual re-establishment of the social and political predominance of landowners over merchants. In an agrarian ex-kingdom 'healing and settling' could not be achieved any other way.

This is one context for understanding the republican masterpiece of the interregnum: James Harrington's *The Commonwealth of Oceana* (1656). Underlining his maritime title Harrington's Introduction contained a

---

[48] Oppenheim, *Administration* p. 355.
[49] Marchamont Nedham, Epistle Dedicatorie, in John Selden, *Of the Dominion, Or, Ownership of the Sea* (London, 1652).

flourish: 'The Sea giveth law unto the growth of *Venice*, but the growth of *Oceana* giveth law unto the Sea.' To take as his model Venice, rather than Amsterdam, was to open a door to aristocratic republicanism. Like More's *Utopia*, and more explicitly, *Oceana* was a geographic figure for England.[50] Yet, like *Utopia* again, and to a far greater extent, what is striking about Harrington's model is its absence of maritime reference. Indeed, unlike More, Harrington was in favour of not only agriculture but aristocracy; and against money, maritime states and economies.

This is partly because Harrington was a gentleman.[51] Sharply critical of the Rump parliament, *Oceana* was dedicated to 'the Lord Protector of The Common-Wealth of *England*; *Scotland*, and *Ireland*' by a former confidant of Charles I.[52] If Harrington's model was a republic, it was one led by a landowning nobility (and cavalry). 'There is something first in the making of a *Common-wealth*, then in the governing of her, and last of all in the leading of her Armies ... peculiar unto the Genius of a Gentleman.'[53] One cannot imagine this last claim being made by Cromwell, let alone Gibson. 'Mechanic' republics (Athens, Holland, Switzerland and the Rump) were unfavourably contrasted by Harrington with aristocratic ones (Sparta, Rome, Venice).[54]

This stance distinguished Harrington not only from most contemporary English republicans, but from his most important sources. Machiavelli's preference for social 'equality' had been one of his few points of agreement with More.[55] This was the point that 'Machiavel hath missed ... very narrowly and more dangerously ... [when] he speaks of the gentry as hostile to popular governments, and of popular governments as hostile to the gentry'. The cause of this error was Machiavelli's ignorance of the doctrine of the balance of dominion. In fact, 'a nobility or gentry in a popular government, not overbalancing it, is the very life and soul of it'.[56]

Urban and maritime republics (Athens and the United Provinces) were dismissed by Harrington as prone to turbulency. The political economy

---

[50] Nelson, *The Greek Tradition* pp. 103–6.
[51] A description applied during Harrington's interrogation after the restoration which he agreed 'I value'. *The Examination of James Harrington*, *The Political Works of James Harrington*, (ed.) J.G.A. Pocock (Cambridge, 1977) p. 856.
[52] James Harrington, *The Common-Wealth of Oceana* (London, 1656) Title Page.
[53] Harrington, *Oceana* (1656) p. 25.
[54] James Harrington, *The Commonwealth of Oceana*, (ed.) J.G.A. Pocock (Cambridge, 1992) p. 138.
[55] Niccolò Machiavelli, *Discourses*, (ed.) B. Crick (Harmondsworth, 1985) pp. 245–7: 'those states where political life survives uncorrupted, do not permit any of their citizens to live after the fashion of the gentry. On the contrary, they maintain there perfect equality ... where the gentry are numerous, no one who proposes to set up a republic can succeed unless he first gets rid of the lot.'
[56] Harrington, *Oceana*, (ed.) Pocock (1992) p. 15.

of *Oceana* was agrarian ('the Country way of life, though of a grosser spinning ... [is] the best stuffe of a Common-wealth').[57] *Oceana*'s military model was not Athens or Venice, but Rome ('the Tillage bringing up a good Souldiery, bringeth up a good Common-Wealth').[58] Astonishingly, despite the book's title, Oceana's navy was not discussed. This contrasted strikingly with other celebrations of the republic's 'Arks of War ... An hideous shole of wood-Leviathans' which had defeated the Dutch.[59]

If Harrington liked his military dry, the Lord Protector would not have been shaken, but stirred. One possible explanation for Harrington's title relates to his later claim that the commonwealth was a ship. Another underlined his claim to have identified the medium (a popular balance of dominion) in which Hobbes' 'great LEVIATHAN' must swim.[60] In a world of material in perpetual motion, the best government was not by a single person ('modern prudence') but by a community of citizens within which office rotated.

This was to say that if Harrington accepted Hobbes' natural philosophy (as he did) what he derived from it was an alternative political philosophy. Harrington's Hobbesian assumptions (he used both *Leviathan* and Hobbes' translation of Thucydides) further contextualize his association of Athens and Holland with turbulency. Like *Leviathan*, *Oceana* is suspicious not only of democracy, but of merchants and trade. These are economies where the wealth is like water; they lack solidity.[61] Istvan Hont has remarked upon Hobbes' 'anti-commercial' stance.[62] John Pocock has generalized from the case of Harrington concerning a broader republican tension between virtue and commerce. However, most English republican writers were in favour of maritime, commercial and naval power. In classical materials, particularly relating to Athens and Phoenicia, they found plenty to support this position.[63] Among republicans it was Harrington who was peculiar, and one of the reasons was Hobbes.

Where Harrington was at one with other republicans was in his commitment to empire. On this point, partly no doubt to assist Cromwell, he

[57] Harrington, *Oceana* (1656) Introduction p. 2.   [58] Ibid. p. 4.
[59] Marvell, *The First Anniversary* pp. 111–12.
[60] Scott, *Commonwealth Principles* pp. 165–6, 184; Hobbes, *Leviathan* pp. 9, 120; see Jonathan Scott, 'James Harrington's Prescription for Healing and Settling', in Michael Braddick and David Smith (eds.), *The Experience of Revolution in Seventeenth Century England* (Cambridge, 2011).
[61] Scott, 'James Harrington's Prescription'; Jonathan Scott, 'The Rapture of Motion: James Harrington's Republicanism', in Nicholas Phillipson and Quentin Skinner (eds.), *Political Discourse in Early Modern Britain* (Cambridge, 1993); Scott, 'Peace of Silence' (2000).
[62] Istvan Hont, *Jealousy of Trade: International Competition and the Nation-State in Historical Perspective* (Cambridge, Mass., 2005) pp. 17–19.
[63] Scott, *Commonwealth Principles* pp. 93–8, and chapters 2 above and 8 below.

even broke with Hobbes.[64] *Oceana*'s empire began with the absorption already effected of two neighbouring kingdoms. Ireland, 'soft mother of a slothful and pusillanimous people ... almost depopulated for shaking the yoke', had now been 'replanted with a new race. But (through what virtues of the soil, or vice of the air soever ...) they come still to degenerate.'[65] Harrington's solution was to settle the island with 'Jews, allowing them their own rites and laws ... [with] a fruitful country and good ports too, they would be good at both' agriculture and trade.

Rather than being expropriated, Scotland was 'incorporated' with England, with representation at Westminster and privileges of free trade. This 'federation' was based on the Roman model recommended by Machiavelli, of 'unequal leagues'. Harrington approved this arrangement, specifying, however, that for the incorporation to work, like the Dutch the Scots would have to manifest an interest in 'the liberty of mankind' (not just the liberty of themselves) and that the Scottish nobility ('who [had] governed that country much after the manner of Poland') would have to be destroyed.

In line with Cromwell's own perspective, Harrington's defence of empire was godly and apocalyptic. 'For which cause ... the orders last rehearsed are buds of empire, such as, with the blessing of God, may spread the arms of your commonwealth like an holy asylum unto the distressed world, and give the earth her Sabbath of years or rest from her labours, under the shadow of your wings.'[66] Harrington wrote this at a time when the establishment of the Protectorate was leading other godly republicans to worry that military power was corrupting the cause.

Many men has war made great whom peace makes small ... Unless you expel avarice, ambition, and luxury from your minds, yes, and extravagance from your families as well, you will find at home and within that tyrant who, you believed, was to be sought abroad and in the field ... In fact many tyrants, impossible to endure, will from day to day hatch out from your very vitals.[67]

It was, in the view of others, by this tyrant within that the republican experiment had been destroyed in 1653. Meanwhile, Harrington described 'islands' (British, Irish and Venetian) as having been 'designed by God for a commonwealth'. Finally, as a good Platonist Harrington

---

[64] Hont, *Jealousy of Trade* p. 18. Hont correctly sees this move as Machiavellian but doesn't note that the language in which it is celebrated comes from the Old Testament. David Armitage, 'The Cromwellian Protectorate and the Languages of Empire', *The Historical Journal* 35, 3 (1992).

[65] Harrington, *Political Works* p. 6.   [66] Ibid. p. 323.

[67] John Milton, *Second Defence of the English People* (1654), in *Complete Prose Works* vol. IV pp. 680–1.

understood his constitution itself as a ship. It was the fabric of timbers which would keep the passengers from getting wet.

[Y]our orders will be worth little if they do not hold you unto them; wherefore embark. They are like a ship; if you be once aboard, you do not carry them but they you. And see how Venice stands unto her tackling; you will no more forsake them than you will leap into the sea. But they are very many [Oceana had thirty orders], and difficult. O my lords, what seaman casts away his card because it hath four and twenty points of compass? And yet those are very near as many and as difficult as the orders in the whole circumference of your commonwealth. Consider how we have been tossed with every wind of doctrine, lost by the glib tongues of your demagogues and grandees in our own havens![68]

These assumptions about shape and movement (the commonwealth a circle, its citizens in perpetual rotation) were fundamental to Harrington's natural philosophy and physics. The novelty of his doctrine of constitutional navigation only became clear during debates with other republicans in 1659.

Harrington's summary of the arguments of *Oceana* in that year was *The Art of Lawgiving* (20 February 1659). Its analysis of the contemporary economic and political situation was supported in Richard Cromwell's parliament, and within the restored Rump, by Henry Neville among others. Neville was a co-author of *The Armies Dutie* (1659), which had reiterated *Oceana*'s argument that 'it is essentially necessary to the securitie of freedome, that the same assemblie should never have the debating and finally resolving power in them, least it suddenly degenerates into an Oligarchie or Tyrannie of some few … as … in the long Parliament, who exercising both the debating and determining power, were strongly tempted to have made themselves perpetually legislators'.[69]

On 13 May the Rump received a *Humble Petition and Address of the Officers of the Army*, requesting that the government 'may be in a Representative of the People, consisting of a House successively chosen by the People in such a way … as this Parliament shall judge meet, and of a select Senate, Co-ordinate in Power, of able and faithful persons, eminent for Godliness, and such as continue adhering to this Cause'.[70] In advancing this proposal the officers' most important ally was Henry Vane (supported by Milton). Three days later the *Humble Petition* was attacked by Harrington in *A Discourse upon this saying: The Spirit of the Nation is not yet to be trusted with Liberty; lest it introduce Monarchy, or invade the Liberty*

---

[68] Harrington, *Political Works* p. 145.   [69] Ibid. p. 25.
[70] Austin Woolrych, 'Historical Introduction', in Milton, *Complete Prose Works* vol. VII p. 72.

of Conscience (16 May 1659). The officers were instructed to 'Detest the base itch of a narrow oligarchy. If your commonwealth be rightly instituted, seven years will not pass ere your clusters of parties, civil and religious, vanish.'

This would follow both from the balance of dominion, established by God, and from 'the frame of your commonwealth'.

> The mariner trusteth not unto the sea, but to his ship. The spirit of the people is no wise to be trusted with their liberty, but by stated laws or orders; so the trust is not in the spirit of the people, but in the frame of those orders, which, as they are tight or leaky, are the ship out of which the people, being once embarked, cannot stir, and without which they can have no motion.[71]

Oceana's orders were the timbers enabling motion across the sea. For Milton, when the ship was sinking, after a decade of 'disturbances, interruptions and dissolutions', it was utterly perverse to continue arguing about the future relationship of the crew. 'The ship of the Commonwealth is alwaies under sail; they sit at the stern; and if they stear well, what need is ther to change them; it being rather dangerous?'[72] Later Algernon Sidney named Plato as his source for the view that it was 'a most desperate and mischievous madness, for a company going to the Indies, to give the guidance of their ship to the son of the best pilot in the world'.[73]

For Harrington, by contrast, the only foundation of 'peace and safetie' was an adequate constitutional settlement. 'A commonwealth ... swerveth not from her principles, but by and through her institution ... a commonwealth that is rightly instituted can never swerve.'[74] Amid the present storm, what was needed was not expert seamanship (or military strategy) but the launching of a vessel so technically sophisticated as to be capable of securing its own course.[75] 'To say that a man may not write of government except he be a magistrate, is as absurd as to say that a man may not make a sea-card unless he be a pilot. It is known that Christopher Columbus made a card in his cabinet that found out the Indies.'[76]

---

[71] James Harrington, *A Discourse upon this saying*, in *Political Works* pp. 737–8.
[72] Milton, *Readie and Easie Way* pp. 433–4.
[73] Algernon Sidney, *Discourses Concerning Government*, in *Sydney on Government: the Works of Algernon Sydney*, (ed.) J. Robertson (London, 1772) pp. 61–2.
[74] James Harrington, *Oceana*, in *Political Works* p. 321.
[75] 'But ... if it be discovered once unto common understanding that monarchy is impracticable, then in cometh the commonwealth, not by halves, but with all her tackling, full sail, in her streamers, and with top and top-gallant.' James Harrington, *The Art of Lawgiving*, in *Political Works* p. 700.
[76] James Harrington, *The Prerogative of Popular Government*, in *Political Works* p. 395.

A century later this innovation was recognized by David Hume who compared the question of whether 'one form of government must be allowed more perfect than another, independent of the manners and humors of particular men' to the discussion among 'The mathematicians in EUROPE ... concerning that figure of a ship, which is the most commodious for sailing'. In relation to which, 'All plans of government, which suppose great reformation in the manners of mankind, are plainly imaginary. Of this nature, are the *Republic* of PLATO, and the *Utopia* of Sir THOMAS MORE. The OCEANA is the only valuable model of a commonwealth, that has as yet been offered to the public.'[77]

Through Gibson and Harrington this chapter has visited the polarities of republican perspective upon the interregnum. These were pre- and post-1653; practical and theoretical; privately and publicly argued; wet and dry; anti- and pro-aristocratic; Amsterdam (or Athens) and Venice. The continuous themes were war and empire, and ships: arks of war and of peace.

Restoration of British monarchy in 1660 posed a test for the theories of Harrington and Gibson. Given a popular balance of dominion, Harrington believed that monarchy could not last. 'Let ... [the King] come-in, and call a Parliament of the greatest Cavaliers in England, so they be men of Estates, and let them sett but 7 yeares, and they will all turn Common-wealthe's men.'[78] This opinion was not greatly appreciated, and interrogation and imprisonment followed. Gibson had not published his views. But with the return of monarchy came that of gentleman naval officers.

---

[77] David Hume, 'Idea of a Perfect Commonwealth', in Hume, *Political Essays*, (ed.) Knud Haakonssen (Cambridge, 1994) pp. 221–2.
[78] John Aubrey, *Aubrey's Brief Lives*, (ed.) Oliver Lawson Dick (London, 1958) p. 125.

5   Blowing a dead coal

Out of a fired ship, which, by no way
But drowning could be rescued from the flame,
Some men leaped forth, and ever as they came
Near the foes' ships, did by their shot decay;
So all were lost, which in the ship were found,
They in the sea being burnt, they in the burnt ship drowned.

John Donne, *A Burnt Ship*[1]

Gentlemen officers were restored, in the later account of Sir Henry Sheres, to 'Counterballance' the 'Seamen ... very much inclined to favour the party of [Edward Montagu] the Earle of Sandwich'.[2] It was, that is to say, to leaven an opinionatedly republican navy sufficiently to make it an instrument of royal power. Gibson, after becoming clerk to Pepys, was told by him that 'the King + Duke [of York] were for Gentle[me]n to comand in the Navy rather then Seamen'.[3] Following the Glorious Revolution Gibson opined that 'the designe of the Late King Charles ye 2 + James ye 2d [was] to bring Gentlemen into ye Navy to Introduce Arbitrary Govermt + Popery'.[4] In the formulation of Charles II himself: 'I am not for the imploying of men merely for quality, yet when men of quality are fitt for the trade they desire to enter into, I thinke it is reasonable they should be encouraged at least equally with others.'[5]

Both Charles and his brother James took a close interest in the navy. James became Lord High Admiral and saw personal military service, until he was narrowly missed by a cannon shot which killed several colleagues. During secret negotiations with France between 1668 and 1670 the one interest of state Charles showed himself determined to defend

---

[1] John Donne, *The Complete English Poems*, (ed.) A.J. Smith (Harmondsworth, 1986) p. 149.
[2] Sir Henry Sheres, 'A Discourse touching ye Decay of our Naval Discipline by Sr H Sheers' [1694], NMM REC/4 Item 4 p. 3.
[3] Gibson, 'A Reformation' f. 76.   [4] Ibid. f. 85 (and see f. 127).
[5] Quoted in J.D. Davies, *Gentlemen and Tarpaulins: the Officers and Men of the Restoration Navy* (Oxford, 1991) p. 33.

was the navy and English maritime power. Both brothers respected the naval achievements of the interregnum and were determined to preserve them.

Whereas the army was largely disbanded by 1661, the republic's fleet remained intact. While the ships were renamed (the *Naseby* becoming the *Royal Charles*, the *Dunbar* the *Henry* and the *Marston Moor* the *York*), most of the large vessels had been built between 1649 and 1653.[6] The navy became the most expensive department of state, accounting for more than 20 per cent of government expenditure.[7] It was also, employing the group of civil servants around Samuel Pepys, one of the most reform-minded and talented.[8]

The restored Stuarts also understood the political importance of mercantile activity and customs revenue. It was during the period 1660–88 that the gap began to close between the comparative value of imports of the English and Dutch East India companies, in part because of English imports (and re-exports) of Indian calicoes.[9] It was customs revenues which permitted Charles II to reign from 1681 until 1685 without parliament. England's presence in India as well as the Mediterranean had been enhanced by the territorial acquisitions attached to Charles' Portuguese marriage (Bombay and Tangiers).

In 1660 the Duke of York co-founded the Royal African Company, which immediately took a share of the Atlantic slave trade (forty-thousand African captives in the first six years).[10] If the restored Stuarts were not sufficiently merchant-minded (or Dutch-minded) to replace customs revenues with excise tax, nor were they administratively reactionary. There was no attempt to restore parliamentary subsidies (or crown lands). Assessment and excise were lowered but retained, and supplemented by new taxes like 'chimney money' (1662). Valuable interregnum political figures like Anthony Ashley Cooper, military ones like Montagu and civil servants like George Downing were kept on.

In 1660 Downing rewrote and improved the commonwealth's Navigation Act. In 1663 this was supplemented by the 'Act for the Encouragement of Trade', or Staple Act, which extended to European exports to the plantations controls similar to those now applying to

[6] Frank Fox, *Great Ships: the Battlefleet of King Charles II* (Greenwich, 1980) pp. 55–7.
[7] Davies, *Gentlemen* p. 15.
[8] Pepys found Gibson in particular 'mighty understanding and acquainted with all things in the Navy': *Diary*, vol. IX p. 16.
[9] Niels Steensgaard, 'The Growth and Composition of the Long-Distance Trade of England and the Dutch Republic before 1750', in James Tracy (ed.), *The Rise of Merchant Empires: Long Distance Trade in the Early Modern World* (1990).
[10] Philip Curtin, *The Atlantic Slave Trade, a Census* (Madison, Wisc., 1969) pp. 119, 216.

Map 4 The facing estuaries of the Scheldt, Maas, Rhine and Thames
constituted a single zone of maritime interaction. Map based on 'The
southern North Sea and the narrow seas', in N. A. M. Rodger, *The Command
of the Ocean: a Naval History of Britain, 1649–1815* (New York, 2005) p. xxx.

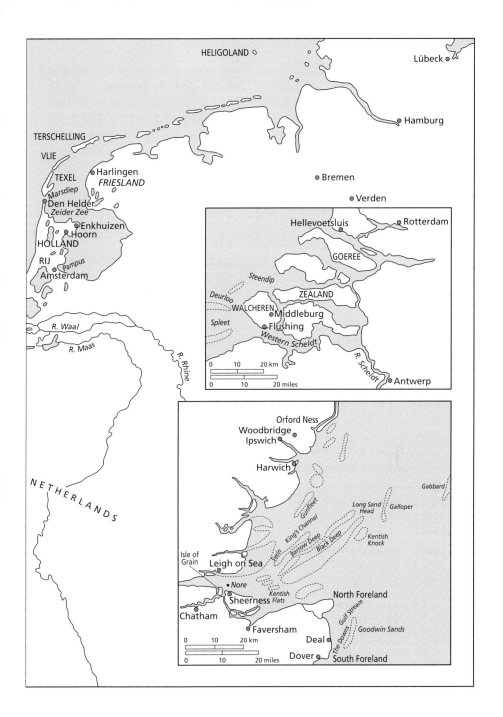

imports. During a reign in which American settlement was vigorously pursued, Cromwell's conquest of Jamaica (1655) became in 1661 the first new crown colony since Virginia, and Ashley Cooper as Earl of Shaftesbury helped found the new territory of Carolina. While the King's wish to establish liberty of conscience in England was twice frustrated (1662, 1672), enough of the new colonies allowed it (Maryland, Carolina, Pennsylvania) to furnish not only additional destinations for nonconformists, but the impression of an alternative colonial royal religious policy.[11] The republic's Council of Trade was retained. In 1673 the Plantation Act gave customs commissioners and their deputies greatly enhanced powers in relation to colonial governments reminiscent of the English republic's trade legislation of 1649–51.[12]

All this would appear to have established a promising context for the regime's first naval war, against the Dutch between 1665 and 1667. For members of the Anglican Cavalier parliament, this was religiously and politically motivated against a 'fanatic [religiously heterodox] republic'. It was supported by the mercantile community in London, and emboldened by a belief in England's strategic geographical advantage (in relation to the routes of Dutch trade) and by memories of the victory of 1652–4. It was a notably cynical act of aggression, not to say piracy, animated by Downing and supported with extraordinary generosity by parliament to the tune of more than two million pounds.[13] It became a disaster from which not only the reign of Charles II, but the Cavalier conception of restoration never recovered.[14]

It was naive to expect a repetition of 1652–4 not only because the English military-fiscal-political situation was very different. The Dutch had given that earlier devastating conflict much thought and were engaged in an energetic programme of shipbuilding. There was also the problem – though in practice it turned out to be a detail – that the United Provinces were allied to France. The first year of the war was closely fought, despite the worst outbreak of bubonic plague in London's history

[11] Ogilby, *America* pp. 185, 212.
[12] Bliss, *Revolution and Empire* p. 174; Hilary Beckles, 'The "Hub of Empire": the Caribbean and Britain in the Seventeenth Century', in Canny (ed.), *The Origins of Empire* p. 236; Scott, 'Good Night Amsterdam' pp. 351–2; Games, *Web of Empire* pp. 290–2.
[13] Scott, 'Good Night Amsterdam'.
[14] Scott, *England's Troubles* chs. 17–18. In 'The Impeachment of the Earl of Clarendon', *Cambridge Historical Journal* 13, 1 (1957) Clayton Roberts argued that the fallout from this crisis permanently diminished royal autonomy in England by exposing it to more effective and continuous scrutiny by the House of Commons. However, in 1689 a Dutch invasion proved necessary to allow a 'parliament' to be summoned and to inaugurate the war against France which members had been demanding since 1673. In the short term the fallout from Chatham involved a diminution of the autonomy of the entire English government as the country became a client of France.

killing a quarter of its population (100,000 people). The following year, however, the military tide began to turn, money ran out, and London was decapitated by fire (described by Edward Hyde, Earl of Clarendon, as 'the highest calamity this nation hath ever felt'[15]).

These developments had already seriously affected public confidence – reviving alarms about the ever-present popish plot – even before the hammer blow which ended the war in 1667. Piloted by English republican exiles, the Dutch fleet sailed unopposed into the mouth of the Thames, then up the Medway, where it set fire to a barely defended fleet at Chatham dockyard and towed the flagship *Royal Charles* back to the Netherlands. 'The dismay that is upon us all in the business of the kingdom and Navy at this day', wrote Pepys, 'is not to be expressed.'[16] Pepys gave his alarm concrete expression by sending Gibson to Huntingdon with a thousand guineas in cash to bury in his back garden 'under colour of [sending] an express to Sir Jer: Smith'.[17] In the words of Jeremy Bentham, 'There is general consternation and wonder that we were in no readiness to receive the enemy ... how strangely were all our counselors lulled into a dead sleep of security that nothing less than so mortal a blow and irreparable loss should awaken them.'[18]

More than the Glorious Revolution, Chatham was England's anti-1588. With a war on, the government had taken the day off. With the loss of fourteen great ships, including some of the best in the fleet, the raid was a military as well as political catastrophe.[19] What the prospects were for an administration which could not send its fleet to sea in wartime, or defend it on the edge of its own capital city, were far from clear.

It was very lucky for all concerned that the Dutch administration of Johann De Witt saw fit to exploit this triumph by making peace (though, needless to say, on Dutch terms).[20] It was the official doctrine of the De Witt regime, expounded in a tract of which a manuscript translation survives in Pepys' papers, that the lifeblood of the Dutch republic was trade, for which the imperative was peace.[21] Nevertheless, the descent on Chatham demonstrated something which remained lodged in minds on both sides of the channel. Without 'mastery of the seas', the most important fact about English geography was not its supposed insularity.

---

[15] Quoted in Pincus, *Protestantism and Patriotism* p. 346.
[16] Pepys, *Diary* vol. VIII: 1667 pp. 268–9.   [17] Ibid. p. 263; Ollard, *Pepys* p. 165.
[18] Quoted in Pincus, *Protestantism and Patriotism* pp. 417–18.
[19] Fox, *Great Ships* pp. 92–4.   [20] Pincus, *Protestantism and Patriotism* pp. 402–3.
[21] Pepys Library, Magdalene College, Cambridge, MS 2888: 'The political grounds and maxims of the Republic of Holland and West Friesland', translation by Toby Bonnell of *Aanwysing der heilsam politike Gronden en Maximen van de Republicke van Holland en West-Vriesland* (Leiden and Rotterdam, 1669).

It was the location of the Thames estuary opposite those of the Scheldt, the Maas and the Rhine, creating a single maritime zone of cultural, economic and military interaction.[22] When Dutch political circumstances changed, adding alongside the peacemongering regents a reinstated and militarily ambitious Stadtholder, the consequences for England might be dramatic.

Following his return from Huntingdon where he had delivered most of Pepys' money (save for what sadly fell out of a broken bag[23]), Gibson composed a blistering analysis of Chatham. This repudiated charges which had been levelled at 'inferior officers' within the naval administration such as himself.[24] These were 'either for not bringing up the great shipps, especially the Charles, in ye midst of the consternation … or for using his Mats boates to save theire goods at such a time as … those very Boates being well mann'd might have preserved his Mats Shipps from burning'.[25] Gibson found little merit in these charges, 'nor matters it much in wch stable ye Horses stood when ye Principll Doore leading to every roome was left open'. Nobody 'imagined that ye Enemy would have sent up 5 or 6 Fireshipps above Upnor Castle without some men of Warr to defend them'.[26] What then was the explanation for this astonishing audacity, or perhaps intelligence? By far the most important problem was the negligence of 'Principll Officers' in preparing and fortifying the waterway.

Core defence was 'Five Guard shipps & a Chaine the meanest contrivance against an Ennemy wth a Briske Easterly winde that could ever bee thought on'.[27] 'Fireshipps … would have proved of great use but they were (by whose Councell I know not) sunk under pretence of stopping up the River wch also proved frivolous.' A 'Fort at ye Ness' ordered to be built a year earlier was three days before the raid 'to ye Seaward … not 12 inches high', equipped with eight guns without firing platforms. At Tilbury 'the carriages being rotted & the Guns dismounted', there was anyway 'a very insufficient quantity of powder'. All of this suggested 'supineness, insufficiency or treason in some of our Prime Officers'.[28]

[22] Haley, *The British and the Dutch* p. 9.
[23] Gibson estimated the number of lost coins as one or two, Pepys as up to twenty. Ollard, *Pepys* p. 167; Pepys, *Diary* vol. VIII: 1667 pp. 268, 272–3, 473–4, 487.
[24] Ollard, *Pepys* p. 167; [Richard Gibson], 'The Dutch Action at Chatham Examined', BL Add MS 11684 ff. 31–3. Gibson's authorship is not certain. The document is signed 'JM'. But it is among Gibson's papers, apparently in his hand, and the tone is vintage Gibson. Both the existence of the manuscript and some indeterminacy regarding authorship are presumably explained by Gibson's (and Pepys') liability for investigation.
[25] [Gibson], 'The Dutch Action' f. 32a.   [26] Ibid. f. 32b.
[27] Ibid. f. 31a.   [28] Ibid. f. 31b.

Anticipating 'ye enquirys that would best become ye wisdome sagacity & grandure of our king & Parliamt' (a pattern of capitalization characteristic of republican writing), Gibson became specific.[29]

Who braged of ye Strength & safety of that Port in ye midle of Aprill in case ye Enemy attacks it wth 40 Men of Warr; who wrott … to Sr Wm Coventry ye beginning of June assureing ye strength and safe condition of that place; Who permitted a Vessell of Flaunders with … 15 Pipes of choice Canary Wines … whereof ye licencer had one pipe for his share wch hee sold for 55 pounds to come up that River contrary to Orders from ye Councell … who was ye author of sinkeing our 5 Fireshipps … in such places as did not at all hinder ye Enemys approach. Who placed our Two Guardshipps so neare wthin ye Chaine ignorantly or traitorously that … the enemys Fireshipps burnt them without ever passing over the Chaine[.] Who should have provided Boates to have saved the many hundreds of Brave Men aboard ye Guardshipps … Who carried away ye Henrietta & Jemmy pleasure Boates wth a few gazeing Principll Officers & other Idle Spectators at ye very moment when those Boates might … have saved ye life of many a brave Man who for want thereof was either drowned like ye Old World or burned like Gomorra.[30]

Decades earlier the possibility of just such a disaster at Chatham had been predicted by Sir William Monson, should the Dutch 'become enemies to us'.[31] Monson had counselled powerful coastal fortifications, constant vigilance and heavily armed ships. Meanwhile, several aspects of Gibson's post-mortem, with names added, were echoed by Andrew Marvell's *Last Instructions to a Painter*. This lamented the Thames, where

> … our sick Ships unrigg'd in Summer lay,
> Like molting Fowl, a weak and easie Prey …
> Once a deep River, now with Timber floor'd,
> And shrunk, lest Navigable, to a Ford.
> Now (nothing more at *Chatham* left to burn)
> The *Holland* Squadron leisurely return:
> And spight of *Ruperts* and of *Albemarles*,
> To *Ruyter*'s Triumph lead the captive *Charles* …
> When aged *Thames* was bound with Fetters base,
> And *Medway* chast ravish'd before his Face …
> Sad change, since first that happy pair was wed,
> When all the Rivers grac'd their Nuptial Bed;
> And Father *Neptune* promis'd to resign
> His Empire old, to their immortal Line![32]

The captive *Charles* was a powerful metaphor. After touching savagely upon most public figures, female and male, Marvell showed the King

[29] Ibid. f. 33b.   [30] Ibid. ff. 32b–33a.   [31] Monson, *Tracts*, Book V pp. 12, 5–15.
[32] Marvell, *Poems and Letters* vol. I pp. 154, 158–9.

tormented by visions of his murdered predecessors, Henry IV of France and Charles I:

> *Harry* sits down, and in his open side
> The grizly Wound reveals, of which he dy'd.
> And ghastly *Charles*, turning his Collar low,
> The purple thread about his Neck does Show:
> Then, whisp'ring to his Son in Words unheard,
> Through the lock'd door both of them disappear'd.[33]

The other bestselling satire inspired by Chatham was Henry Neville's *The Isle of Pines … A late Discovery … near Terra Australis Incognita* (London, 1668). George Pines was an Elizabethan book-keeper ship-wrecked on an uninhabited island in the East Indies with four women: his merchant Master's daughter, two maids and an African slave. '[T]hey were all handsome Women, when they had Cloathes', which was not for long, and they clung to George excessively, he 'being now all their stay in this lost condition'. Their condition could have been worse, since the island was large, 'ever warm … always … green', devoid of harmful animals, and blessed with food. It could have been much worse for George, for whom 'Idleness and fullness' led to sex, first with two women, and then with all, initially in private, and then 'more openly'.[34] By the time the island was rediscovered a hundred years later its population was two thousand. Readers trying to determine whether Neville's anonymously published story was a spoof might have found their first clue here: such a rate of increase is not possible in a human population where the children are being breastfed. The same readers would have been on solid ground in deducing that the author was male.[35]

This story found a lively market. It was quickly translated into Dutch, French, Italian, German and Danish. While one German scholar considered learnedly the moral status of Pines' *menage à cinq*, another unscrambled the title as *Penis Island*.[36] While laughing all the way to the

---

[33] Ibid. p. 163.

[34] Onofrio Nicastro (ed.), *Henry Neville e L'isola di Pines* (Pisa, 1988) pp. 67, 69, 81–9.

[35] I am grateful to Melanie Good for this point. Seventeenth-century demographers have established that in England, combined with a late average age of marriage, the temporary infertility accompanying breastfeeding (lactational amenorrhoea) was the leading means of controlling the number of births. Average duration of breastfeeding was twelve to nineteen months. E. A. Wrigley, R. S. Davies, J. E. Oeppen and R. S. Schofield, *English Population History from Family Reconstitution 1580–1837* (Cambridge, 1997) pp. 446, 465, 478.

[36] Gaby Mahlberg, 'Republicanism as Anti-patriarchalism in Henry Neville's *The Isle of Pines* (1668)', in John Morrow and Jonathan Scott (eds.), *Liberty, Authority, Formality: Political Ideas and Culture, 1600–1900* (Exeter, 2008). The following discussion is indebted to Mahlberg's analysis.

bank, Neville's point was serious. Like Marvell he was a product of the interregnum. Like Henry Vane and Algernon Sidney, Neville had been a member of the Rump parliament. This was the government which had run, and won, the first Anglo-Dutch war.

The ship by which Pines' island was rediscovered was Dutch. The ostensible author of the published account was its captain. What Henry Cornelius Van Sloetten's crew found was a people which, although they 'could speak *English* ... yet go naked'. Great numbers 'flock ... about us ... admiring ... our Cloaths ... [and] wondering at our ship, as if it had been the greatest miracle of Nature'.[37] Their 'Prince' William Pine, grandson of George, was a good-natured idiot who lived in a 'Pallace' made of 'rough unhewn pieces of Timber'. His hundred-year-old axe was 'blunt and dulled', he ate like a 'peasant', drank only water (not for want of Dutch trying), and was 'altogether ignorant [of] ... ships, or shipping'. His people live in a state of 'Nature' without 'the benefit of Art'.[38]

When they saw someone playing bagpipes they thought he was blowing into 'a living creature'.[39] When the Dutch came 'to discharge a piece of Ordnance, it struck him into a wonder ... to behold the strange effects of Powder'. When William faced domestic disorder and persuaded the Dutch to intervene, they countered 'Clubs and Stones' by 'discharging ... three or four Guns', which caused the offenders to run away.[40]

Neville's account resembled Columbus' description of the inhabitants of Hispaniola as 'naked and with no experience of arms and very timid'.[41] The Dutch could enter Penis Island any time. Since Elizabeth it had reverted to the military stone age. It was not only pre-technological but post-maritime. Leaving his kingdom naked, Charles II cavorted with his mistresses. These semi-public couplings produced no legitimate issue. In another reversal of both Elizabethan and Cromwellian situations, royal sexual promiscuity stood for military impotence. Marvell made even more of this *conjuncture*, including spectacular ridicule of the Duchess of York:

> Happy'st of Women, if she were but able
> To make her glassen *Dildoes* once *malleable*!
> Paint her with Oyster Lip, and breath of Fame,
> Wide Mouth that Sparagus may well proclaim:
> With *Chanc'lor*'s Belly, and so large a Rump.
> There, not behind the Coach, her Pages jump.[42]

---

[37] Nicastro (ed.), *L'isola di Pines* p. 73.   [38] Ibid. p. 105.
[39] Ibid. p. 119.   [40] Ibid. pp. 109, 111.
[41] Quoted in Elliott, *Empires of the Atlantic World* p. 18.
[42] Marvell, *Poems and Letters* p. 142.

In this and other ways *Last Instructions to a Painter* was an inversion of Marvell's *First Anniversary*, which had reflected upon Cromwell credit for his own victories and those of the fleet.[43]

It was from the same post-Chatham doldrums that another floating island hove into view. Richard Head's *The Floating Island: Or, A New Discovery* (London, 1673) was a spoof travel narrative of still less subtle hue. Its apparently complex geographical co-ordinates turned out to describe a crossing from the south to the north bank of the Thames (*Lambethana to Villafranca* alias *Ramallia*). At least Head scored full marks for making the purpose of publication clear. This was a voyage 'Under the Conduct of Captain *Robert Owe-much*' to flee the consequences of debt.

The resulting scatological tour of the City concentrated on the area around Ram Alley and the Inns of Court where a warren of public houses proved suitable for the evasion of creditors. On the first vessel encountered during the crossing (a *Canary-man*) the crew appeared to be 'Sea-sick ... [being] perceived ... ever and anon to *cast over board*'. At '*Cape-verd*, or *Green's Wharfe* ... the youth ... have an unlimited freedom, especially such who are known and try'd to be men of *great natural parts*, though they have but *slender understandings*'. On the 'floating Island, called the Summer Island ... the Inhabitants are a lazy sort of people, and not given to Tillage; and yet sometimes they will *plow with another mans Heifer*'.[44]

What the King himself thought about Chatham may be determined not only from the policy *volte face* of the next three years, and thereafter. Throughout the secret negotiations leading to the Treaties of Dover in 1670, English documents began with the matter 'de plus Important ... Le Roy de la grand Bretagne estoit convaincu de la verite de la Religion Catholique et resolu de se declarer Catholique et de reconcilier avec l'Eglise de Rome'.[45] This conversion was to be the centrepiece of a dramatic reorientation of Stuart religious, political and foreign policy to establish a 'paix, union, vraye confraternite' and 'confederation perpetuelle' with France which would annihilate the Netherlands and secure the future of the Stuart monarchy and dynasty.[46]

---

[43] Ibid. pp. 111–12.

[44] [Richard Head], *The Floating Island: Or, A New Discovery Relating the Strange Adventure on a late voyage, From Lambethana to Villa Franca* (London, 1673) pp. 11, 13, 15.

[45] Ministère des Affaires Etrangères, Paris, Archives Diplomatique, Correspondence Politique Angleterre vol. VC, pp. 235–6; also 241, 247–8, 258–9.

[46] Ibid. p. 229. For the shared Anglo-French perception of a continued English republican danger see Colbert to 'Sire' [the King] 19 August 1669 pp. 57–8. Scott, 'England's Houdini: Charles II's Escape from Worcester as a Metaphor for his Reign (1660–1685)', in Morrow and Scott (eds.), *Liberty, Authority, Formality*.

Fear not only of popery, but for the security of monarchy, had been a constant of seventeenth-century English politics.[47] How much more reason for this was there in the mind of a King, once a hunted fugitive, then penniless exile, whose father had been publicly murdered by the people over whom he now reigned? 'We are bound to *honour* our Kings and Princes ... and how have we done it? *Murder the Father!* Banish the *Son!*'[48] Once again, in the aftermath of Chatham, Pepys reported 'people make nothing of talking treason in the streets openly'.[49]

Eighteen years later, not long before the King's death, Henry Sheres recorded an account given him by Charles 'alone in his Closet' of Chatham,

with Soe feeling a Sense of ye Misfortune, Such Admirable Observations upon the Motives the Enemy had to the Attempt ... together with what was done and Attempted on Our Part, What false Stepps and Judgements were made and by whom, Descending to every Remarkable Particular ... That a Stranger to the Story would by ye Relation have Guess'd It to have just then hapned; soe lively and lasting an Impression had that fatall Success made in his Mats Mind ... [A]s his ... Matie ... observed to me ... the People on the Occasion of ... [that] Attempt ... were frighted almost out of their Obedience, and the Successe of that action threatened even a Convulsion of the State.[50]

The disaster on the Medway was followed by predictions of another civil war. Should such a thing occur '(which God forbid)', Sir William Coventry told Pepys,

that which must save the Crown in every other particular will do it also in this, namely, the securing to itself the City of London, the being master of that and of the River ... particularly the fleet, which cannot ... reasonably be supported by any power of this nation that hath not London, where lie not only the maga-zines of provisions and stores, but which is the general home to the seaman and his relations. And in proof of this he very well observed that the losing of London did not discover itself of prejudice to the late King in anything more than in his fleet.[51]

Sheres had been in Spain at the time of the Chatham raid, but after his return made 'an Inquisitive Searche after the Reasons ... of that Great Calamity ... An Action how much to the Glory of that People [the Dutch], and the Disgrace (to say noe more) of the English Nation'.[52] For most of

[47] Scott, *England's Troubles* pp. 62–5.
[48] Francis Gregory, *David's Returne From His Banishment* (Oxford, 1660) pp. 11, 14.
[49] Pepys, *Diary* vol. VIII: 1667 pp. 268–9.
[50] Sir Henry Sheres, 'Sir H Shere's [*sic*] proposal to King James for preserving the Naval Royal in Port from any Insult', 4 May 1688, NMM REC/6 Item 24 pp. 343–4, 353.
[51] Pepys, *Samuel Pepys and the Second Dutch War* pp. 225–6.
[52] Sheres, 'Shere's proposal' p. 343.

the period between 1669 and 1681 Sheres was in Tangiers building and
defending the mole (he became surveyor general in 1676, partly thanks
to the support of Pepys).[53] Meanwhile, if for Charles II the focus of the
Treaties of Dover was religious – a planned owning of his own Roman
Catholicism – the priority for Louis XIV was war against the United
Provinces.[54] Declarations of Indulgence and of War were issued in 1672.

For Charles II the war, with the support of France, offered the possibility of revenge for Chatham. In England's share of the proposed dismem-
bering of the United Provinces might lie not only security against another
such raid in the future, but the reacquisition (only a few years after the
sale of Dunkirk) of English territory on the other side of the channel.
In 1673 the Earl of Shaftesbury built upon John Milton's 1660 image
of England as 'a new Rome in the West' by applying to the Dutch state
Cato's mantra that it was necessary to destroy Carthage. Unlike Milton's,
Shaftesbury's political-geographic analysis of England's situation (and it
was that of England, not Britain) was insular and maritime.

When you consider we are an Island, 'tis not Riches nor Greatness we contend
for, yet those must attend Success; but 'tis our very Beings are in Question; we
fight *pro aris & focis*, in this War, we are no longer Freemen, being Islanders and
Neighbours, if they Master us at Sea: There is not so Lawful or Commendable
a Jealousie in the World, as an *English Man's*, of the growing Greatness of any
Prince or State at Sea.[55]

This was a glance back towards the naval policies of the English republic, as well as forward to geographic perspectives to be developed in the
eighteenth century (not including the, in this case, royalist claim that the
Dutch 'government must be brought down').[56] Although the Dutch government was not brought down, it was a close-run thing, thanks to the
overwhelming of southern and eastern land defences by France. Later
the same year Protestant and parliamentary outrage forced English withdrawal from the war, and replacement of the Declaration of Indulgence
with an Anglican Test Act.

The near-fall of the United Provinces prompted a famous analysis by Sir William Temple, who described the spectacular growth and

[53] J.D. Davies, 'Sheres, Sir Henry 1641–1710, Military Engineer and Author', in *Oxford Dictionary of National Biography* vol. L pp. 289–90; Letter from Pepys to Sheres, 11 December 1677, BL Add MS 19872 ff. 31–6.
[54] Scott, 'England's Houdini' p. 73.
[55] Quoted in Hont, *Jealousy of Trade* p. 1 (apparently incorrectly dated 1663). Shaftesbury gave the *Delenda est Carthago* speech on 5 February 1673, though in it he did refer to parliamentary opinion of the 1660s. K.H.D. Haley, *The First Earl of Shaftesbury* (Oxford, 1968) pp. 316–17; Spurr, *England in the 1670s* p. 36.
[56] Hont, *Jealousy* p. 316.

decline of Dutch wealth and power as tidal, like the sea upon which it depended. He criticized the overconcentration of the De Witt administration on maritime affairs and trade at the expense of land defences. But he also observed that the Dutch governmental assumption that every state followed its own interest left it incapable of predicting England's abandonment of the Triple Alliance (1668) for the Treaty of Dover, not understanding that the English constitution gave the monarch control of war and peace, regardless of the interest of the state.[57] Meanwhile the focus of English military effort, such as it was, shifted to the western Mediterranean. There were naval campaigns against Tripoli (1674–6), Algiers (1677–83) and Sally (1684–8).[58] In 1680 Henry Sheres anonymously published *A Discourse Touching Tanger*, pleading the town's usefulness, indeed indispensability in this context, and within the larger framework of European naval rivalry.

This Mediterranean emphasis was evident as early as 1674, in John Evelyn's *Navigation and Commerce, Their Original and Progress*, dedicated to the King. Applying Temple's tidal image to the ancient world ('this Vicissitude is unavoidable'), Evelyn claimed that '*Tingis*, which of old deriv'd its Name from *Commerce*, was a renown'd *Emporium* near three hundred Years before *Carthage* was a City, was lately the Desolate *Tanger*; though now again, by the Influence of our glorious Monarch, raising its aged head with fresh vigour.'[59] More generally Evelyn mused of the Mediterranean Sea,

That if the *Hollanders* themselves (who of all the Inhabitants in it, are the best skill'd in making Canales and Trenches, and to derive Waters) had joyn'd in Consultation, how the scatter'd parts of the Earth might be rendred most Accessible, and easie for Commerce; They could not have contriv'd, where to have made the In-let with so much advantage, as GOD and Nature have done it for Us; Since by means of this Sea, we have admission to no less than Three Parts of the habitable World.[60]

Part of the purpose of Evelyn's work was to assert royal 'DOMINION' over the seas surrounding the British Isles since medieval times. In addition to a long history, this entailed another extended lament over a Dutch fishing industry employing 'above fourty thousand Fisher-men, and one hundred and sixteen thousand Mariners' in British waters.[61] Evelyn calculated that the Dutch owed the British crown a million pounds sterling

---

[57] Temple, *Observations Upon the United Provinces* chs. 7–8.
[58] Sari Hornstein, *The Restoration Navy and English Foreign Trade 1674–1688: a Study in the Peacetime Use of Sea Power* (Aldershot, 1991) pp. 9–23.
[59] Evelyn, *Navigation and Commerce* p. 45.   [60] Ibid. p. 3.   [61] Ibid. p. 107.

in 'Rent' and customs duties for the fish taken. Like Monson before him, he deplored that

to our shame be it spoken, we blush not to buy our own Fish of them, and purchase that of Strangers, which God, and Nature has made our own, inriching others to our destruction, by a detestable sloath; whilst to encourage us, we have Timber, Victuals, Havens, Men, and all that at our dores, which these people adventure for in remoter Seas, and at excessive charges.[62]

The broader purpose of Evelyn's work, as these remarks suggested, was to assert the divinely ordained primacy of navigation and commerce, and the special advantages given to England to dominate it worldwide. As in other later such accounts, this entailed an ancient as well as modern history of navigation including, in this case, an emphasis upon the invention of the sail, a spectacular description of the Venetian Silk Road, and a discourse on the carrier pigeons of Aleppo (Syria). Most interestingly, Evelyn gave his ancient history two moderate royalist twists. In the first, while paying due regard to the maritime achievements of the Phoenicians and Greeks, he asserted:

Yet it was *Solomon* doubtless, who open'd the Passages to the *South* [that is, beyond the Mediterranean to the Red Sea and Indian Ocean], when animated by his directions, and now leaving-off their Rafts, and Improving their Adventures in Ships, and Stouter Vessels, they assay'd to penetrate the farthest *Indies*; and visit an Unknown *Hemisphere*.[63]

In the second place, after describing the epic struggle between Rome and Carthage from Polybius, Evelyn turned to Suetonius to sketch an Augustan golden age of maritime power. Rome learning the lesson of the Punic Wars that they 'Onely might be said to speed Conquerors of the World, when they had Conquer'd the Sea, and subdu'd the Waters', it was under Augustus that 'the World by Sea … [was] first subdu'd to the Empire of a single Person. What discoveries this mighty Prince made, did as far exceed his Praedecessors, as the frozen *North*, and horrid Coasts of *Cimbria*, the milder Clime of our *Britain*, which was yet in those daies esteemed another World, and her Boundaries, as much unknown, as those of *Virginia* to us' (this latter point again from Virgil).[64] Augustus had one fleet

at *Ravenna*, as a constant Guard of the *Adriatic*; and another riding at *Misenum*, to scowr the *Tyrrhen*-Sea … The *Misenian*-Fleet lay conveniently for *France*, *Spain*, *Morocco*, *Africk*, *Aegypt*, *Sardinia*, and *Sicily*; That at *Ravenna*, for *Epirus*, *Macedon*, *Achaia*, *Propontis*, *Pontus*; The *Levantine* parts, *Creete*, *Rhodes*,

---

[62] Ibid. p. 109.   [63] Ibid. p. 26.   [64] Ibid. pp. 33, 35.

and *Cyprus*, &c. So as by the Number of their Vessels, and Arms, they made a Bridge (as it were) to all their Provinces, and Vast Dominions at what distance soever.[65]

Thus this monarchy was maritime, Mediterranean and imperial. Not only that but '*Marine* Laws and Customes they also had', and foreign vessels were required 'to strike Sail to the Ports of the Empire ... So early was the claim to the Flag, and the ceremonies of Naval-Honour stated'.[66]

Two years later a dramatically alternative account of ancient history, and British history, emerged from the pen of Aylett Sammes, 'of Christ's Colledge in *Cambridge*' and 'the *Inner-Temple*'. Sammes was also a royalist, and a proponent of trade and navigation, offering a prescription for British empire. However, as his ancient model was not Rome but Phoenicia, so his modern worry was less about the United Provinces than about France (despite the fact that this account of Phoenicia was substantially French in origin).[67]

Sammes' *Britannia Antiqua Illustrata ... Derived from the Phoenicians* (1676) was dedicated to Heneage Lord Finch and licensed by Roger L'Estrange. Engaging critically with Camden's *Britannia*, and relying on similar etymological evidence, Sammes challenged his predecessor's findings in two notable ways. First, he attempted to demolish what was, as we have seen, the widely held view (as well as fact) that Britain had once been 'joined to the Opposite Continent, by a narrow Isthmus'. These words 'Opposite' and 'Britain' (rather than England) may be thought to align Sammes politically with Speed, though his text is actually highly critical of Speed. More importantly, whereas Camden had claimed that the ancient Britons had migrated from Gaul, the principal purpose of Sammes' work was to establish that they had in fact been Phoenician. These two arguments were related, for underlying the question '*Whether* BRITAIN *was ever part of the* Continent?' was another: '*Whether the First Planters of this Island came by Sea, or Land?*'[68]

Sammes listed those who had failed the isthmus test (building an unnecessary isthmus), including several of Camden's sources.[69] He admitted that according to notable authorities (Pliny, Lucan, Virgil) 'most Islands in the World' (Cyprus, Eubea (*sic*) and Sicily) had once been similarly attached. However, whereas in the cases of Sicily and the

---

[65] Ibid. p. 34.   [66] Ibid. p. 36.
[67] Parry, *The Trophies of Time* ch. 11. Sammes acknowledged his French source Bochartus: Aylett Sammes, *Britannia Antiqua Illustrata: Or, The Antiquities of Ancient Britain, Derived from the Phoenicians* (London, 1676), 'The Preface to the Reader' p. 3.
[68] Sammes, *Britannia* p. 25.   [69] Ibid. pp. 25, 36.

Isle of Wight there was linguistic evidence of such detachment (Wight signifying 'in the *British* Tongue, SEPARATION'), contrary to Camden's opinion there was none on either side of the channel. Indeed the word '*Dover* … as it is derived in great probability, by Mr *Lambard*, it comes from the word DURYRRHA, which in the *British* Language betokeneth, a place *steep* and *upright*, an evident sign of the Antiquity of those Cliffs'.[70] As for Verstegan's observations concerning the great geological and topographical similarities between the nearest parts of 'England and France, *not exceeding Twenty four miles*', given that the same similarities were observable under as well as on either side of the water, these were of no historical significance.

Sammes' channel fortifications were bolstered by '*Des-Cartes* his *Hypothesis* concerning the *forming of the Earth*'.[71] He argued that seas were receding rather than rising (hence the success of land reclamation in the Netherlands), so that 'there are many more Examples in the World of *Peninsula's* [sic] made, than destroyed'. The hostage to fortune offered by this argument appeared no more evident to its author than that offered by Charles II in agreeing to help France absorb most of the Netherlands. As for the question of how wolves and foxes came to England without a land bridge, the obvious answer was that they were imported by humans as game. In short,

> It was ever the Glory and Safety of GREAT BRITAIN to be environed by the Sea, and to command those Waters that encompass it, and whilst other Nations are subject to daily Incursions, being separated only by *Rivers*, *Hills*, or *Valleys*, and imaginary *Lines*, by turns, one Kingdom often Elbows out another, but Nature has set BRITAIN such distinct Bounds and Limits, that its Empire is preserved entire; and as it abounds in All things … and needs not the World to sustain it, so it was always esteemed, and called, *Novus Orbis*, & *Orbis* BRITANNICUS, by reason of its *Greatness*, and especially Separation from the *Continent* … That it ever was joined Eastward to the Continent of *France*, as there is no Tradition for it, so there is no real Truth in it, and so I shall leave it, as I found it, encompast by the Sea.[72]

As previously the continent had been 'Opposite', so now it was '*France*'. For 'if this *Isthmus* were admitted, then it would seem beyond dispute, but that the *Gauls* peopled this Nation, which, for the Reasons before mentioned can not be imagined. It seems more glorious for this excellent part of the Earth to have been always a distinct Nation by it self, than to be a dependent Member of the Territory to which it hath often given Laws.'[73] The point was of course that since 1670 Britain had indeed become

---

[70] Ibid. p. 26.   [71] Ibid. pp. 27–30.   [72] Ibid. pp. 36–7.   [73] Ibid. p. 16.

a 'dependent member' of that large part of Europe under the influence of France. Specifically Sammes' work, with its high-level patronage, may be contextualized within the campaign of Thomas Osborne,
Earl of Danby (both cavalier and Anglican), the purpose of which was
to distract attention from this fact. This is not to suggest that Danby (or
Sammes) approved of the King's Francophile policies. Danby's actual
achievement, however, was temporarily to disguise, rather than moderate
or counteract them.

According to Sammes, similarities between the Gaulish and British
languages derived primarily from Phoenician trade between them.[74]
(Evelyn had noted that 'the ancient Gaules had great Commerce with
those of Carthage (as appears out of *Polybius* and *Livy*)' but said nothing
of Britain in this connection.[75]) The first Britons might have been Cimbri,
from Germany, or Phoenicians from Tyre and Sidon. What Sammes
argued strenuously, particularly against Camden's 'fallacious' supposi-
tions to the contrary, was that the oldest linguistic record was entirely
Phoenician; that the Phoenicians had preceded the Greeks; and that all
Greek descriptions and place names were themselves Phoenician in origin. Camden's mistake, followed by most subsequent writers including
Evelyn, in believing the island unknown before the Greeks, derived from
a misreading of Polybius, as well as inattention to subsequently lost por-
tions of Polybius' text quoted by Strabo.[76]

Thus Bretanica or Bretania derived from the Phoenician Bretanac,
meaning 'A Country, or Field of *Tynn*'. This tin, and also lead, these diligent traders mined in the Scilly Islands, Cornwall and Devonshire, 'so
that the *Graecians* had none but what was brought from thence'.[77] Albion
derived from the Phoenician Alban (white) or Alpin (mountainous).[78]
Ireland had also been discovered and settled by the same Phoenician
'Fleet of Threescore Sail ... accompanied with Thirty thousand Men'.[79]
The Phoenician word Kern, meaning promontory, which had led them
to call Corsica Carnatha, earned Cornwall the name Kernaw.[80] Not '*only
the Name of* Britain *it self, but of most places therein ... are purely derived
from the* Phoenician *Tongue, and that the Language itself for the most part, as
well as the Customes, Religion, Idols, Offices, Dignities, of the Ancient* Britains
are all clearly Phoenician'.[81] It was scarcely a coincidence that there were
only two places in the world where ancient history recorded the use of a
drink ('which we call *Ale*') made from barley.

[74] Ibid. pp. 61–70.   [75] Evelyn, *Navigation and Commerce* p. 46.
[76] Sammes, *Britannia* pp. 53, 70.   [77] Ibid. pp. 41–3, 51, 53.
[78] Ibid. pp. 48–9.   [79] Ibid. p. 50.   [80] Ibid. p. 59.
[81] Ibid., 'The Preface to the Reader' p. 4.

Now, why may not this Custome be thought to come from them by the means of the *Phoenecians*, who found *Britain* very fruitful in that Grain, and not inferiour to *Egypt* it self in the wonderful production of it. For as *Egypt* was esteemed the Granary of those parts, so was *Britain* of these; yea, as *Orpheus* calls it, The very Seat of the Lady *Ceres*, so that the usefulness of this Invention of the *Egyptians* ... was not less to the *Britains*.[82]

Thus Sammes launched a British historical mythology which would have a vibrant eighteenth-century, and subsequent, history.[83] But his purpose in this was not, as that of others would become, to lay claim to a specifically mercantile and manufacturing national pedigree. Nor, while connecting Britain to the ancient 'Masters and Instructers in the Art of *Navigation*, as well as in all other Arts and Sciences whatsoever', did he invest the island as a whole with a navigational culture. Within Bretanac the Phoenicians mined. From it they traded. But other inhabitants farmed grain and animals, hunted, consulted Druids and drank ale.

In addition to fortifying his nation's insular geography, Sammes' objective appears to have been to add to the depth, and therefore prestige, of its history. It was, that is to say, to improve dramatically upon Camden's achievement in restoring Britain to its antiquity, and its antiquity to Britain. This ambition had an imperial as well as national context. In an interesting twist on recent contemporary history, Sammes opined that the Phoenicians imported Iberians to work their mines. More generally, 'The cause of making the *Phoenicians* so early Marriners, was not only through their ambition of Empire, and particular genius to Navigation and Merchandize, but through necessity of inventing the best and safest way of escaping the hands of *Joshua*, who persecuted them with an Army of *Israelites*.'[84]

Before the contemporary European empires there had been Rome; before Rome the Greeks; before Greeks the Phoenicians (who, according to Sammes, were Syrians); before them Egyptians and Sumerians. Lacking this imperial context, the first phase of Britain's antiquity had entirely escaped Camden's attention. Not only had he omitted Phoenician settlement, but the Greeks also had arrived 'far earlier than Mr *Cambden* will acknowledge them'.[85] This was despite his own confession

That the Syrians, *meaning the* Phoenicians, *sending out so many Colonies, left great part of their Language in most places of the World*; Now if he had seriously considered, and not have deceived himself by misunderstanding *Polybius, That* Britain *was but lately known*, certainly he would have given a more exact account of this most Renowned Island, and never have derived its name from Bryth,

[82] Ibid. pp. 108–9.   [83] Parry, *Trophies of Time* p. 330, note 29.
[84] Sammes, *Britannia* p. 73.   [85] Ibid. p. 74.

[body] *Painting*, a Custome among very few of them, and that many hundred years after it was called *Bretanica*.[86]

Ancient Britain had not been America, off Europe's western edge, a primitive new world of body painters waiting to be discovered. Rather it had been part of a Syrian/Phoenician world empire which imported Spaniards to work its mines. This was a historical understanding far more in keeping with '*a Nation great in its Infancy, and like* Hercules ... *deserving an History even in its Cradle*'.[87]

By the end of 1678 the crown's continuing secret relationship with France had become exposed, precipitating a major crisis. It was the withholding by the House of Commons, within this context, of funding for the garrison at Tangiers that had produced the pamphlet on that strategic outpost by Henry Sheres. The work mentioned that 'We are just Alarm'd with the News of *Tanger*'s being sold to the *French*,' as earlier Dunkirk had been. However, Sheres argued, while the cost of defending Dunkirk had been insupportable, in this case 'we have a wise Prince, learned beyond his Predecessors in the Interests and Advantages of Navigation and Commerce ... Nor is his Royal Highness ... so ill possess'd of the value of this Place, [as] to concur in any deliberations of that kind.'[88] Yet partly because of the crisis resources could not be found to defend Sheres' mole, which he was instructed to raze.[89] Not only was he required personally to oversee its demolition, but to compose a report improving 'the ordinary objections made against the Mole ... the most he could to justify the King's destroying of it, though he did tell me [Pepys] privately that he is able to answer them all'.[90] In April 1679 one of Sheres' correspondents (Sir Palmer Fairborne) wrote: 'Whilst wee [are] thus striving to destroy one another for reformation and security to the king and kingdome, most sober men who sitt not att the helm stand amazed att our slackness in making preparations to secure us from the French who has apoynted his rendevous with his fleet att Dunkirk.'[91]

---

[86] Ibid. p. 70.   [87] Ibid., 'The Preface to the Reader' p. 2.

[88] [Sir Henry Sheres], *A Discourse Touching Tanger* (London, 1680) p. 33. Sheres' authorship is confirmed by Sir William Trumbull, who accompanied him and Pepys on the 1683 mission to raze the fortifications. 'Sir H. Sheres had written a book in commendation of Tangier and so was sent with us to confute every article had he so industriously praised.' Pepys, *Naval Minutes* p. 269.

[89] BL Add MS 19872 f. 63, letter 14 February 1681 for Sheres' frustration at parliament's withholding over Tangier (also, on 8 June 1680 Pepys was sent to the Tower).

[90] Samuel Pepys, *The Tangier Papers of Samuel Pepys*, (ed.) Edwin Chapell (London, 1935), pp. 36–7. Pepys himself hated Tangiers, which was no Club Med (Ollard, *Pepys* pp. 270–3).

[91] BL Add MS 19872 f. 46.

In 1700 Sheres appended to his publication of *A Discourse of Seaports; Principally the ... Port of Dover*, attributed to Sir Walter Ralegh, certain *Useful Remarks* of his own on that subject, *Never before made Publick*. These recalled why, after

severall Essays to awaken his late Majesty King *Charles* out of the Lethargie he seem'd to me to be under, upon the *French* King's so loudly Alarming us by the Profuse Expence he had been at in Fortifying his Coast, making Artificial Ports, and sparing no Coast where he had the least Prospect of Compassing *Harbour* and Defence for Shipping ... I grew at length convinc'd, that I labour'd in Vain, and had been all the while Blowing a Dead Coal.[92]

Sheres recounted a conversation with Charles II in 1682 in which

I had often hinted to him how busy the *French* King was on his *Coast*, and what Vast Designs he had conceiv'd for the Improvement of his *Naval* Power ... Visible by his Fortifying of *Dunkirke* ... making *Peers*, *Channels*, *Basins*, and every Provision that Art can Suggest, and Money Compass ... and other Places where nature and Situation had given them some Help and Encouragement to Prosecute their *Maritim Projects* ... which, as I had often told his Majesty, seem'd to me to have a very Evil Aspect on all the Maritin States of *Europe*, but more especially his Majesty ... [the French] Coast not yielding him one good *Port* on all that *Frontier* which Regards us, which he [Louis XIV] most Providently weighing, had from an Harbourless, Inhospitable Shoar, by Art, Industry, and a most Lavish Expence of Treasure ... Repair'd ... in Despight of Nature.[93]

This echoed Ralegh on the Dutch a century earlier. Now again,

While we on our Coast, where Providence is so bountiful, have been so very little on our Guard, that tho' *Navigation* be the Prime Jewel of the Crown, and is the Fountain and Foundation of both our Wealth and Safety; and without which we shou'd be a Contemptible Nation, have not only omitted to Improve the Tenders which Nature makes us for the Increase and Cultivation of our *Naval* Power; But have in this last Age consented to see many of our useful *Ports*, Run to Decay, and at length to Ruine, and to become totally lost ... which a very little Foresight, and as little charge might have prevented ... Among which Ports I instanc'd *Sandwich, Dover, Rye, Winchelsea* &tc.

According to Sheres, the King took this dressing down on the chin and resolved that nothing would be more effectual in easing his people's 'Jealousy' of France than the attempted 'Recovery of *Dover Haven*'.[94] He dispatched forthwith his overjoyed interlocutor to survey the port and return with 'a *Plan* and State of the present Peer ... and how with least

---

[92] Raleigh, *A Discourse of Seaports* p. 9.
[93] Ibid. pp. 9–10.   [94] Ibid. pp. 10–11.

Charge it might be Repair'd and Render'd useful again'. This Sheres performed, returning almost certainly too soon 'with Evidence enough to oblige his *Majesty* at that time to say that he was so well satisfy'd, that he was Resolv'd he wou'd not Defer the Work a Day'.[95]

Sheres' plan would pay for itself (through revived customs duties) and boasted 'a New and very Demonstrable Invention' capable of securing 'the Depth of Water for ever'.[96] Dover was the port 'nearest of all others to a *Great, Dangerous* and *Aspiring Neighbour* ... which whenever his Majesty shou'd Chance to have a War with that People, wou'd be found to turn ... Offensively and Defensively to Marvellous account'. Yet inexplicably, and despite several reminders from Sheres, nothing happened, until finally the King told him that 'it was a *Noble Project* indeed, but that it was too big for his present Purse, and wou'd Keep Cold'.[97]

Since Sheres had, to his own satisfaction at least, dealt with the problem of cost he did not take this explanation seriously. Rather he remembered that the long audience in which he had presented his plans

chanc'd to be in a certain great Ladies Apartment in *White-Hall* [that of Louise de Keroualle, the Duchess of Portsmouth], where I had no sooner begun my Discourse ... when Mons. *Barillon*, the *French* Ambassador came in, who I observ'd to Listen with great Attention ... asking the said *Lady* very earnestly many Questions ... who I perceiv'd to Interpret to him every thing that was said on that occasion, as did the King afterwards in my hearing ... whereupon making Reflection ... I was no longer in doubt touching the cause of my Disappointment; but that it was not the *French* King's Interest, and therefore not his Pleasure, that we shou'd proceed on this Work.[98]

This story of the fortification of Dunkirk, sold to Louis XIV by Charles II in 1662, and a simultaneous French veto over the recovery of Dover, was convenient enough to tell in 1700. But it is in such conformity with the known behaviour of Charles, and the political situation in England in 1682, as to be likely to be true.[99]

Richard Gibson later claimed: 'Ever since the year 1660 ... Our Gentleman Captaines have had the honour to bring in Drinking, Gameing, whoring, swearing, and all Impiety into ye Navy; and banish all order and sobriety out of their ships.'[100] '[S]ince the Restoration the Design of popery has bin by Raiseing our Customs and ill Guarding

[95] Ibid. pp. 12–13.
[96] For Sheres the marine engineer see *Sir Henry Sheere's Discourse of the Mediteranian Sea, And The Streights of Gibraltar*, in *Miscellanies Historical and Philological: Being a Curious Collection of Private Papers* (London, 1703).
[97] Raleigh, *A Discourse of Seaports* pp. 14–15.   [98] Ibid. p. 15.
[99] Scott, 'England's Houdini' p. 84.
[100] Gibson, 'Discourse on our Naval Conduct' f. 261.

our Trade.' 'From the Restoration to this day there have been two stocks Raised to set on foot a Royall Fishery; And both have failed ... As all publicke undertakeings have hitherto done when converted to Private profitt.'[101]

Upon the whole, if the Number of daies a Gentleman Captaine layes in Port unnecessarily, his supernumeraries, over=Manning, over Gunning, and Spoyling the Sayling of his Shipp; The small Care he takes + Jdgement hee has to Increase Seamen, Secure them from Drowning, + his ship from Stranding, Annoy his Ennemy, or Secure his Convoys; or prevent the great Wast + Theft of stores made by his Officers, through his Ignorance to signe, and Interest to get them past bee put together; the Crowne will at all times be better able to Secure Trade, [and] Prevent the Growth of ... our Enemy with 100,000 under a naturall Sea Admiralty and Seaman Captaines (witness the Dutch) then with three times that sum under Land Admiralty, and Gentlemen Captaines, not bredd Tarpawlins.[102]

On 31 December 1684 it fell to Pepys as the new Secretary of the Admiralty to report to the King on 'The State of the Royal navy of England'. Throughout the administration, Pepys now explained to Charles, in Navy yards as in ships at sea he found regulations ignored, corruption and graft, wages three years in arrears and mariners' families starving.

[V]iewing at once your whole Navy both at sea and in Harbour, I find not one Article of this Discipline left unshaken ... even at this Day among those, upon whom the weightiest Part of its Good *Government* ... depends; Discords betweene Commanders at Sea; Hardships Exercised upon Inferiours ... strangers unquallifyed, introduced (for by-Considerations) into office; while others longest bred and best deserving in your service have been over looked ... Intemperence everywhere and unthriftinesse ... a Generall Debauchery of Manners, Violation of Discipline, and soe Universall an Indigence, that ... those of the best, as well as lowest Ranckes at sea, are now a dayes rarely found to dye with ... Reputation sufficient (for Sobriety and Thrift) to recommend themselves to the Merchants.[103]

Once again the discipline of the sea had been lost. This King had a relationship to the sea, but (partly because he was a King) not to discipline. Pepys begged Charles to consider that the generation of experience inherited from the interregnum was dying: 'the Race of your Old Commanders being now by Death almost worne out, the support of your service must 'ere long of Necessity fall into younger hands; upon whom

[101] Gibson, 'A Reformation' f. 66.
[102] Gibson, 'Discourse on our Naval Conduct' f. 41.
[103] Samuel Pepys, 'The State of the Royall Navy of England at the Dissolution of the late Commission of the Admiralty' 31 December 1684 NMM REC/6 Item 14 ff. 232–3.

Impressions of VIRTUE + good DISCIPLINE will take easier Place, while in a state of OBEDIENCE'.

Earlier during their voyage to Tangiers, Pepys and Sheres had talked about the indiscipline of the navy and the corruption of its officers.[104] To Sheres Pepys had been more personal about the root of the problem. 'The King's familiarity with commanders and under-officers makes them insolent, presuming upon their access to the King, and frights poor commanders or others their superiours from using their just authority (especially poor tarpaulins) considering ... the King's familiarity with those that offend.'[105] Macaulay expressed horror at the 'degradation and decay' revealed by Pepys' report 'such as would be almost incredible if it were not certified to us by the independent and concurring evidence of witnesses'. He was still more horrified that a few months later the French King sent his own envoy, Bonrepaux, to ascertain independently the state of the English navy, producing a second report 'to the same effect'.[106]

This chapter has considered the work of public and private intellectuals (Evelyn was a prominent member of the Royal Society, Sammes a maverick), satirists, critics of government policy, senior and junior public servants. Many of their concerns are familiar, deeply affected by the republican experience and problems restored with the Stuart monarchy itself. J. D. Davies has rightly questioned the impartiality of the tarpaulin perspective on this reign produced by dominance of the archival record by Pepys and his associates. If it was such a mess, he asks, 'how did the royal navy manage to hold its own in two wars with arguably the best-commanded naval force of the age, the Dutch fleet'?[107] But did the navy, burning at anchor in 1667, hold its own? Davies himself judges the English performance in 1665 poor and that in 1666 worse. The road downhill accelerated thereafter and there was worse – much worse – to come.

---

[104] Pepys, *Tangier Papers* pp. 95–6, 100, 112–13, 144–6, 149–50.
[105] Pepys quoted in Ollard, *Pepys* p. 275.
[106] NMM REC 28/1, History of the Navy, quoting Macaulay p. 5.
[107] Davies, *Gentlemen and Tarpaulins* pp. 34–5, 138, 144.

6   The British empire in Europe

> ... the Face of Things so often alters, and the Situation of Affairs in
> the *Great British Empire* gives such new Turns, even to Nature itself,
> that there is Matter of new Observation every Day presented to the
> Traveller's Eye.
>
> Daniel Defoe, *A Tour Thro' the Whole Island of Great Britain*[1]

Lamenting the 'Popular Discontents' which 'have ravaged and defaced
the noblest Island of the World', Sir William Temple remarked:

> The Comparison between a State and a Ship, has been so illustrated by Poets
> and Orators, that 'tis hard to find any point in which they differ; and yet they
> seem to do it in this, That in great Storms and rough Seas, if all the Men
> and Lading roll to one side, the Ship will be in danger of oversetting by their
> Weight: But on the contrary in the Storms of a State, if the Body of the People,
> with the Bulk of Estates, roll all one Way, the Nation will be safe. For the rest,
> the Similitude holds.[2]

Like Camden, Temple worried that England's internal instability would
furnish the occasion for 'some new Revolution, and perhaps final Ruine
of the Government, in case a Foreign Invasion enters upon the Breaches
of Civil Distractions. But such fatal Effects of popular Discontents, either
past or to come, in this floating Island, will be a worthy Subject of some
better History than has been yet written of *England*.'[3]

Sheres' account of Charles II's memory of Chatham was composed
in mid-1688 in an urgent letter to James II. With the rest of the country,
both men were watching the assembly of a massive Dutch fleet. '[I]f wee
look into the Greek Roman and Carthaginian Storyes ... Wee may learne
there what Stupendous Workes were performed by those Great Nations ...
how Religiously Jealous, and Chary they were of their Navall Power.'[4]
Now, against such a 'skillfull Dareing and Powerfull Enemy that shall be

---

[1] Defoe, *A Tour* vol. I, The Author's Preface p. 2.
[2] William Temple, *Of Popular Discontents*, in *Miscellanea. The Third Part* (London, 1701)
pp. 44, 90–1.
[3] Ibid. pp. 50–1.   [4] Sheres, 'Shere's Proposal' f. 345.

116

Master of the Sea', Sheres advised, no faith whatsoever could be placed in ground-mounted cannon and artillery. Harbour fortifications had less firepower than ships and were less mobile. The same went for 'such other Projects as are usually made, and put in Execution in Emergencys of this Kind', such as chains, booms, ships sunk in the harbour mouth, fireships and guardships. None could 'deter a formidable Enemy from attempting soe Glorious an Action, as the Insulting yor Maties Ports, and burning and Destroying a Navy Royall of England (a Calamity that I am sure needs noe Exaggeration to yor Matie)'.[5] Assuming that once again the Dutch objective was to destroy the fleet, Sheres had as usual an ingenious solution.[6] This was to divide the fleet between several defensible harbours and focus that defence upon the ships themselves, rather than sending the navy to sea. Still thinking of Chatham, Sheres had no inkling how much more 'Dareing' the real Dutch plan now was. For the republic was remembering, not 1667, but 1672. Then, in the disaster analysed by Temple, the United Provinces had almost been annihilated.

Now the Dutch project was to land a major army in England and force the summoning of a 'free' parliament. Judging by the anti-French sentiment on display since 1673, and improved by Dutch propaganda, this would not only pre-empt the possibility of another Anglo-French alliance, but bring England into a European war against France.[7] By February 1689 a new Anglo-Dutch monarchy had been installed. This devoted itself to a military struggle against France for the Protestant religion and liberties of Europe which was a culmination of both Dutch and English troubles. Within this context was completed the process of Anglo-Dutch military-fiscal state-building which had been in progress for more than half a century.

The power which emerged was not only Anglo-Dutch, then Anglo-Scottish, and ultimately British-Hanoverian. It was also imperial, both within Europe and outside it. Throughout the following century British military interests in Europe and in the New World were closely intertwined.[8] In 1665 Algernon Sidney had written in the Netherlands: 'if those [United] provinces encompassed with such difficulties opposed with the vast power of Spain ... have with small helps attained so great prosperity, England, if so governed, may promise itself incomparably more, abounding in all they want, and being free from all inconveniences they suffered or feared, apprehending no opposition but that of the Stuart family'.[9] After 1689, England became 'so governed' fiscally (the

---

[5] Ibid. ff. 347, 350, 352.   [6] Ibid. ff. 352–3.
[7] K.D.H. Haley, *William of Orange and the English Opposition 1672–4* (London, 1953); Israel, 'Dutch Role'; Scott, *England's Troubles* chs. 20–1.
[8] Simms, *Three Victories.*   [9] Sidney, *Court Maxims* p. 162.

'Financial Revolution'), militarily (Dutch-led military reconstruction), religiously (Protestant liberty of conscience) and politically (Britain becoming the only major power other than the United Provinces to be governed by Estates).[10]

Crucial, in 1688–9 as in 1648–9, was the military occupation of London. Occupation was important because it quickly secured the transfer of political authority necessary to commit large-scale resources to war against a foreign enemy. London was important, not only as the key to those resources, but because they drew upon the wealth not only of nation, but of empire. It was the collaboration of London, and of its whig City government, which gave William of Orange the government, and eventually the crown. As Stadtholder of a republic of cities he exhibited an appropriate sensitivity to London's sense of its own importance, as well as a crucial capacity to keep his troops under control.[11] Power acquired, London multiplied and co-opted the resources of a landed aristocracy. No less important, as Coventry had observed to Pepys, was the relationship of the capital to surrounding waterways.

Within late seventeenth-century north-western Europe the motors of development were not nation-states, but cities. Of radical Enlightenment Jonathan Israel has written that this 'was not inspired by any single nation, be it France, England, or the Netherlands, but rather had its centre of gravity in north-western Europe and particularly in the inner circuit linking Amsterdam, the other main Dutch cities, Paris, London, Hamburg and Berlin'.[12] Not only economic developments like agricultural, financial or commercial revolution, or military ones like the Dutch revolt and the Glorious Revolution, but cultural phenomena like northern humanism, Protestant reformation and Enlightenment, can be understood to have occurred within such regional contexts. In the words of David Hume:

If we trace commerce in its progress through TYRE, SYRACUSE, CARTHAGE, VENICE, FLORENCE, GENOA, ANTWERP, HOLLAND, ENGLAND etc, we shall always find it to have fixed its seat in free governments. The three greatest trading towns now in the world, are LONDON, AMSTERDAM, and HAMBURGH; all free cities, and protestant cities; that is, enjoying a double liberty.[13]

[10] Scott, *England's Troubles*; Scott, 'What the Dutch Taught Us' pp. 4–6.
[11] Robert Beddard, 'The Unexpected Whig Revolution of 1688', in Robert Beddard (ed.), *The Revolutions of 1688* (Oxford, 1991); Israel, 'Dutch Role'; Charles-Edouard Levillain, 'London Besieged? The City's Vulnerability during the Glorious Revolution', in McElligott (ed.), *Fear, Exclusion and Revolution*.
[12] Jonathan Israel, *Radical Enlightenment: Philosophy and the Making of Modernity 1650–1750* (Oxford, 2001) p. 141.
[13] David Hume, 'Of Civil Liberty', in Hume, *Political Essays* p. 54.

In relation to the nation of which it was capital, the role of London was unprecedented. Asked Fernand Braudel:

How can one begin to describe the role played by London in making Britain great? The capital city created and directed England from start to finish. London's outsize dimensions meant that other cities hardly began to exist as regional capitals ... In no other western country, as Arnold Toynbee remarked, did one city so completely eclipse the rest.[14]

The Dutch invasion, and the collaboration it secured, did not settle the question of England's internal constitution. Was the resulting early eighteenth-century state a parliamentary monarchy or a crowned republic? Looking at the constitution, who had won the English civil war? If this was, in party terms, infinitely arguable, that was the point. This point could be made by calling the state a mixed constitution. Alternatively, if it was either a monarchy or a republic it was very different from its seventeenth-century predecessors. Formally, while the United Provinces was a republic, England remained a monarchy. Yet this monarchy was no longer a government of persons but one of laws. Institutional structures regulated the economy, the state and their relationship. This became the only monarchy in Europe with a legislatively governed national bank. Dynastic continuity was subordinated, in 1689 and 1701, to confessional and military security.

What the revolution secured was that England would be Protestant, London-centred and imperial. Every aspect of this outcome had been anticipated in 1649, along with the appropriate modes of taxation and mechanisms for directing these resources towards effective military power. It was during the 1690s that Gibson's advice on the navy was first solicited directly by a Minister of State. His first account for John Trenchard of 'Defects and Remedies' was signed at 'Colchester Street neer Great Tower hill 25th July 1693'. 'If what is here wrot in any measure answer your Honours Expectation it will Atone for the Hazard I Run in doeing it.'[15] 'The Charge of this Warr with France not diminishing but Increasing', Gibson explained, there was 'nothing left us to hope for seeing through it [sic] more than (as the Athenians of old) to stick to our Wooden Walls'. The priority in defending these must be

to Change most of the Admiralty and Navy Board; And put the former into the hands of Merchants of Good Estates and Affection to the Government ... And the Latter fill up with Men able and more hearty to the Government than some

---

[14] Braudel, *Civilisation and Capitalism volume III* p. 365.
[15] BL Add MS 11684 ff. 37–42.

of them are; (who possibly had something else to recommend them thither then their fitness to serve their Majesties in that Station).[16]

As Henry Sheres put it, more tactfully but no less emphatically:

[A]s by a surprising Revolution of State we are come to pay obedience to one Head and Governour in the Person + Character of his present Majesty King William, who presides in ... the Conduct of our Affairs in Comon, So it would be monstrous ... should wee be found to go by other Maxims than such as may denote us one Collective Body ... the only Remedy that appears left to withstand ye Torrent that hath already broken so many Banks to invade Us.[17]

This was the third extraordinary moment of Anglo-Dutch political proximity. Once again, as in the 1580s and 1650s,

England is become the Cittadel ... of Europe, where the Keys of her Libertys are deposited, & may be defended ... In which [respect] ... Holland is become so much a piece with us, is so necessary & indispensable an outwork to this great Fortress; being placed as by Nature's hand & improved by infinite Art and Expence to Cover us, & be defended by a Reciprocation of Strength mutually to be imparted by Land & Sea.[18]

The first of these Anglo-Dutch moments (1584–5) had emerged from extreme Dutch need. The second (1649–54) had demonstrated that, with English government under the sway of London's merchants, co-option of Dutch policies would be voluntary, not coerced. Now the necessary material and military resources were secured by Dutch-inspired mechanisms of public credit rather than confiscations. The result was equally revolutionary.

As in 1649–54 the revolution settlement had to be defended on land and at sea. This meant in Ireland, England, Scotland and further afield. On this occasion, by 1707 Scotland had been brought into a political union peacefully. By comparison to the English republic, the legitimacy of the state was underpinned not only by institutional continuity but by such innovations as limited religious toleration, annual parliaments and (from 1694) legislatively regularized parliamentary elections. Nevertheless, as in the 1650s Anglo-Scottish union was a by-product of the security needs of the English state. Half a century later William Pitt

---

[16] 'Defects and Remedies in the present management of the royal navy' BL Add MS 11602 ff. 57–61 (quotes here from f. 57) became 'Memorials for the King About the Fleet, Flagg-Officers, Admiralty, Navy-Bord, Victualling, and Sick and Wounded Comissioners, Wrot at the Command of Sr John Trenchard the Secretary of State; by Richard Gibson', London 5 October 1693 BL Add MS 11684 ff. 51–7. This in turn furnished the basis for the Georgian 'A Reformation'.

[17] Sir Henry Sheres, 'Of Navall Warr', in Bodleian Library Rawlinson MS D 147, 'Navall Essays written by Sr Hen: Shere Knt Whilst a Prisonr in ye Gate-House Anno 1691'.

[18] Ibid.; see Scott, *England's Troubles* pp. 476–9.

would say: 'it is our interest, to have the peace of Europe preserved, and as we cannot do this by ourselves alone, we must unite with … the Dutch and the Empire of Germany, both'.[19] He did not mention Scotland, though only six years earlier in 1745 England had been invaded from Scotland with only 16,000 troops to defend it while 28,000 struggled to hold the front line against France in Flanders.[20]

From the War of the Spanish Succession emerged the United Kingdom of Great Britain. It was during successive military struggles, primarily against France, that inhabitants of the island began to think of themselves as British.[21] This was a product not only of state but of empire formation.[22] Attracted by the cultural and economic benefits of empire, Wales and Scotland became core participants in these processes. 'I might enlarge here', wrote Daniel Defoe,

Upon the Honour it is for *Scotland* to be a Part of the *British* Empire, and to be incorporated with so Powerful a People under the Crown of so great a Monarch; their being united in Name as one, *Britain*, and their enjoying all the Privileges of, and in common with, a Nation who have the greatest Privileges, and enjoy the most Liberty of any People in the World. But I should be told, and perhaps justly too, that this was talking like an *Englishman*.[23]

To this union Scotland would also bring its own European identity and relationships. In addition to the '"Auld Alliance" with France and the Calvinist … links with Universities in Germany and the Netherlands', it was from the south-west of Scotland, rather than any part of England, that one could see Ireland.[24] England, too, had to be persuaded to the marriage. It was the failure to move his English audience which had doomed the earlier attempted union of James VI and I. The most important factor in bringing English minds to union was consolidation of the security of the Hanoverian succession. Bearing in mind the Anglo-Dutch union negotiations of 1650–2 it is notable that in 1706 English envoys categorically rejected Scottish proposals for a federal union. What was achieved was an 'incorporating union' which created a parliament of Great Britain, and aligned the two economies, but left Scottish and English legal and ecclesiastical institutions intact.[25]

Addressing English readers in 1706 Defoe put the case for union both positively and negatively. On the one hand, since the English and Scots

---

[19] Quoted in Simms, *Three Victories* p. 355 (1751).
[20] Ibid. p. 340.   [21] Colley, *Britons*.
[22] Bayly, *Imperial Meridian* pp. 77–99.   [23] Defoe, *A Tour* vol. II p. 541.
[24] Fania Oz-Salzberger, 'Introduction', in Adam Ferguson, *An Essay on the History of Civil Society*, (ed.) Fania Oz-Salzberger (Cambridge, 1995) p. xii.
[25] Levack, *Formation of the British State* pp. 48–51, 67.

inhabit one Island, neither separated by dangerous Seas or unpassable Mountains, neither bounded with vast Deserts or great Rivers, by which either the Communications of Peace and Trade, or the Access of War might be rendred difficult, the on-looking World has beheld with no less Wonder than Pleasure, that they have not to this Day been able to unite in one Body.[26]

This was particularly true given that both nations 'are Protestant[,] both Orthodox in Principle, and equally opposite to Popery'.[27] To those who thought England was now strong enough to do without Scotland's support, Defoe replied that when England's power 'is by the Addition of *Scotland* so fortify'd ... it must be her own Fault, if she does not make a different Figure in ... *Europe*, to what she ever did before.'[28] To those who worried that the union might undo the religious or political settlements in either country he replied: '*tis no Way the Business of a Union, TO ALTER*, but *TO CONFIRM*, secure, and render impregnable, the present Settlements in both kingdoms'.[29] Like the Glorious Revolution itself, union was an instrument of restoration.[30] To those who worried that it might make Scots wealthier, Defoe replied that this would be to make Britons wealthier.

At the same time, particularly in wartime, there was a negative way to make the case. In the words of an earlier work, remembering the rebellions of 1638 and 1641, 'Scotland and Ireland are two Doors, either to let in Good or Mischief upon us.'[31] Defoe claimed:

I have heard that when the *Spanish Armada* in 1588 was, *after all our fabulous Stories of Sir* Fr. Drake, *and his Wonders*, by the meer hand of Providence, Storm and Tempest, *More than our Opposition* dispers'd scatter'd, and by various Disasters render'd useless to the Design ... Q. *Elizabeth* was often heard to say, that *had they enter'd the Mouth of the Thames*, and been joyn'd by the Ducke of *Parma* from *Flanders*, who lay ready to come over with 32,000 Men of the best Troops the World ever saw *England must have submitted*, and she had been undone.

In the event of a successful French invasion those still opposed to union would 'see things with a different Aspect, will have their Opticks extended, and see the Gulphs and Precipices, which they, blinded by Ignorance and Prejudices, are now willing to push the Nations upon'.[32] In the analysis of Sheres,

[26] [Daniel Defoe], *An Essay at Removing National Prejudices Against a Union with Scotland* (London, 1706) p. 3.
[27] Ibid. p. 17.   [28] Ibid. p. 27.   [29] Ibid. p. 24.   [30] Scott, *England's Troubles* ch. 20.
[31] *An Account of Divers remarkeable proceedings* (1679) quoted in Scott, *England's Troubles* p. 165.
[32] [Defoe], *An Essay at Removing National Prejudices* p. 26.

Such a Disaster to us with respect to the Enemy with whom we have now to deal would ... give a Period to the War + our Liberty together: for so Lysander finish'd the Peloponnesian Warr by burning + destroying the Athenian Fleet at Aegos=Potamos; which was loss of their Dominion by Sea, and that being the Basis of their Empire by Land left them at the mercy of an insulting Enemy who thought [of] no less a Fine than their captivity and the Dissolution of their State.[33]

Fear of invasion was at a peak in the early 1690s. It would return throughout the eighteenth century, especially following the French revolution and loss of the thirteen American colonies, eventually underpinning a broadening of the union to one of Great Britain and Ireland.[34]

Imprisoned in the Gate-House as a suspected Jacobite, in 1691 Sheres credited himself with invention of the genre 'Navall Essays ... from its Propriety, as I am an Englishman, + from its Novelty; as having been never yet publickly handled to any tolerable purpose'.[35]

Within the existing European and global contexts, to explore England's maritime potential was to underline its Anglo-Dutch, rather than Anglo-French, or -Spanish, future. The British empire in Europe was to be 'Protestant, commercial, maritime and free'.[36] If by 1730 Dutch maritime and mercantile supremacy had itself been eclipsed by that of Great Britain, this was a development partly financed by Dutch and Huguenot immigrants to south-eastern England.[37] Like that for the Anglo-Scottish union, this case for Protestant and commercial empire could be made both positively and negatively.

A remarkable example of the latter came from a Scot, Andrew Fletcher. According to Fletcher, on the eve of a Spanish succession crisis the future of the Spanish empire was the most pressing political problem facing humankind.[38] Under Philip II an obstinate determination to retain the Spanish Netherlands had been accompanied by the depopulation and enervation of both Iberia and the Americas. Philip did not

introduce among the people of Spain ... any sort of industry, whether in agriculture, in manufactures, in commerce or in navigation ... Instead the little ships of the English traversed his seas with impunity; [and] attacked his

[33] Sheres, 'Navall Essays', Bodleian Library Rawl MS D 147 p. 64.
[34] Hilton, *A Mad, Bad and Dangerous People?* pp. 82–106.
[35] Sheres, 'Navall Essays' p. 3.
[36] Armitage, *Ideological Origins* p. 173; see Reeve, 'Britain or Europe?' p. 301.
[37] Peter Spufford, 'Access to Credit and Capital in the Commercial Centres of Europe', in Karel Davids and Jan Lucassen (eds.), *A Miracle Mirrored: the Dutch Republic in European Perspective* (Cambridge, 1995) p. 328; Charles Wilson, *Anglo-Dutch Commerce and Finance in the Eighteenth Century* (Cambridge, 1966); Murray, 'Cultural Impact'.
[38] Andrew Fletcher, *A Discourse concerning the Affairs of Spain: written in the month of July, 1698,* in *Political Works,* (ed.) J. Robertson (Cambridge, 1997).

greatest carracks, which his subjects did not know how to sail ... That King and his Spaniards lived entirely on the mines of the Indies; the gold and silver of which, passing out of their hands, served only to enrich their enemies, the English, the French and the Dutch, who provided the Spanish with their manufactures, and other necessities of life.[39]

The present solution to the empire's problems was two-fold. It required, in the first place, territorial rationalization. The key to this was abandonment of what remained of the Spanish Netherlands and consolidation of control of the strategic corridor between the Mediterranean straits and the Americas. One contribution to this might be the ceding of Flanders to England in exchange for Jamaica. This would make sense for Spain, but also for England. The Low Countries were still the outworks defending English religion and liberties. Geographical proximity, economic and military ties, and a foothold on both sides of the channel still counted for much more than Caribbean sugar.

The other necessity for Spanish recovery was change in government policy. What was necessary was an 'increase of population [which] will in turn lead to an increase in agriculture, the mechanical arts, commerce and navigation'. The 'increase of commerce and navigation will [in turn] add to the number of seamen'. Following the latter policy Fletcher described as 'imitating the orders of the English, the Dutch and [until recently] the French'.[40] During the 1670s William Penn had lamented that 'our Forreign Islands yearly take off so many necessary Inhabitants from us', reaching like Fletcher for a Dutch-style solution:

so let the Government of *England* but give that prudent Invitation to Forreigners, and she maketh her self Mistress of the Arts and Manufactures of *Europe*: Nothing else hath hindred *Holland* from truckling under the *Spanish* Monarchy, and being ruin'd above threescore Years ago, and given her that Rise to Wealth and Glory.[41]

The foreigners Penn had in mind were Protestants dissenting from the Church of England who, he took it, dominated the nation's 'Arts and Manufactures', as well as the numbers of its emigrants to America. Thus, for Penn, as the Dutch example had long since demonstrated, the key to post-agricultural prosperity was liberty of conscience. For Fletcher this should be an important part of a broader political and economic policy. In 1673 William Temple had also claimed that the key to Dutch prosperity was policy-sponsored population density. In the following decade, perhaps while he was an exile in Rotterdam, John Locke mused:

---

[39] Ibid. p. 90.   [40] Ibid. p. 115.

[41] [William Penn], *England's Present Interest Discover'd With Honour to the Prince and Safety to the People* (London, 1675) pp. 12–13.

'[I]n the beginning all the World was *America.*' Yet as "'tis *Labour* ... that *puts the difference of value* on every thing ... Land that is left wholly to Nature, that hath no improvement of Pasturage, Tillage or Planting, is called ... *wast* ... This shows how much numbers of men are to be preferred to largeness of dominions.'[42] By 1681 Penn had given up waiting for liberty of conscience in England and acquired his own colonial charter.

Thus for Fletcher, following the Glorious Revolution, the English had belatedly taken the correct (Dutch) path, while the French had followed Spain, making 'this fatal error of government, of tormenting and persecuting peoples on account of their religion, and not wishing to have subjects who differ in their opinions on the highest and most difficult mysteries'.[43] In the later words of his countryman William Robertson:

It was towards the close of the seventeenth century, before toleration, under its present form, was admitted first into the republic of the United Provinces, and from thence introduced into England. Long experience of the calamities flowing from mutual persecution, the influence of free government, the light and humanity acquired from the progress of science, together with the prudence and authority of the civil magistrate, were all requisite in order to establish ... [this] regulation.[44]

Yet if such liberty was important, much remained to be done to establish a Dutch-style society and economy in England. This required, in the first place, attention to the disastrous policies and corruption of the period since 1660. One sign of this was a decline of English ships, the old and 'nimble Frigats' having been replaced by 'great ungovernable Two-Deck-Ships' which wore themselves out at sea. Another was a longstanding neglect of 'Navigationall Science':

if a petty Tyrant of Syracuse thought it worth his while to ... employ the greatest man in Learning + Practice of that or any Age before ... (namely Archimedes) in the Study and Exercise of Naval Architecture ... What Negligence ... what Poverty of Council will be found due to the Character of the English Nation, wch has all the helps of Nature we can wish ... if we shall be found chargeable with any omission in ye use + Improvement of such means + motives so essential to our Safety?[45]

Pepys too 'owned our ignorance in sea affairs; as also appears [by] our never having had any Lectures for Navigation', despite Hakluyt's attempts

---

[42] John Locke, *Locke's Two Treatises of Government*, (ed.) Peter Laslett (2nd edn, Cambridge, 1967) pp. 314–15, 319.

[43] Fletcher, *A Discourse* p. 114.

[44] William Robertson, *History of the Reign of the Emperor Charles V* quoted in J. G. A. Pocock, *Barbarism and Religion, volume II: Narratives of Civil Government* (Cambridge, 1999) p. 296.

[45] Sheres, 'Navall Essays' pp. 15–16, 35, 38.

to establish them in 1582. He recorded that the French and Dutch knew English coasts as well as the English, and that 'We [are still] beholden for our maps ... to the Spaniards and Portugueses.'[46]

For Sheres, as for Gibson, by far the most dangerous symptom of national malaise was the decline of naval discipline underlined by Pepys. During the Nine Years War, closely echoing his analysis of Chatham, Gibson did not hesitate to call the resulting problems treason. How else to explain the 'settled Generall Rule That no Captaine shall be Imployed in ye King's Service ... that hath been bred at Sea But Cheifly Land Officers'? How else to explain the captains of brand new ships re-employing men discharged for cowardice ('they Encourage all cowards as much as they can') and staying in port throughout the summer ('That either through Ignorance or Trechery there hath never been the like')? The roll call of 'Disaffected Persons', cowards and 'Greatest Jabobites' in the fleet included 'one Pickard ... Pettitt ... Guy'. The commissioning and building of vessels was so riddled with corruption and incompetence it was no wonder they were 'all built so Clouterly, and saile so heavy'. This treachery extended beyond the yards, and fleet, to the Admiralty itself. How else did 'French Privateers ... knowe what orders are sent to our cruising Frigatts' before the captains themselves? As for those captains, 'if the[y] knew the Rocks and Shoales as well as the[y do] dressing themselves, and abuseing their Men' the war would now be over.[47]

Sheres agreed that the problem was the 'wresting that Plain home=spun Profession of Life off the Hinges of old order and wholesome Discipline' by replacing 'our true bred Seaman' with unqualified Gentlemen.[48] Of his ten prison essays, only 'Of Navall Discipline' was developed over the next three years into a much-circulated manuscript tract.

Our Navy is the Soul of our Government, without which, we should languish into the State of Old Brittains, and be as easy a Prey to the French as we were heretofore to the Romans ... Upon what Slender Threads in hostile tymes may the fate of a Nation hang? ... the fortune of England is Im=bark'd in the Navy of England ... We are a Gallant People, but the most Careless of all mankind ... Let us fear a little more, that we may do a great deal better.[49]

---

[46] Pepys, *Samuel Pepys' Naval Minutes* pp. 229–30, 342–5.

[47] NMM CAD/D/20, 'October 1693. Reasons to prove There hath been, Negligence, Ignorance, or Treachery in ye Lds of Admiralty and Commissioners of the Navy' Items 1–50.

[48] I must here dissent from the conclusion of Capp, *Cromwell's Navy* p. 393 that 'By 1688 ... the [tarpaulins versus gentlemen] debate had lost its earlier political overtones.' The analysis of Halifax, which took those overtones as its starting point, was written in the early 1690s. For many turn-of-the-century arguments on both sides of this issue see British Library Harleian MS 6287 Naval Tracts.

[49] Sheres, 'A Discourse touching ye decay' pp. 1–2, 9–10. There is another copy in BL Egerton MS 3383 ff. 116–37.

There is no life so full of Labour, no Mens Minds more justly Anxious than a Seamans. The Sea, the Land, the Winds, Rocks, Sands, Tempests, Fire, and Water, Foul Weather and Fair, Calms, Currents, Tydes, are all Friends and Enemyes as they may be Manag'd and Improv'd by the good or Ill behaviour of an Officer.[50]

Morality was 'the Basis of good Discipline'.

And tis no wonder so many young Gentlemen come to nothing at Sea … who are sent so late abroad, and go Rakehells out of Town brimful of Lewdness and debauchery, who, instead of learning … teach others what they have acquir'd in Taverns, Ordinaryes, And Bawdy houses.[51]

This might subject a fleet to 'the Conduct of a Proud, lazy, self-willed Fool, perhaps a Coward: This [was] intolerable' because the 'Fate of a whole nation' could hinge on the 'bare Example of one bad commander'.[52] A captain

is a Governour of a Moving Fortresse with a Garrison of 500 or 1000 men under his command, that Act, move, fight, or Run=away, are Cowards or brave Men, as he inspires them … As every Sea Comander … being Head of that little Comon wealth should be a Man of Example in all the nicest Points of discipline, so every ship should be a Seminary … of Virtue and Instruction … where their tender Bodyes and Minds should be broken and beat betimes to those virtues and austerities that … go to the Composition of an able sea officer.[53]

'Twas not among the … [Romans] a Point of debate between Patrician and Plebean in actions of Glory … virtue was considered for her own single sake.[54]

Such morality had been lost in England by the effect of 'a gentle Prince, a lazy Court, and a generall vicious administracon of Government'. It was idle to pretend to sovereignty over, while lacking elementary competence in, the seas.

[W]e of this Nation enjoying all ye helps of Nature's Situation that can be … have nevertheless (in contempt as it were of Providence) slighted ye use of those aids, + by a proud Sloth (incident to a fierce + opulent People) … consented to sink beneath ourselves, + see our Rivals by a different Spirit + Conduct growing upon us, + threatening to mate us in that Element, wherein we have pretended to so long a Tenure of Sovraignty.[55]

---

[50] Sheres, 'A Discourse touching ye decay' p. 25.   [51] Ibid. p. 7.
[52] This was not an abstract opinion. During their Tangiers visit Sheres and Pepys were scandalized by the 'stupendous … tyranny and vice' of Captain Kirke. Pepys, *Tangier Papers* pp. 95–7, 100–1, 138–40.
[53] Sheres, 'A Discourse touching ye decay' pp. 15, 22–3, 24.
[54] Ibid. pp. 12–13.   [55] Sheres, 'Of Navall Discipline' p. 5.

Thus, despite the huge military effort also being made on land (in Ireland and on the continent), the war against France of 1689–97 saw a revival of the maritime political debates of 1625–9. Given the recent unresisted Dutch invasion, and the subsequent scale of naval commitment, this was not surprising. The war also produced a debate concerning the comparative merits of land and sea warfare.

Land Armyes, 'tis true are proper for Conquest, and to Spread Dominion to oppose an Invader, and perhaps to humble a proud-incroaching Neighbour; But Conquest is no where Recorded among the felicities of the English Nation, and Extent of Territoryes and Dominion would render us as Spain is, the less by being greater.[56]

This was Tory blue-water policy in the bud, although we have seen that Sheres accepted that for England's immediate security land and sea defence had to be intertwined. Within this context the emphasis of Sheres, as of Gibson, was upon England's special maritime vulnerabilities and resources. 'Our commerce breeds our Seamen, and lends them to the publick when Occasion calls.' Gibson even proposed republican-style election of naval officers: that 'all Pretenders to Comand of 1st, 2nd + 3te Rat[e]s, bee chosen by ye Venetian way of ye Ballotting Box', thus 'putting the Navy into ye hands of Seamen Recommended to yr Majesty's Choice … by a Balloting Box for every hundred volunteer Seamen in each Customhouse Port'.[57]

George Savile, Earl of Halifax, agreed with Sheres that 'The Navy is … the life and Soule of the Government,' and 'that England hath its root in the Sea, and a deep root too, from whence it sendeth its branches into both the Indyes'.[58] Halifax, however, like Shaftesbury before him, reflected less even-handedly on the merits of land war, claiming that England's 'Allegiance … to the Sea is due from [the fact that] … by that … alone wee are to be protected; and if wee have of late suffered the usurpation of other methods, contrary to the homage wee ow to that which must preserve us, it is time now to restore the Sea to its right'. Halifax agreed that the 'Corner Stone' of the naval building was 'the choice of Officers … [which] immediately leadeth us to the present Controversy between the Gentlemen and the Tarpaulins'.[59] However, unlike Sheres and Gibson, Halifax did not focus on the needs

---

[56] Ibid. pp. 26–9.
[57] BL Add MS 11602 [Gibson], 'Notes for better manageing war against the French' f. 103; Gibson, 'A Reformation' f. 166.
[58] Savile, *A Rough Draught of a New Modell at Sea*, in George Savile, *The Works of George Savile Marquis of Halifax*, (ed.) Mark N. Brown (3 vols., Oxford, 1989) vol. I p. 297.
[59] Ibid. pp. 297–8.

of the navy, from which conclusions might follow for the state. Instead he reversed this formula.

In the first place 'England must bee ... [an] Absolute Monarchy, A Commonwealth, or a Mixed Monarchy, as it now is'. Liberty being 'the vitall strength that should support us', absolute monarchy was out of the question. Republics requiring 'Vertue, Morality, diligence, Religion ... a Commonwealth is not *fit* for us, because *Wee* are not *fit* for a Commonwealth'.[60] Since it followed that the nation must remain a mixed monarchy 'there must bee a mixture in the Navy of Gentlemen and Tarpaulins'. However, this did not mean that the navy should be governed by unqualified officers. 'To Expect that *Quality* alone should waft Men up into places and Imployments, is as unreasonable as to think that a Ship, because it is carved and gilded, should bee fit to go to sea, without Sayles or tackling.' Rather,

Gentlemen, shall not be capable of bearing Office at Sea, except they are Tarpaulins too ... so trained up by a continued habit of living at Sea, that they may have a right to bee admitted free Denizens of Wapping ... and indeed here lyeth the difficulty, because the Gentlemen brought up under the connivance of a looser discipline ... will take it heavily to bee reduced within the fetters of such a new Modell ... [yet] When a Gentleman hath learnt how to obey, hee will grow much fitter to command ... When the undistinguishing discipline of a Ship hath tamed the *Young Mastership* ... hee then groweth proud in the right place ... In plaine English, Men of quality in their severall degrees must either restore themselves to a better opinion both for morality and diligence, or else *Quality* itself will be in danger of being extinguished.[61]

Thus, in Halifax's model, the discipline of a ship, far from dissolving the English aristocracy, might help to save it.

What both Sheres and Gibson wanted was an Anglo-Dutch revolution not only in politics, the military and finance, but in the attention paid to the 'infinite Liberalitys of Nature incommunicable to Forreigners improveable to our Naval Power'.[62] These included Britain's situation, climate, 'the genius of the people' and raw materials. Among the latter Sheres emphasized 'the Excellency of English Oak; that is like Golia[t]h's Sword, whereof there is not its like ... [for] Singular Perfection + kindly Growth'.[63] In 1600 an English inquiry into Dutch shipbuilding had reported, 'They think the wood which we use in England for shipping to be better than any wood which they use there, and is better dried

---

[60] Ibid. pp. 301–3. Halifax recorded in a notebook: 'Sunderland Ld: said once to me that a Commonwealth would do very well if it could be had.' BL Add MS 51511 p. 46.

[61] Savile, *Rough Draught* pp. 305–6.

[62] Sheres, 'Of Navall Architecture', Bodleian Library Rawl MS D 147 p. 33.

[63] Ibid.; Sheres, 'Of Timber, Woods and Forests', in 'Navall Essays' p. 39.

and seasoned.'[64] Gibson agreed concerning 'Our Advantages of Oake and Elme Timber the best in the World for Shipping, and wch splints the least by great shot,' though by this time 'Masts and Planke of all Sorts' were also imported from New England.[65]

In 1664 John Evelyn had published *Sylva, Or A Discourse of Forest-Trees* analysing the nation's timber resources, berating the damage done to them during the civil war and interregnum, and emphasizing their centrality to the nation's military security. He claimed that had the Spanish armada force landed, but failed to 'make good their *Conquest*', they had orders 'not to leave a Tree standing in the *Forest* of *Dean*'.[66] Like Defoe's *Robinson Crusoe* (see next chapter), Evelyn's work would prove more influential in France than in England.[67] Following this line of interest, Evelyn's history of *Navigation and Commerce* had paid attention to not only sails, but all other materials necessary for shipbuilding. The result was 'the most Beautiful, Useful, and stupendous Creature ... the whole World has to shew: And if the Winds, and Elements prove Auspicious ... this enormous Machine ... is ready for every Motion, and to brave all encounters and adventures, [and] undertakes to fathom the World it self'.[68]

According to Gibson, these materials included '(as long as our Country will beare hemp to grow) canvas and Cordage, Lead for shot and Iron for Gunns; Shot, Bolts, Anchors and the finest for Locks; Sea Cole to Worke it; Provisions for the Belly of all Sorts in great Plenty'. Sheres had held forth to Pepys in Tangiers concerning the properties of English as opposed to other European types of iron.[69] William Monson had discussed the same issues:

> let me tell you there is never a Lord, Knight, Gentl, or yeomen of any account in England, but is able to furnish ... Timber, Iron, wheat, mault, Beef, Pork, Bakon, Pease, Butter, Cheese, or homespun=cloth out of the woole ... No man that hath or hyreth land, but may as well plant for Hemp, to make lynes, netts, cordage ... as any other graine.[70]

In his later *History of Discoveries* (1725–6) Daniel Defoe offered a broader prescription for the country's future. Like that of Sammes, his

---

[64] NMM REC/3, 'Answers to the demands concerning the Navie of the United Provinces' f. 123.

[65] Gibson, 'Observations Upon Islands in Generall', NMM REC/6 Item 17 f. 280.

[66] John Evelyn, *Sylva, Or A Discourse of Forest-Trees, and the Propagation of Timber* (London, 1664), The Epistle Dedicatory, To The Reader and p. 108.

[67] Richard Grove, *Green Imperialism: Colonial Expansion, Tropical Island Edens and the Origins of Environmentalism, 1600–1860* (Cambridge, 1995) pp. 58, 160.

[68] Evelyn, *Navigation and Commerce* p. 4.

[69] Pepys, *Tangier Papers* p. 307.   [70] Monson, 'Relating to ye Fishery' ff. 15–16.

focus was upon the ancient Carthaginians, as architects, however, not of a British history but of a contemporary model: the inventors of commerce, the original settlers of America. That at the height of its power the empire of Carthage had included north and west Africa, Sicily, Sardinia, Spain and the Americas was clear from 'the Similitude of Manners and Customs, between the *Carthaginians* and the *Americans*'.[71] Hanno 'I take to be the Carthaginian Sir *Walter* Raleigh, as afterwards Sir *Walter* Raleigh was call'd the *English* Hanno'. However, following conquest by 'their cruel Enemies the Romans ... having but little Genius to Trade, and but few merchants among them', the whole Carthaginian edifice disappeared.[72]

The geography which interested Defoe in this work was not that of island or continent (neither Tyre nor Carthage had been islands), but that maritime complex capable of sustaining navigation and commerce. This had, in the ancient world, been predominantly Mediterranean, but was now Atlantic. What mattered was not the geographical totality of a nation's relationship to water, but its quality. Defoe's most substantial account of Britain in these terms, 'a trading, improving Nation' by dedication to manufactures and commerce, had come a year previously in his *Tour Thro' the Whole Island of Great Britain* (1724–5).[73]

Defoe's *Tour* combined the local detail of chorography with the chronological structure of a travel account. Where he diverged from both Camden (to whom he made frequent reference) and Sammes was in his programmatic lack of interest in antiquity. What attracted his attention in the places he visited was what they indicated, not about the past but about the future. In the *Tour*, as in the *History of Discoveries*, the geographical figure of an island was incidental. What was crucial, both to the organization of Defoe's work and its content, was the relationship of British society to water (both salt and fresh). This was because this was crucial to prosperity (improvement).

Thus Defoe's text was divided into Letters, each describing a tour or 'Circuit, if not a Circle'.[74] All of these were predominantly coastal. In the fourth Letter Defoe explained that it had been his original intention

to have coasted the whole Circuit of *Britain* by Sea, as 'tis said, *Agricola* the *Roman* General, did; and in this Voyage I would have gone about every Promontory, and into the Bottom of every Bay, and had provided myself with a good Yacht, and an able Commander for that Purpose; but I found it would

---

[71] [Defoe], *A General History of Discoveries* pp. 102–7.   [72] Ibid. pp. 105, 106, 107.
[73] Defoe, *A Tour* p. 252; Esther Moir, *The Discovery of Britain* ch. 4.
[74] Defoe, *A Tour* vol. I p. 4.

be too hazardous an Undertaking for any Man to justify himself in the doing it upon meer Foundation of Curiousity ... so I gave it over.[75]

Instead Defoe 'satisfied myself, to make the Circuit very near as perfect by Land, which I have done with much less Hazard, though with much more Pains and Expence'. During the resulting overland circumnavigation, Defoe's maritime preoccupations were everywhere evident.

The first Letter was dominated by his account of the coastal towns of Suffolk and Norfolk. Their position between London and the Newcastle colliery, and the trading towns of the Baltic and the United Provinces received much attention. So did reminiscences of the Anglo-Dutch wars. Towns not on the coast, like Bury St Edmunds, turned out to have been overrated ('a Town of which other Writers have talk'd very largely, and perhaps too much').[76] Although in Norfolk 'NORWICH is the Capital ... an antient, rich and populous City', coastal 'YARMOUTH is ... much older ... and at present, tho' not standing on so much Ground, yet better Built; much more Compleat ... and for Wealth, Trade, and advantage of its Situation, infinitely superior'.[77]

Greenwich was 'the most delightful Spot of Ground in *Great-Britain*'. The next twenty pages described the naval infrastructure and history of the south bank of the Thames, and later came that of Portsmouth.[78] 'Liverpoole is one of the Wonders of *Britain*.'[79] '*Newcastle* is a spacious, extended, infinitely populous Place.'[80] An Appendix to Letter III described the Scilly Islands as '*Excrescences* of the Island ... Rocks of ... Reproach' because of 'How many good Ships are, almost *continually* dash'd in pieces there, and how many brave Lives lost, in spight of the Mariners best skill, or the Light-Houses, and other Sea-Marks best Notice'.[81]

Between Yarmouth and King's Lynn Defoe 'resolv'd to pursue my first Design, (*viz*) To view the Sea-side on this Coast, which is particularly Famous for being one of the most dangerous and most fatal to the Sailors in all *England*'.[82] There followed many meteorological, geographic and navigational details to explain this phenomenon. He dwelt upon the calamitous storm of 1692 (as later, in another 'very wild Road, the *Downs*' of 1703, and at Plymouth, 1704).[83] Defoe found 'scarce a Barn, or a Shed, or a Stable; nay, not the Pales of their Yards, and Gardens ... but what was built of old Planks, Beams, Wales and Timbers ... the Wrecks of Ships'.[84] It is no surprise that Robinson Crusoe's first storm and shipwreck was at Yarmouth Roads.

---

[75] Ibid. vol. II p. 254.   [76] Ibid. vol. I p. 49.   [77] Ibid. pp. 63, 65.
[78] Ibid. pp. 94, 95–115, 136–9.   [79] Ibid. vol. II p. 664.   [80] Ibid. p. 659.
[81] Ibid. vol. I p. 244.   [82] Ibid. p. 69.   [83] Ibid. pp. 71–2, 121–2, 229–30.   [84] Ibid. p. 71.

One of the sub-plots of Defoe's book was fish. Around Dunwich 'they begin to talk of Herrings, and ... they Cure Sprats, in the same manner as they do Herrings at *Yarmouth*'.[85] Yarmouth smoke-cured 40,000 barrels of herring a season ('besides all the Herrings consum'd in the Country towns') and exported them to Italy, Spain and Portugal, in addition to their 'Fishing Trade to the North-Seas for White Fish ... called ... Cod'. Dunbar in Scotland processed herring the same way ('*red Herrings*') but because the fish were fatter they didn't keep as well.[86] Nearby, white fish was cured 'for *Bilboa*' (Spain) and 'great Quantities of Oysters' gathered for Edinburgh and Newcastle.[87] In Biddiford (north Devon) herring were cured with brine ('Salt upon Salt') rather than smoke. However, only 'a *Glasgow* Herring is esteem'd as good as a *Dutch* Herring, which in *England* they cannot come up to'.[88] Cromer was not famous for anything 'except good Lobsters'.[89] Milton and Feversham in Kent supplied 'the Fish-Market at *Billingsgate* ... with several sorts of Fish; but particularly ... the best and largest Oysters'.[90] At Bridport in Dorset, '*Mackerell*, the finest and largest I ever saw, were sold at the Sea Side a hundred for a Penny.'[91] At Lake Windermere '*Char Fish* ... as a Dainty, is Potted.'[92] Near Kirkaldy in Fife the locals diverted themselves by 'shooting of Porpoises, of which very great numbers are seen almost constantly ... and sometimes they have Grampuses, Finn Fish, and several Species of the small Whale Kind ... which they always make the best of, if they can take them'.[93]

At Arundel the River Arun was not as swift as Camden had said it was, but at least supplied 'the best *Mullets*, and the largest in *England*'.[94] In the distressingly dozy west Scottish port of Kirkubright 'the Salmon come and offer themselves, and go again' uncaught.[95] At Totness on the River Dart, small salmon ('salmon peal') were driven into a net by a trained dog, and Defoe bought 'six for our dinner, for ... two Pence a piece'.[96] The River *Tivy* in Wales was 'famous for its plenty of the best and largest Salmon in *Britain*'.[97] In a case for the piscine police '*Newcastle* salmon ... pickled or cured ... in Kits or Tubs' turned out to be from the Tweed, and were actually therefore '*Berwick* salmon'.[98] There was a salmon express: from the Derwent in Cumberland 'Salmon (fresh as they take it)' is rushed on 'Horses, which, changing often, go Night and Day

---

[85] Ibid. p. 55.   [86] Ibid. vol. II p. 696.
[87] Ibid. pp. 704–5. Here and throughout I have retained Defoe's spelling of place names.
[88] Ibid. p. 746.   [89] Ibid. vol. I pp. 67, 72, 261–2.   [90] Ibid. p. 113.
[91] Ibid. p. 215.   [92] Ibid. vol. II p. 679.   [93] Ibid. p. 780.
[94] Ibid. vol. I p. 132; Camden got another river wrong on pp. 148–9.
[95] Ibid. vol. II p. 733. 'They have also white Fish, but cure none; and Herrings, but pickle none.'
[96] Ibid. vol. I p. 225.   [97] Ibid. vol. II p. 457.   [98] Ibid. p. 660.

without Intermission ... so that the Fish come very sweet and good to London, where the extraordinary price they yield ... at two shillings ... to four Shillings per Pound, pay very well for the Carriage'.[99]

At John O'Groats in far northern Scotland, by contrast, there was 'Salmon in such Plenty as is scarce credible, and so cheap, that to those who have any Substance to buy with, it is not worth their while to catch it themselves'.[100] At Dartmouth 'a great *Shoal*, or as they call it a *Scool* of *Pilchards* came swimming with the Tide of Flood directly', driven into the river by 'a whole Army of Porpuses'.

We sent our Servant to the Key to buy some, who for a Half-penny, brought us seventeen, and ... with these went to Dinner; the Cook at the Inn broil'd them for us, which is their way of Dressing them, with Pepper and Salt, which cost us about a Farthing; so that two of us, and a Servant Din'd, *and at a Tavern too*, for three Farthings, Dressing and all, and this is the Reason of telling the Tale.[101]

Four shillings per pound versus three farthing for an entire meal: Defoe's London readers could do the maths. For the central theme of Defoe's work was actually the nation-sized economic powerhouse of the metropolis. All empires needed a capital, and London was Defoe's Babylon, Athens and Constantinople.

What Defoe most wished to illustrate, even from the periphery, and especially from it, was the incredible market and trading stimulus of London. Grain was barged, fish ferried, cheese shipped, bullock driven, coal sailed, iron moved, logs floated and geese driven towards its all-embracing maw. Around the outskirts '(as the Inhabitants say) above a Thousand new Foundations have been erected, besides old Houses repaired, all since the Revolution'.[102] The 'Increase of People, as well as Buildings in *London*' required explanation, 'but the Discourse seems too Political to belong to this Work'.[103] Discussing the Thames ('The whole River ... from *London*-Bridge to *Black Wall* is one great Arsenal, nothing in the World can be like it'), Defoe considers, before dismissing, the suggestion 'that there are more Ships ... seen at *Amsterdam*'.[104] One result of London's vitality was the improvement of the entire isle. As for the other:

In a Word, nothing can be more Beautiful; here is a plain and pleasant Country, a rich fertile Soil, cultivated and enclosed to the utmost perfection of Husbandry, then bespangled with Villages; those Villages fill'd with these Houses, and the Houses surrounded with Gardens, Walks, Vistas, Avenues ... the Country adjoining fill'd with the Palaces of the *British* Nobility and Gentry ... looking

---

[99] Ibid. p. 684.   [100] Ibid. p. 825.   [101] Ibid. vol. I pp. 226–7.
[102] Ibid. p. 6.   [103] Ibid. vol. II p. 324.   [104] Ibid. pp. 349–50.

Figure 2 London as a maritime city-state. The River Thames with St Paul's Cathedral on Lord Mayor's Day, c.1747–8 (oil on canvas) by Canaletto (Giovanni Antonio Canal) (1697–1768), Lobkowicz Palace, Prague Castle, Czech Republic/The Bridgeman Art Library.

North, behold, to crown all, a fair Prospect of the whole City of *London* it self; the most glorious Sight without exception, that the whole World at present can show, or perhaps ever cou'd show since the Sacking of *Rome* in the *European*, and the burning the Temple of *Jerusalem* in the *Asian* part of the World.[105]

The world was London's oyster, and it now included not only Europe and the Atlantic, but Asia.

Gibson and Sheres recorded their arguments in manuscripts which did, however, circulate among the political elite. Evelyn, Temple, Fletcher, Halifax and Defoe exercised the prerogative of print, the last-named becoming a phenomenon within more than one such genre. All testified to the continuing relevance of century-old themes, including the 'undistinguishing discipline of a ship' which was a society, and similitude of the state. These themes were revisited in the course of a decisive Anglo-Dutch transformation. As its centre was metropolitan (and cosmopolitan), so the context of this process was European and global.

In the following chapters we consider the consequent geographical redescription of the nation and empire (whether English or British). This brought back into focus the distinction between an island and a continental power. As we have seen, this was as old as Greece, for which the real continental power had been not Sparta, but Persia. Luxurious and despotical, Persia was, for Britain, now France (or China, or Spain).

---

[105] Ibid. vol. I p. 168.

7   The world in an island

We came to Aiolia Island next. Aiolos lived there,
Hippotes's son: the deathless Gods are his good friends.
The island's floating, walls are entirely around it,
Unbreakable bronze, and the smooth-faced cliff is a high one.
Homer, The Odyssey Book 10, lines 1–4[1]

They go to an Island to take special charge,
Much warmer than Britain, and ten times as large:
No customs-house duty, no freightage to pay,
And tax-free they'll live when in Botany Bay.
Ballad, Whitehall Evening Post, 19 December 1786[2]

After an Athenian tweak during the Elizabethan period, islands versus continents had enjoyed a brief early Stuart revival before the mid-century collapse of monarchy. As the revolution of 1689 and its military aftermath transformed national power, and created a British state, so this aspect of self-definition re-emerged. Now, however, the framework was not dynastic but political, military and cultural. All of these developments had national, regional, European and global contexts.

For George Savile insularity equalled circumscription:

Wee are in an island, Restrained to it by God Almighty ... Happy Confinement! That hath made us free, rich, and quiet ... Our Scituation hath made Greatnesse abroad by land Conquests unnaturall things to us. It is true we have made excursions and Glorious ones too ... but they did not last ... Admitt the English to be Gyants in Courage, yet they must not hope to succeed in making warre against Heaven, which seemeth to have enjoyed them, to acquiesce in being happy with their own Circle.[3]

Henry Sheres was more expansive. By comparison with France,

I shall ... shew ... the Necessity Islanders are under to Cherish + Cultivate Maritime Applications, preferable to all others; as being the surest + most

---

[1] Homer, *The Odyssey of Homer*, trans. Edward McCrorie (Baltimore, 2004) p. 135.
[2] Quoted in Hughes, *The Fatal Shore* p. 76.   [3] Savile, *A Rough Draught* p. 296.

natural Bottom whereon to build their Happiness. In which argument I shall do my best to shew, that as People so situate have more native Helps towards ye Improvement of Navigation, than those of the Continent; so, of all Islands in ye World this of Great Britain has ye Right of Superiority.[4]

Another contemporary writer put it similarly: 'Nature has assign'd us an Island, and kind Providence furnish'd us with Materials to build ships, and with men of able Bodies and stout Hearts to man them: nor has the divine Goodness been wanting to supply us with navigable Rivers, and safe Harbours.'[5] Earlier Sir William Temple had mused that while the United Provinces possessed an incalculable advantage for trade 'by those two great Rivers of the *Rhyne* and the *Mose*, reaching up, and Navigable so mighty a length into so rich and populous Countreys of the Higher and Lower *Germany*', when it came to harbours the advantage lay with England.[6] He echoed Gibson in taking the prevailing westerly winds to be 'the natural reason of so many deep and commodious Havens found upon all the *English* side of the Channel, and so few (or indeed none) upon the *French* and *Dutch*; An advantage seeming to be given us by Nature, and never to be equal'd by any Art or Expence of our Neighbours'.[7]

Twenty years later Sheres gave Halifax's image of the ocean as a circle a global redescription. This sketched

a Scheme and Modell of a Maritime Monarchy. Wherin I shall shew how I con- ceive this Nation has by nature all the materials necessary to lay the Foundation of such a Power by Sea, as to entitle us not only to a Dominion of the Narrow Seas, but to the Wide Ocean ... which giving us a Paramount incontestable Power by Sea (which is the Circle that seems appointed by Nature to contain + circumscribe our Ambition) ensures our Safety + Liberty at home.[8]

Halifax had not mentioned the possibility – briefly achieved during the interregnum – of 'Paramount Power by Sea'. Sheres could surely not have imagined that within two generations this would be a reality. Indeed, arguably the image used by both men of the ocean as a sphere of domin- ion belonged to a land power, still actually to witness the sea change from bridge for invaders into gateway to the world.[9] '[H]aving nature so much in our favour', Sheres continued, 'nothing but want of Genius, Art and

---

[4] Sir Henry Sheres, 'Of Navigation + ye Benefit of Nav[igationa]ll Science', Bodleian Library Rawlinson MS D 147 ff. 3–4.

[5] *An Inquiry into the Causes of our Naval Miscarriages* (2nd edn, London, 1707).

[6] Temple, *Observations Upon the United Provinces* p. 129.   [7] Ibid. p. 125.

[8] Sir Henry Sheres, 'A Scheme + Model of a Marit[i]me Monarchy', in 'Navall Essays', Bodleian Library Rawlinson MS D147 p. 67.

[9] Compare Ogilby's description of 'one continu'd Sea, extending itself round the Universal Globe' from an imagined vantage point within the straits of Magellan. Ogilby, *America* p. 1.

Application can be thought to frustrate so vast a Design.' This maritime or navalist account of England's nature, potential or destiny remained a permanent component of eighteenth-century political discourse, ebbing or flooding according to military developments.

One peer in 1735 drew a contrast in these terms with the Dutch. 'They have the misfortune to be situated upon the Continent, and may consequently be suddenly invaded by great armies; they have an extensive frontier to defend ... but as we have the happiness to be surrounded by the sea; as we have the happiness to have a fleet, superior to any that can probably be sent against us; we have no occasion to be worried.' 'The situation of Great Britain,' wrote Lord Bolingbroke two years later, 'the character of her people ... fit her for trade and commerce ... The sea is our barrier, ships are our fortresses, and the mariners, that trade and commerce alone can furnish, are the garrisons to defend them.'[10]

As we have seen, this argument had its origins in the early seventeenth century, or earlier. But before 1763 at least, such complacency about the military self-sufficiency of the navy was relatively rare. Even if the British navy was superior – which was not clear – it would not remain so without maintenance of the balance of power within Europe. As since the sixteenth century England's religion and liberties had to be defended in Europe. 'Notwithstanding we are insulars', observed Lord Bute in 1762, 'we are either by our political or commercial interest connected with every power in Europe.'[11] England could not pull up the drawbridge if there wasn't one. What, asked the Duke of Argyll, echoing Defoe, if the armada had made landfall? What of various French-sponsored invasion attempts? 'Even the happy Revolution [of 1688] ... is an instance how little a fleet is to be depended on ... By this accident we discovered our liberties, but if we should ever resolve to trust entirely to our fleet, the same accident may hereafter be the cause of our losing them.'[12] To put this another way, islands might be less vulnerable than continental powers under some circumstances, but more vulnerable under others. In either case, with a narrow channel, and within the European geopolitical system, geography was not destiny. As ever, what mattered was what was made of natural situation by society, culture and power.

It was therefore entirely appropriate that the first sustained analysis of the properties and potential of England's insular situation looked at its advantages and disadvantages. First Richard Gibson considered 'the Advantages' and 'Disadvantages (wth respect to Defensiveness only)

---

[10] Quoted in Simms, *Three Victories* pp. 235, 253.   [11] Ibid. p. 488.
[12] Ibid. p. 223 (see also pp. 302, 307, 354–6, 366, 369).

ariseing to an Island from the Single Consideration of Its being such'.[13] From this level of generality he turned, like Temple whose work he read, to

the Advantages or Disadvantages ... ariseing to this Island in particular, Circumstantiated as it is, with respect to Its neighbouring Continent ... [the] number and nature of its Ports, Condition of its Seas – And ... Winds ... The number and Quality of Its Inhabitants – Its store of home Materialls for shipping – And provisions for men.

Being of his generation and disposition, Gibson's take was sober and admonitory. The advantages or disadvantages of islands in general were relative to the military and especially naval strength of their neighbours. When another power was master of the sea, islands were vulnerable. This was shown not only by ancient examples but

to come home, the Danes conquer'd this Island by their Navys Ravageing Lincoln, and Yorkshire up the Humber; Kent and Essex up the Thames; Sommerset Shire Glostershire up the Severne, and Cheshire-Lancashire up the Dee ... Our head=Lands + bayes giving receptacle to great Fleets to ride safe, and the many places in this Kingdome to Land at; As Julius Cesar at Deale and Romans Gate, and Wm the Conqueror at Pevensy, and his present Maty at Torbay and since that the French at Tinmouth without opposition. And altho' King Henry the 8th + Queen Elizabeth endeavoured by Building Castles ... to hinder It, yet none of them is of Force but Hull to oppose a formidable Enemy from Landing.[14]

To counter this vulnerability Gibson now counselled a full-scale Dutch-style makeover of English culture, government and demography. This involved fortifying every navigable river mouth and harbour (he listed twenty-eight), appropriating

soe many of the Inland Parishes adjacent, as to bring their Impotent and Idle people thither to be set on worke upon the Fishing Trade, spinning carding weaving, Dressing hemp ... for shipping; [they] will in halfe a century ... be brought to see the sweetness of Trade and Sea Voyages; That and their Fish Dyet +c will multiply them to double the number a like quantity of People in Inland Townes can arrive to, and as Holland, Increase to 26 cittys in a County. That with Immunitys to Trade separate from other Ports, as in Holland, will (this way) divert all pretentions to an Invasion, even by a Royall Army; and lay the foundation of a lasting greatnesse by such seminarys for sea men, the want of which in a little time more may undoe us, before we know how.[15]

---

[13] Gibson, 'Observations Upon Islands in Generall' f. 271.
[14] Ibid. ff. 275–6.   [15] Ibid. f. 276.

This was in conformity with Gibson's earlier praise of Dutch naval government. He also noted the importance of Athenian and other examples. For 'where they are an overbalance to ye naval strength of their neighbours ... the advantages touching Islands ... are many'.

As History informs us of the Athenians, Rhodians, Carthaginians, Romans, Venetians – Genoveses, Danes, Portugueses, Spaniards, Dutch, English ... and to come nearer home, The Dutch recovered the Briel and their Freedome from the Spaniard (as the Athenians ... formerly did from the Persians) by their Sea Conduct and Courage. As the Prince of Orange raised the Siege of Leiden by the help of Flat botom'd Boates and Seamen, and they and our selves became secure by destroying the Spanish Armada in 1588. And while the Rochellers were Masters by Sea they were above the French King's Power of subjecting them ... To give a present Instance ... the Riches and Navall strength of the Little Island of Walcharen (alias Zeland) compar'd with the Kingdomes of Spaine Portugall ... Muscovia +c, being much more than an equall match at sea to either.[16]

Islands had more ports 'than other Countrys, where but part of It lye toward the sea' and so 'better opportunities to breed Seamen'. 'Navigation where it fflourishes, by getting ... food out of the sea, and worke for the Poore, Increases the Inhabitants along the Sea Coasts', as might be seen by comparing Spain with Holland. In England's case the same maritime infrastructure made possible a trade to

all our Plantations, with thinges of our owne Growth; In returne for Furrs, Masts, Tobacco, Sugars, Cotton, Indigo – Ginger +c From Hudsons bay, New found Land, New=Jersey, New York, Mary=Land, Virginia, Carolina, Bermudas, Barbados, Caribbee Islands, Jamaica ... soe as when ever wee leave off our wanton appetite for wines, silkes, spices and toyes; our home Trade and Colonies (having secured Ireland and Scotland) will be enough to support us without Dependence on or Trade wth any other People of the World, And noe hurt to us by those Colonies taking away our People, were not the love of Cele=bacy become a Mode more in this Age, than ever was knowne since the Days of Popery.[17]

We encountered this perception of colonies 'taking away our people' in Penn. From about 1640 the English population growth attracting public attention in Hakluyt's time had ceased and yielded to moderate decline. In 1741, however, by which time the increase had resumed, John Oldmixon dismissed the anxiety that plantations depleted the metropolis of people on the grounds that the key to prosperity was not population anyway, but productivity (industry). The antithesis of both was idleness. By this criterion the most productive part of the world was Barbados, a

---

[16] Ibid. ff. 271, 277.   [17] Ibid. f. 272.

fact necessary to make practicable the extreme cost and inefficiency of slave labour.[18] Over and above such factors, Oldmixon argued that to Britain colonial activity had its own special value. For 'as we in *England* are the Inhabitants of an Island, we have no Ways of conveying our Product and Manufactures abroad, but by Navigation'. For acquisition of this skill the activities of 'the Merchant, the Mariner, or the Planter' were equally to be encouraged.[19]

While no less alert to the importance of navigation, Gibson's interest in colonies hinged upon mercantile self-sufficiency. He was, after all, a product of the English republic which had set in place the system anchored by the Navigation Act (1651, 1660) and developed by the Staple Act (1663). Like Sheres his greatest concern remained the absence of industry and good government at home. Thus 'the decay of our Sea Trades and Sea Port Townes since anno. 1660 came by our many great Warrs since, with bad Paym.t of the Navy … neglecting Harbours as at … Harwich, Dover, Rye' and the 'great Evill of putting our Naval Strength into the hands of our Gentry'.[20] Any advantages furnished by nature were useless without appropriate cultivation. Hence the need for 'wholesome Incitements to a greater Application + Vigilance than we seem disposed to practice in the Polishing + Ensuring our Navall Strength'.

In the same decade John Flamsteed, first Astronomer Royal at the new Observatory at Greenwich, lamented the tendency of 'our modern Sailors' to 'look upon fortune as ye sole disposer of wealth and Advancement' and to appeal to 'Fatality' to excuse and cover faults. There was no substitute among seamen, and especially Masters, for proper education in geometry, trigonometry, geography and astronomy. Flamsteed praised the achievement of Hipparchus the Rhodian 'for finding Latitude of the ships at sea', thus encouraging 'ye Rhodians to adventure to sea more boldly then those that had not ye Like'. He noted that Americus Vespucius was the first European to study the skies of the southern hemisphere, and 'tis remarkable that he who first observ'd ye stars … and not he who first discover'd ye Land, gave his name to ye vast Western continent'.[21]

According to Gibson the pre-eminent importance of art, experience and education applied even though the natural advantages being

[18] A claim later expanded upon by Adam Smith, *An Inquiry into the Nature and Causes of the Wealth of Nations* (2 vols., Homewood, Ill., 1963) vol. I pp. 299–320. In fact plantation agriculture worked by slaves remained extremely profitable. See Bayly, *Birth of the Modern World* pp. 40–1, 51–5.

[19] [Oldmixon], *The British Empire in America* 'Introduction' pp. xvi–xvii.

[20] Gibson, 'Observations Upon Islands in Generall' ff. 277–8.

[21] PL MS 2184, 'April 21 1697 Mr Flamsteed's Acct of ye Beginning, Progress + present State … in ye Doctrine + Practice of Navigation' ff. 8, 18–21.

neglected in England's case were greater than those of 'any other Spot of Ground in the World'.

> As that the Tydes of Flood[,] from Cape cleare round Ireland to the Wes[t]-ward, and then through St Georges Channell and both about Scotland one way, and alsoe up the channel ye other, both meeting at the long sand head Joyntly runn up the River of Thames. Besides the Winds blowing westerly for more than 3 quarters of the year makes all our Cape Lands and Bayes, oppos-ite to the French and Dutch=Coast, good Roades for All our great Shipps to ride with Security out any winter storme beyond any Port of France Flanders or Holland.[22]

In addition Gibson spoke from experience in claiming that the English coast yielded a superior anchor hold to the French, 'being generally a stiff clay, chalk or hard Gravell, when theirs is only a hard Rock or loose sand'. The Flemish and Dutch coast was too shallow for 'great Shipps' and 'choak'd up with Quicksands ... Their Ports alsoe are oft Frozen up 2 months or more in a yeare.' In addition all 'French, Flemings, Dutch, Hamburgers, Danes, Swedes Poles +c must ... pass in sight of our Islands to France Spaine Portugal, the Streights Guinea, East and West Indies or fetch a Circum=Navigation round Scotland + Ireland'.

Finally, 'The Quality of England's Inhabitants is by all Historians ... agreed to be Martiall, whether from the Quantity of flesh eaten by Its Inhabitants ... or its often being at Warr with its Neighbours, or from our many great intestine Warrs; or from the Freedome enjoyed by Its inhabit-ants or from our Air.'[23] In 1678 Pepys had recorded pages noted to him 'by Mr Gibson ... from Sir William Temple's book ... touching the confessed courage of the English, his imputing much of it to their diet'.[24] On that occasion Gibson followed up with instances of English sea courage within his memory.[25] Yet here his conclusion was melancholy. 'And is it not a great Pity that our Courages should be soe often baulkd by ill Conduct?'[26]

Defoe had his say on islands in the anonymous *Life and Strange Surprising Adventures of Robinson Crusoe, of York, Mariner*. Crusoe began by revisiting Hakluyt's theme of an appeal to God for rescue from a tur-bulent ocean. Having ostensibly just left Hull on his first sea voyage on 1 September 1651 (an interesting date), Crusoe experienced the terror

---

[22] Gibson, 'Observations Upon Islands in Generall' f. 273.
[23] Ibid. ff. 273–4, 283.
[24] Pepys, *Samuel Pepys' Naval Minutes* p. 27 (and see pp. 23, 25). Temple, *Observations Upon the United Provinces* pp. 157–8: '[T]he Yeomanry and Commonalty of *England* are generally braver than in other Countreys ... Their ... constant food, being of flesh', a fact which Temple attributed to low English taxes.
[25] Gibson, 'A few Instances of English Courage and Conduct at Sea'.
[26] Gibson, 'Observations Upon Islands in Generall' f. 283.

of a storm, causing him to 'Vow ... that if it would please God here to spare my Life this one Voyage ... I would ... never set ... my Foot ... into a Ship again'.[27] When the wind dropped, however, and this promise was neglected, a second worse storm sank his ship off Yarmouth. Still Crusoe could not mend his ways. It was only many years later, shipwrecked and subsequently marooned on an island, that he was brought to attend to the words of scripture: '*Call on me, and I will deliver you.*' At that point Crusoe realized that the 'Captivity I was in' was not simply that of 'the Island ... [and] my solitary Life ... [which] was certainly a prison to me'. In exchange for '*Repentence*', what made Crusoe's internal storm a calm was the promise of 'Deliverance from Sin'.[28]

Observing that Crusoe's predicament as 'a prisoner locked up with the eternal bars and bolts of the Ocean' was prefigured by enslavement by Barbary corsairs, Linda Colley has seen in Defoe's work a parable of the vulnerability of early empire.[29] Yet it should also be observed that Crusoe's first island prison was not the 'uninhabited wilderness' upon which he was cast away, but Britain. Within Britain it was his unquenchable longing to escape from those shores ('I would be satisfied with nothing but going to Sea') which separated him from his family and exposed him to all his subsequent misfortunes. In this sense it was not even the island which isolated Crusoe, but his absolute need to leave. It was in the context of an emerging empire that Crusoe's 'Thoughts ... [were] entirely bent upon seeing the World'.[30] Yet family and community give way to solitude. The 'World' Crusoe eventually discovered was the divinely wrought reality of himself.

Thus within the genre of travel narrative, what was new about *Crusoe* was its internal voyage. Longing to get out, eventually Crusoe got in. This was one explanation for the book's success. For all of its drama, and exotic locations, it offered familiarity, domesticity and routine. One result was an intimate, and informal, subject–reader relationship. A consequence of this intimacy was universality. Thus, although it has been suggested that *Crusoe* appealed particularly to a nation of islanders, and Virginia Woolf declared it a cultural production 'of the race', in fact '*Crusoe* ... enjoyed a far more enthusiastic reception in France than it had in England,'[31] and it was Jean-Jacques Rousseau who wrote

---

[27] Daniel Defoe, *Robinson Crusoe: an Authoritative Text Contexts Criticism*, (ed.) Michael Shinagel (2nd edn, London, 1994) p. 8.

[28] Ibid. p. 71. In 1788 a convict in the new penal colony at Port Arthur, New South Wales, lamented his 'Crusoe-like adventures'. Quoted by Hughes, *The Fatal Shore* p. 103.

[29] Colley, *Captives* p. 1.   [30] Defoe, *Crusoe* p. 6.

[31] Grove, *Green Imperialism* pp. 233–4; Virginia Woolf, *The Common Reader* (1925) p. 125: *Crusoe* so 'resembles one of the anonymous productions of the race itself' that

in *Emile* in 1762 that *Crusoe* was the one book 'that should be required reading for all children'.

> This is the first book Emile will read; and for a long time it will form his whole library ... Robinson Crusoe on his island, deprived of the help of his fellow-men, without the means of carrying on the various arts, yet finding food, preserving his life, and procuring a certain amount of comfort; this is the thing to interest people of all ages ... The surest way to raise him above prejudice and to base his judgements on the true relations of things is to put him in the place of a solitary man.[32]

To speak to the imagination of the reader thrown on to their own resources was to dissolve the communities of nation and age. In France, '[T]he cult of Crusoe became so well developed and its themes so frequently imitated that it was probably fundamental to the formulation of the tropical island as the location for complex Utopias and a focus for ideas about social reform and even revolution in mid-eighteenth-century France.'[33] Across Europe *Robinson Crusoe* became 'a work whose ... impact is so pervasive as to be almost unthinkable ... it was to assume an educational importance, an overwhelming popularity and an unquestionable literary influence ... perhaps unrivalled by any other single work'.[34]

Nineteenth-century classics with explicit references to Defoe like Jules Verne's *The Mysterious Island*, Wyss's *Swiss Family Robinson*, *Masterman Ready*, and Robert Louis Stevenson's *Treasure Island* emerged from France, Switzerland, England and Scotland respectively.[35] This reinforces the suggestion that the European imaginative force of the island, from More and Shakespeare to Stevenson, had little to do with national geography. It could be suggested, in the nineteenth century at least, that it stood as a metaphor for modern individualism. But as islands were connected by water, none of these works depicts or advocates a self-containment at odds with Christianity. To lose 'the world' was to discover reality. They instead depict the island as a world, or microcosm, and island experience, like individual experience, as universal.

Aside from the latter work's identified author, there was little obviously to distinguish *The Life ... of Robinson Crusoe ... Who lived Eight and Twenty Years, all alone in an un-inhabited Island on the Coast of America* (London, 1719) from Captain George Shelvocke's *A Voyage Round the World By Way of the Great South Sea, Perform'd in the Years 1719, 20, 21,*

'the name of Daniel Defoe has no right to appear upon the title-page'. The name of Daniel Defoe did not appear on the title page.

[32] Rousseau, *Emile* quoted by Loxley, *Problematic Shores* p. 7.
[33] Grove, *Green Imperialism* p. 229.
[34] Loxley, *Problematic Shores* pp. 7, 73.   [35] Ibid. chs. 1–3.

22, in the Speedwell *of* London ... *till she was cast away on the Island of* Juan Fernandes, *in May 1720* (London, 1726). Both were sold 'at the *Ship* in *Pater-Noster-Row*'. Both accounts shared aspects of their form (typography) and content (comparable veracity effect), though only one of the voyages took place. Both, that is to say, were contributions to the process of textual navigation by which English readers had explored and mapped their relationship to the world, in time and space, since Hakluyt and earlier.

Defoe's work, though relocated to the Atlantic, had been inspired by the marooning on Juan Fernandes island (off Chile) of Alexander Selkirk in 1709.[36] Several accounts of Selkirk's experience were published, some suggesting that, like Crusoe later, for the castaway his loss (of the world) had been his salvation. According to Richard Steele, Selkirk later 'frequently bewailed his return to the world, which could not, he said, with all its enjoyments, restore him to the tranquillity of his solitude'.[37] Guillaume Raynal took Selkirk's experience to furnish a lesson about the dubious benefits of contemporary civilization. Selkirk 'was happy as soon as he was so taken up with supplying his wants, as to forget his own country, his language, his name, and even the utterance of words'.[38]

George Shelvocke's actual arrival on Juan Fernandes eleven years later, like that of Crusoe, involved destruction of his vessel. Unlike Crusoe, however, Shelvocke did not arrive alone. Relatedly, and unlike Crusoe, all of his thoughts were bent upon escape. Devoid of introspection, and despite company, Shelvocke expressed the singularity of his condition in a remarkable passage:

In short, every thing that one sees or hears in this place is perfectly romantick; the very structure of the island, in all its parts, has a certain savage irregular beauty, which is not to be expressed; the many prospects of lofty inaccessible hills, and the solitariness of the gloomy narrow valleys, which a great part of the day enjoy little benefit from the sun, and the fall of waters, which one hears all around, would be agreeable to none but those who would indulge themselves, for a time, in a pensive melancholy. To conclude, nothing can be conceiv'd more dismally solemn, than to hear the silence of the still night destroy'd by the surf of the sea beating on the shore, together with the violent roaring of the sea-lions repeated all around by the echoes of deep vallies, the incessant howling of the seals, (who according to their age, make a hoarser or a shriller noise) so

---

[36] Howe, *Nature, Culture and History* p. 12.

[37] Steele in *The Englishman* no. 26, 3 December 1713, pp. 121–4, quoted in Grove, *Green Imperialism* p. 227.

[38] Guillaume Raynal, *A Philosophical and Political History of the Settlements and Trade of the Europeans in the East and West Indies*, trans. J. Justamond (4 vols., Dublin, 1776) vol. IV p. 182.

that in this confused medley, a man might imagine that he heard the different tones of all the species of animals on earth mix'd together.[39]

If Shelvocke was not alone, his island was. If its topography enveloped him, it remained inaccessible. Yet like Crusoe, in an entirely different way, in it Shelvocke discovered the world.

The roaring of Juan Fernandes' seals and sea-lions was understated in the context of the violence committed against those blameless animals by Shelvocke and his colleagues. Consequently it also abated. When the castaways arrived 'on the beach ... [seals] lay so thick that we were obliged to clear our way of them as we went along'.[40] In due course the men erected 'dwellings ... cover'd ... with the skins of Seals and Sea-lions'. They passed their 'time in the evening in making a great fire before my tent ... roasting craw-fish in the embers'.[41] These were 'the largest craw-fish [Pacific ocean lobsters] I ever saw; it requir'd no other trouble to catch them than to knock down a seal, take out its entrails, make them fast to a line, and stand on the rocks, where you might take them at discretion'.[42] More generally,

At first the weather not permitting us to go a fishing for some time ... necessity drove us to make use of seals; but [we] could not, for a pretty while venture upon their flesh, and therefore began by their entrails, which are really palatable. This was the destruction of great numbers of those amphibious creatures, who, in short, were so alarm'd by such continual slaughters of them, and being offended by the stench, or terrified by the sight of so many of their putrified carcasses, that from the innumerable shoals we had of them at the beginning, they diminish'd so much, by taking refuge in other parts of the Island ... that they appear'd very thin in our bay; which ... oblig'd us to eat of their flesh.[43]

Forty years earlier, in 1683, William Dampier had visited the same island, describing 'thousands, I might say possibly millions of them [seals], either sitting on the Bays, or going and coming in the Sea round the Island', and also sea-lions 'making a hideous noise'.[44] Three years after Shelvocke's

---

[39] George Shelvocke, *A Voyage Round the World By Way of the Great South Sea* (London, 1726) pp. 257–8. Compare Bougainville on the Malvinas (Falkland Islands) fifty years later: 'the horizon terminated by bald mountains, the land lacerated by the sea ... a vast silence, now and then interrupted by the howls of marine monsters'. *A Voyage Round the World ... By Lewis de Bougainville*, trans. John Reinhold Forster (London, 1772) pp. 44–5. For a more upbeat account of Juan Fernandes see George Anson, *Voyage Round the World, 1740–44*, comp. Richard Walter, extract in Jonathan Lamb, Vanessa Smith and Nicholas Thomas (eds.), *Exploration and Exchange: a South Seas Anthology 1680–1900* (Chicago, 2000), pp. 39–45.
[40] Shelvocke, *A Voyage* p. 208.   [41] Ibid. pp. 211–12.   [42] Ibid. p. 253.
[43] Ibid. pp. 243–4.
[44] William Dampier, *A New Voyage Round the World, Describing particularly, The Isthmus of America* (London, 1697) pp. 89, 91.

appeared another island travel account: *Madagascar; Or, Robert Drury's Journal, During Fifteen Years' Captivity On That Island* (London, 1729). Entailing a story of shipwreck (that of an East Indiaman) and subsequent enslavement, this contained Crusoe-like elements, and appeared with an anonymous editor's Preface stating:

> At the first Appearance of this Treatise, I make no Doubt of its being taken for such another Romance as 'Robinson Crusoe'; but whoever expects to find here the fine Inventions of a prolific Brain will be deceived; for so far as every Body concerned in the Publication knows, it is nothing else but a plain, honest Narrative of Matter of Fact.[45]

In general the work's authenticity seems to have been accepted, though an alternative interpretation developed that it had been edited or even written by Defoe. According to an edition published in 1890, the first damaging attacks on Drury's veracity appeared in France, source of most genuine early modern accounts of Madagascar, including De Flacourt's *Histoire de Madagascar* (1661), to parts of which *Madagascar* bore a striking resemblance.[46] Although this editor did not doubt the existence of Drury or his shipwreck, he thought the account of his slavery a charming but improbable romance, and either execution or piracy a much more likely fate. In 1943 the work was 'proved' to have been written by Defoe; in 1991 it was pronounced by a marine archaeologist to be 'a largely accurate historical document'.[47]

Like the fictional Crusoe, and in very similar language, Drury emphasized his longing for 'the sea'.

> And I well remember that, from eleven years of age, my mind had taken such an unhappy bent this way that it grew with my stature, and at length became an obstinate resolution; and not all the tender insinuations of my dear and indulgent mother, though she once entreated me on her knees, nor the persuasions of my tender father and other friends, could make any impression on me.[48]

Thus, as in *Crusoe*, that by which Drury was first isolated, if not yet marooned, was his determination to leave home. In the other work of fiction comparable in stature to *Crusoe*, Lemuel Gulliver similarly confessed his 'insatiable Desire of seeing foreign Countries ... the Thirst I had of seeing the World, notwithstanding my past Misfortunes, continuing as violent as ever'.[49] *Gulliver's Travels into Several Remote Nations of the World* also began with shipwreck (following 'a violent Storm to the

---

[45] Robert Drury, *Madagascar; Or, Robert Drury's Journal, During Fifteen Years' Captivity On That Island*, (ed.) Capt. Pasfield Oliver (New York, 1969) Preface p. 31.

[46] Ibid., Oliver's 'Introduction' p. 15.

[47] Colley, *Captives* pp. 14–15.   [48] Drury, *Madagascar* p. 40.

[49] Swift, *Gulliver's Travels* pp. 5, 147; Part 3 p. 3.

Northwest of *Van Dieman's* Land'). Gulliver claimed to be a cousin of William Dampier, whose bestselling *New Voyage Around the World* had introduced English readers to north-west Australia.[50] There followed, if not slavery, then capture and constraint. Even having escaped Lilliput for England, and then later Brobingnag, Gulliver kept going back to sea.

What is one to make of this fictional and non-fictional longing to sail? It was obviously a symptom of Britain's new global connectedness and centrality. It was also a reflection of how many were now actually travelling, in the maritime trades or to and from the colonies, the hazards notwithstanding. Nor were these travellers only men.[51] At last water had indeed set the country in motion. Defoe's and Swift's parables both had their morals. In his *Tour Thro' Great Britain* Defoe laid down as one of four 'few Things' needed to raise Scotland to a pitch of prosperity: '2. A Change in the Disposition of the common People, from a Desire of travelling abroad, and wandring from Home, to an industrious and diligent Application to Labour at Home.'[52] Crusoe's experience on his island was in part a warning about wandering abroad. It was equally testimony to the rewards of 'diligent Application to Labour'.

In 1737 there appeared a pamphlet in support of British seamen which would have heartened Gibson. This imputed the country's mastery 'of the greatest Number of Ships of War ... [and] the best and most considerable Body of able Seamen, both to Fight and Navigate them, of any Prince or State in the World ... entirely to its being an Island, together with the Greatness of its Trade'.[53] It quoted from *An Act for the Encrease and Encouragement of Seamen* of William's reign, and two acts *for the Encouragement of ... Trade* of the sixth year of Queen Anne, to say that although much had been done for seamen by British parliaments, they needed to do much more.[54] Specifically it claimed that nothing had been done for seamen between 1660 and 1710, and offered its own largely republican chronology of the rise of British naval power.[55]

This began with the achievements of Elizabeth in encouraging '*Drake, Forbisher, Hawkins, Cavendish,* and others', and beginning the settlement of America.[56] It continued by quoting from legislation passed by 'The Parliament of *England* ... so sensible of the Advantages which must accrue to the Nation by giving Rewards ... in the Year 1649, for

---

[50] Thomas Keneally, *Australians: Origins to Eureka, volume I* (Sydney, 2009) pp. 13–14.

[51] Linda Colley, *The Ordeal of Elizabeth Marsh: a Woman in World History* (New York, 2007).

[52] Defoe, *A Tour* vol. II p. 690.

[53] *Reasons for Giving Encouragement To The Sea-Faring People of Great Britain, In Times of Peace or War* (London, 1739) p. A2.

[54] Ibid. pp. 10–19.   [55] Ibid. p. 10.   [56] Ibid. p. 14.

the Encouragement of Seamen ... to apply themselves the more willingly to the Service of the Commonwealth'.[57] It praised 'the taking of
the Island of *Jamaica* ... and so many *Spanish* Ships of War ... in the
Time of *Cromwell*'.[58] It quoted the observations of 'Monsieur *de Wit* ...
long ago' on the admirable improvement of English colonial and naval
power. Most extensively it quoted from Camden's *Annals* on the exploits
of Cavendish and Drake, and from Burnet's and Clarendon's *Histories* on
those of Blake, concluding from the latter:

> He [Blake] was the first Man that declined the old Track ... and despised
> those Rules which had been long in Practice, to keep his Ship and his Men out
> of Danger ... as if the principal Art requisite in the Captain ... had been ...
> to come home safe again ... He was the first that infused that Proportion of
> Courage into Seamen, by making them see by Experience, what mighty Things
> they could do, if they were resolved ... he was the first that gave the Example of
> that kind of Naval Courage, and bold and resolute Atchievements.[59]

By the middle of the eighteenth century British reflections upon insularity incorporated Asia. Swift had already located his flying island of
Laputa just to the east of Japan.[60] Ptolemy, it will be recalled, had listed
as the three most notable islands and peninsulas Taprobane (Sri Lanka),
Albion and the Golden Peninsula (peninsular Malaysia).[61] In 1760 Tory
satirist John Shebbeare published a scathing assault upon the British government under the title *History ... of the Sumatrans*. The most sustained
and outrageous such satire came a few years later from Tobias Smollett.

Smollett's *History and Adventures of an Atom*, first published in 1769,
focused upon the relationship between a sovereign ('Dairo Got-hama-
baba') and a ministry which amounted to 'the strangest phenomenon
that ever appeared in the political world. A statesman without capacity,
or the smallest tincture of human learning; a secretary who could not
write; a financier who did not understand the multiplication table; and
the treasurer of a vast empire, who never could balance accounts with his
own butler.'[62]

In particular Smollett anatomized the King's unusual relationship with
his first minister, or Cuboy, Fika-kaka. This depended, in the first place,
upon the minister's preparedness to

> submit ... personally to his [Majesty's] capricious humours with the most pla-
> cid resignation. He presented his posteriors to be kicked as regularly as the
> day revolved; and presented them not barely with submission, but with all the

---

[57] Ibid. p. 10.   [58] Ibid. p. 15.   [59] Ibid. pp. 19–32, quote on p. 32.
[60] Swift, *Gulliver's Travels* Part 3 (and page 1 Plate III).
[61] *Ptolemy's Geography* p. 110.
[62] Tobias Smollett, *The History and Adventures of an Atom* (London, 1786) p. 10.

appearance of fond desire: and truly this diurnal exposure was attended with
such delectation as he never enjoyed in any other attitude.[63]

Fika-kaka's itch 'to receive the Dairo's ... pedestrian digitation' was
not simply political, but medical. It was stimulated by the warring of 'two
atoms quarrelling for precedency, in this the Cuboy's seat of honour'. To
this condition the daily royal boot – the minister concerned might have
been Newcastle, Pitt the Younger or Lord Bute – administered comfort,
until one day, when 'Got-hama-baba performed the exercise with such
uncommon vehemence, that first his slipper, and then his toe-nail, flew
off, after having first made a small breach in the perineum of Fika-kaka',
the minister was driven to the services of a 'venerable doctor' with a

grizzled beard ... and taking him into his cabinet, proposed that he should
make oral application to the part affected. The proposal was embraced without hesitation, and the effect even transcended the hopes of the Cuboy. The
osculation itself was soft, warm, emollient, and comfortable; but when the ner-
vous papillae were gently stroked ... by the long, elastic, peristaltic, abster-
sive fibres that composed this reverend verriculum, such a delectable titillation
ensued, that Fika-kaka was quite in raptures.
   That which he intended at first for a medicine, he now converted into an article of luxury. All the Bonzas [secondary ministers] who enrolled themselves
in the number of his dependants, whether old or young, black or fair, rough or
smooth, were enjoined every day to perform this additional and posterior rite
of worship, so productive of delight to the Cuboy, that he was every morning
impatient to receive the Dairo's calcitration ... after which, he flew with all the
eagerness of desire to the subsequent part of his entertainment.[64]

Soon all the Bonzas were ranked and 'preferred according to the colour
of their beards ... The sensation ensuing from the contact of a grey beard
was soft and delicate, and agreeably demulcent ... a red, yellow or brin-
dled beard was in request when the business was to thrill or tingle: but a
black beard was of all the others most honoured by Fika-kaka, not only
on account of its fleecy feel, equally spirited and balsamick', but also its
phosphorescent capacity to 'emit ... sparkles upon friction'.[65]
   The geographical setting of this startling analysis of a nation of butt-
kickers and arse-lickers came to Smollett as a result of editorial work on
a sixty-volume *Universal History*. In a review of volume IX, containing
an account of Japan, what struck him were three things. There was the
geographical analogy:

Japan ... is but small in point of extent. It consists of three ... islands, on the
most eastern verge of Asia ... if England and Scotland were divided from each

[63] Ibid. p. 11.   [64] Ibid. p. 12.   [65] Ibid. p. 13.

other by an arm of the sea, Japan might be aptly compared to Britain and Ireland ... The coasts of Japan are dangerous and rocky; so are those of Great Britain. The climate of Japan is wet, stormy, and variable; so is that of Great Britain.

Secondly there was

a resemblance in the genius and disposition of the people: the Japanese, like the English, are brave and warlike, quick in apprehension, solid in understanding, modest, patient, courteous, docile, industrious, studious, just in their dealings ... sincere in their professions ... proud, supercilious, passionate, humorous, and addicted to suicide; split into a multitude of religious sects, and so distracted by political factions, that the nation is at last divided between two separate governments.

Yet 'still more remarkable' than both these resemblances was Japan's relationship to its continental neighbour. For 'China ... in divers respects, may be compared to France ... China is more populous, powerful, and extensive ... its palaces are more grand ... its armies are more numerous ... But what Chinese have invented, the Japanese have improved ... The Chinese are more *gay*, the Japanese more *substantial* ... The Chinese are remarkable for *dissimulation, complaisance*, and *effeminacy*; the Japanese are famous for their *integrity, plain-dealing*, and *manly vigour*.'[66]

Smollett's obscene lampooning of Britain's government during the Seven Years War was not accompanied by a questioning of national stereotypes. Nor, however, did it lack an offshore perspective (the work was composed in Italy).

The Japanese value themselves much upon their constitution, and are very clamorous about the words Liberty and Property; yet ... the only liberty they enjoy is to get drunk whenever they please, to revile the government, and quarrel with one another. With respect to their property, they are the tamest animals in the world; and ... undergo, without wincing, such impositions, as no other nation in the world would bear ... Notwithstanding ... the Japanese are become a wealthy and powerful people, partly from their insular situation, and partly from a spirit of commercial adventure ... conducted by repeated flashes of good sense, which almost incessantly gleam through the chaos of their absurdities.[67]

---

[66] Smollett, review published in September 1759 quoted in Robert Adams Day, 'Introduction', in Tobias Smollett, *The History and Adventures of an Atom* (Athens, Ga., 1989) pp. xliii–xliv.

[67] Smollett, *History and Adventures* pp. 7–8.

8   Anti-continentalism

> The rise of a city, which swelled into an empire, may deserve, as a singular prodigy, the reflection of a philosophic mind. But the decline of Rome was the natural and inevitable effect of immoderate greatness. Prosperity ripened the principle of decay; the causes of destruction multiplied with the extent of conquest ... the stupendous fabric yielded to the pressure of its own weight. The story of its ruin is simple and obvious; and instead of inquiring why the Roman empire was destroyed, we should rather be surprised that it had subsisted so long.
>
> Edward Gibbon, *Decline and Fall of the Roman Empire*[1]

Within Gibson's discussion of plantations had reappeared the image of an imperial archipelago on an Atlantic rather than simply Aegean scale. After the Seven Years War (1756–63) the framework of the British empire was increasingly global and, militarily, maritime.[2] The subsequent loss of the thirteen American colonies barely dented its growth. However, especially during its struggle with revolutionary France, Britain's territorial priorities became increasingly oriented towards the Pacific, the Mediterranean and Asia.[3]

Only during and after the victory of 1756–63 was the 'distinction ... into island and continent' regularly discussed by British writers in terms of the defensive superiority of the former. In 1759 a Venetian observer commented: 'The island ... appears to be completely different from the Continent ... all the inhabitants have a peculiar character, and they feel themselves superior to any other people.'[4] William Falconer (a Scot)

---

[1] Edward Gibbon, *The History of the Decline and Fall of the Roman Empire*, (ed.) J.B. Bury (7 vols., London, 1896) vol. IV 'General Observations on the Fall of the Roman Empire in the West' p. 161.

[2] Alan Frost, *The Global Reach of Empire: Britain's Maritime Expansion in the Indian and Pacific Oceans 1764–1817* (Melbourne, 2003) pp. 31–42; Richard Harding, 'The Royal Navy', in H.T. Dickinson (ed.), *A Companion to Eighteenth-Century Britain* (Oxford, 2002) p. 483.

[3] Bayly, *Birth of the Modern World* p. 45.

[4] Giacomo Casanova quoted by Simms, *Three Victories* p. 501.

quoted Montesquieu (who knew his Thucydides) to the effect that 'The inhabitants of islands ... have a higher relish for liberty than those of a continent.' In fact Montesquieu's remark that in the case of 'island peoples ... the sea separates them from great empires, and tyranny cannot reach them'[5] bore at least as plausibly on the relationship of islands to empire, as to liberty. Yet, taking an opposite tack to Gibson, Falconer went on to argue that in the Mediterranean the Sardinians, Corsicans, Sicilians and islanders of the Aegean had successfully resisted Athens, Carthage and Rome. The same was true of 'the East Indian islands; which still remain mostly under the dominion of the original inhabitants, whilst the continent has always been, and still is, a prey to every invader'.[6]

According to Falconer there were many reasons for this: islands did not conquer and were not conquered ('conquerors are stopped by the sea'); the surrounding seas rendered islands temperate, and so the people 'less timid indolent and servile'; on an island a standing army ('always necessary to the support of a despotism') was impractical, and the people on the contrary were 'employed on fleets and a maritime force', a circumstance favourable to liberty, as in Holland, Venice and Athens. Moreover, 'What has been said of islands, may in great measure be applied to countries that approach islands in their situation.' Falconer went on, drawing from Aristotle ('Aristotle advises to chuse a situation for a city, if possible adjacent to the sea'), to posit an inverse relationship between sea water and barbarism.

Thriving and independent nations were accordingly scattered on the banks of the Pacific and Atlantic oceans; they surrounded the Red-sea, the Mediterranean, and the Baltic; whilst (a few tribes excepted, who retire among mountains bordering on India and Persia, or who have found some rude establishment among the creeks and shores of the Caspian and Euxine seas) there is scarcely a people in the vast continent of Asia that deserves the name of nation.[7]

This was the second revival, on a greatly extended geographical scale, of ancient maritime orientalism. The purpose now was not to mobilize on deck a dozy population of grain- and sheep-farming villagers. It was to appropriate for western Europe what Athens had once claimed for itself: cultural superiority based on a relationship to the ocean. Falconer took this one step further, replacing Athens' pretence at being an island with Britain's actual status as one. Quoting Xenophon to the effect that

[5] Montesquieu, Charles-Louis de Secondat, Baron, *The Spirit of the Laws*, (eds.) Anne Cohler, Basia Carolyn Miller and Harold Samuel Stone (Cambridge, 1989) p. 288.
[6] William Falconer, *Remarks on the influence of climate, situation, nature of country ... on the disposition and temper* (London, 1781) pp. 170–1.
[7] Ibid. p. 172.

had Athens really been an island, instead of simply allowing Pericles to persuade it to think of itself as one, it might have kept its liberty and power indefinitely, he added: 'One would imagine, says Mr Montesquieu, that Xenophon was speaking of England.'[8]

The potential result of this argument was not only a geographically organized ranking of cultures with Europe at its apex. It was also a geographically organized ranking within Europe with Britain at its head. Among all European nations, this could claim, Britain was freest, its economy richest and its empire largest because it was an island.

In fact if Britain was free that was not because it was an island, but because for the first time since the Roman conquest its inhabitants had acquired the capacity to defend it. That defence had become global in scale. Thus far had British writing come from Elizabethan and early Stuart anxiety, and even Gibson's weighing of advantages against disadvantages. A new myth of islands was taking shape. It did so within the context of a broader maritime orientalism which, in addition to being Athenian in origin, was both anti-Asian (Europe detaching itself from Eurasia) and anti-continental (this chapter of Falconer's book being titled 'Effects of an Insular or Continental Situation').

As Edward Said argued, orientalism was a culturally constructed 'other' designed by Europeans to give expression to their claim to be 'the West'. Though we have discussed its Elizabethan prehistory, this blossomed in the heyday of European global empires (the eighteenth as well as nineteenth and twentieth centuries). All of the moral tropes identified by Said were present. However, to repeat, the geography of this construct was not 'a line … drawn between two continents'.[9] It was a line drawn between a continent (following Ptolemy) called Asia and something claiming to be alternative to it. In the case of Athens that alternative had been water in general and islands in particular. In some writings of Enlightenment western Europe it became a line drawn between Europe, or Britain, and all continents everywhere.

Apart from claiming to distinguish Europe within the world, and/or Britain within Europe, this imagined geography acquired a further use. This was to underpin, during the heyday of empire, an argument against empires, especially during the crisis over the American colonies.[10] To this extent orientalism might yield not simply a discourse of power, including imperial power, over non-European peoples.[11] It might furnish a

---

[8] Ibid. pp. 172–3.   [9] Said, *Orientalism* p. 57.

[10] David Armitage, *The Declaration of Independence: a Global History* (Cambridge, Mass., 2007) p. 101.

[11] Anna Suranyi, *The Genius of the English Nation: Travel Writing and National Identity in Early Modern England* (Cranbury, N.J., 2008) pp. 20–2.

discourse of cultural superiority which criticized empire as barbaric, continental and non-European. It is no accident that so many pro-Athenian-and-Carthaginian ancient histories in this period were also anti-Roman. Many, but not all. For within orientalism in general, which could see Roman arms and law as the foundation of European civilization, existed maritime orientalism in particular.

A recent collection of essays takes issue with

the cultural myth that the ocean is outside and beyond history, that the interminable, repetitive cycle of the sea obliterates memory and temporality, and that a fully historicized land somehow stands diametrically opposed to an atemporal, 'ahistorical' sea. Such a mythical view of the sea – as a symbol of madness, irrational femininity, unruly or romantic anti-civilization – arguably serves only to consolidate the dualistic structure of Western modernity whose definition of knowledge and reason has a remarkably *landed* quality, as Foucault suggested long ago in *Madness and Civilization*.[12]

This perception is precisely the opposite of that discussed here. Chapter 1 above considered suggestions that Europeans possessed a 'continental' territorial or material imagination, as well as contemporary depictions of the ocean as dangerous, agitated or transgressive. The following chapter (9) will revisit in a different context the suggestion that early modern European writers imagined *empire* as continental. Thereafter the feat of redescription to be accomplished in the British case was to turn an empire of continents (American, Asian and African) into a (Pacific-style) sea of islands. But this is some way short of disclosing the entirety of a culture's spatial imagination. Early modern depictions of wilderness could be oceanic or 'landed'. Europe's own geography, of plains, peninsulas, oceans and islands, transcended the boundaries between sea and land. The differing distances between European islands and Pacific islands had cultural consequences. But so, as we will see, did their relationship to changing technology.

Far from associating the sea with 'anti-civilization', many of the writers discussed here did the opposite. The result was a coastal perspective upon Eurasian and American history, geography and culture. According to this, civilization was oceanic, and continents barbaric. That the whole of the indented passage above quoted from Falconer was lifted without acknowledgement from Adam Ferguson's *An Essay on the History of Civil Society*, first published in 1767, gives us some insight into this process.[13] Ferguson's account 'Of the Influences of Climate and Situation', also

---

[12] Bernhard Klein and Gesa Mackenthun, 'Introduction', in Klein and Mackenthun (eds.), *Sea Changes: Historicizing the Ocean* (New York, 2004) p. 2.
[13] Ferguson, *An Essay* p. 117.

indebted to Montesquieu and his Greek sources, had not given special attention to islands. As Falconer's lifted quote suggests, however, it was both pro-maritime and anti-continental. It was also global: for Ferguson, the outlook for liberty and virtue was as dim in Africa and America as in Asia. The reasons for this, however, had not only to do with the relationship of land to water, and were handled with more subtlety and complexity than by Falconer or Defoe.

For Ferguson the prospects for moral life and development depended upon not only situation, but climate, and the interaction between them. He began with the longstanding tripartite distinction between frigid, temperate and torrid zones. For Bodin (1573), author of this schema in its modern form (it was of ancient origin), these temperatures, primarily a function of latitude, affected behaviour through their impact on the humours.[14] Post-humorally, Ferguson argued that 'under the extremes of heat or cold, the active range of the human soul appears to be limited … In the one extreme, they are dull and slow, moderate in their desires, regular and pacific in their manner of life; in the other they are feverish in their passions, weak in their judgements, and addicted by temperament to animal pleasure.'[15] It was therefore the 'intermediate climates' which most seemed to favour man's nature.

[I]n whatever manner we account for the fact, it cannot be doubted, that this animal has always attained the principal honours of his species within the temperate zone. The arts, which he has on this scene repeatedly invented, the extent of his reason, the fertility of his fancy, and the force of his genius in literature, commerce, policy, and war, sufficiently declare either a distinguished advantage of situation, or a natural superiority of mind.[16]

So far more-or-less Bodin, for whom the most temperate part of the world had been Europe, the most temperate part of Europe France and, it seems reasonable to suspect, the most temperate part of France somewhere between Toulouse (where he was born) and Paris (where he was educated and worked). Like Bodin, Ferguson amused himself with accounts of the human relationship to sex, elocution and alcohol changing as humans crossed the Mediterranean, the Alps or (a new twist) the Mississippi. In Louisiana, ominously, 'The female sex domineers.'[17]

[14] Jean Bodin, *Six Bookes of a Commonweale*, a facsimile reprint of the English translation of 1606, (ed.) K.D. McRae (Cambridge, Mass., 1962), Book Five, Chapter One. William Robertson, *The History of America* (2 vols., Dublin, 1777) vol. I p. 23 explained that 'according to this theory' in its ancient form 'a vast portion of the habitable earth was pronounced to be unfit for sustaining the human species', because frigid and torrid zones were both considered uninhabitable.
[15] Ferguson, *An Essay* p. 110.   [16] Ibid. p. 106.   [17] Ibid. pp. 112–13.

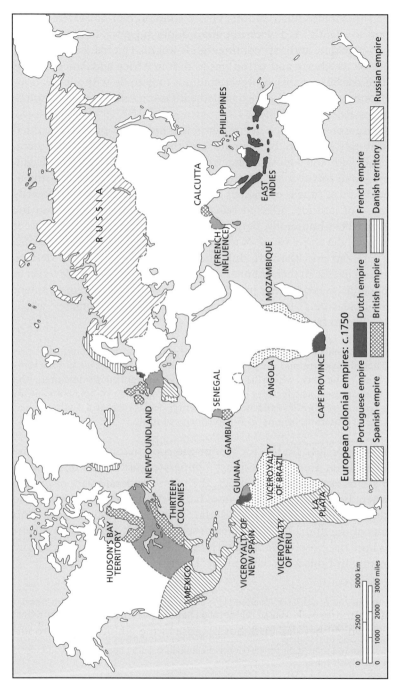

Map 5 Most European empires were both continental and maritime. Map based on 'European colonial empires, c.1750', in Paul Kennedy, *The Rise and Fall of the Great Powers, 1500–2000* (New York, 1987) p. 112.

European colonial empires: c.1750

Portuguese empire

Spanish empire

Dutch empire

British empire

French empire

Danish territory

Russian empire

RUSSIA

PHILIPPINES

CALCUTTA

EAST INDIES

(FRENCH INFLUENCE)

MOZAMBIQUE

SENEGAL

ANGOLA

GAMBIA

CAPE PROVINCE

NEWFOUNDLAND

THIRTEEN COLONIES

HUDSON'S BAY TERRITORY

MEXICO

GUIANA

VICEROYALTY OF NEW SPAIN

VICEROYALTY OF BRAZIL

VICEROYALTY OF PERU

LA PLATA

2500   5000 km

0

1000   2000   3000 miles

0

However, for Bodin, cultured Europe had included its own torrid and frigid extremes. Whatever their addiction to lassitude and cruelty, no one could deny the achievements of Mediterranean peoples in pure sciences (including mathematics, philosophy, theology). Despite their habitual insobriety northern Europeans were manufacturers to the world and superior soldiers. For Ferguson, however, relative to the rest of the world, the whole of Europe was temperate. Most importantly this, and temperature in general, was not simply a function of latitude.

> These and character, do not indeed correspond with the number of degrees that are measured from the equator to the pole; nor does the temperature of the air itself depend on the latitude. Varieties of soil and position, the distance or neighbourhood of the sea, are known to effect the atmosphere, and may have signal effects in composing the animal frame.[18]

If there was more to temperature than latitude, there was more to 'atmosphere' than temperature, including the presence or absence of 'heavy and noxious vapours'. Thus to consider climate aright was to consider, within particular latitudes, the relationship between air, land and sea.

Here Ferguson observed that by comparison with the same latitudes in Europe 'The [northern] climates of America' suffered 'a double asperity to the winter, and during many months, by the frequency and continuance of fogs, snow, and frost, carry the inconveniences of the frigid zone far into the temperate'. Elsewhere 'the Mexican, like the Asiatic of India, being addicted to pleasure, was sunk in effeminacy; and … had suffered to be raised … a domineering superstition, and … despotic government'.[19] Similarly,

> Great part of Tartary lies under the same parallels with Greece, Italy, and Spain; but the climates are found to be different; and while the shores, not only of the Mediterranean, but even those of the Atlantic, are favoured with a moderate change and vicissitude of seasons, the eastern parts of Europe, and northern continent of Asia, are afflicted with all their extremes. In one season, we are told, that the plagues of an ardent summer reach almost to the frozen sea; and that the inhabitant is obliged to screen himself from noxious vermin in the same clouds of smoke in which he must, at a different time of the year, take shelter from the rigours of the cold.[20]

Finally, no (European-type) civilizations had been found in the temperate latitudes of southern Africa or South America. Continents, then, were uncivilized not only because of who galloped over them, and the territory over which they galloped, but because of the temperatures through

---

[18] Ibid. p. 113.   [19] Ibid. pp. 113–14.   [20] Ibid. p. 114.

which they galloped. The basis of Ferguson's maritime orientalism was not (as in Defoe) a belief in commerce as the motor of advanced civilization (though he was not against it). It was a belief in water as a moderating influence on climate.[21]

From this standpoint it could be seen that Europe's cultural achievements were an effect, not only or mainly of its latitude, but of its maritime geography. This was, as has been noted, a geography of islands, peninsulas, rivers and inland seas. 'While the shores of the Baltic became famed for the studies of Copernicus, Tycho Brahe, and Kepler, those of the Mediterranean were celebrated for giving birth to men of genius in all its variety, and for having abounded with poets and historians, as well as with men of science.'[22] No less important, and perhaps related, was political geography. Europe was highly developed in arts and sciences (including 'policy') because it was internally divided into 'distinct and independent communities'.

The society and concourse of other men, are not more necessary to form the individual, than the rivalship and competition of nations are to invigorate the principles of political life in a state. Their wars, and their treaties, their mutual jealousies, and the establishments which they devise with a view to each other, constitute more than half the occupations of mankind, and furnish materials for their greatest and most improving exertions. For these reasons, clusters of islands, a continent divided by many natural barriers, great rivers, ridges of mountains, and arms of the sea, are best fitted for becoming the nursery of independent and respectable nations ... The most respectable nations have always been found where at least one part of the frontier has been washed by the sea. This barrier, perhaps the strongest of all in the times of barbarity, does not, however, even then supersede the cares of a national defence; and in the advanced state of arts, gives the greatest scope and facility to commerce.[23]

In the formulation of John Pocock, for Ferguson 'Geography determines what humans can do, but culture determines what they do do, with their terrestrial situation.'[24] This is correct if it is understood that in this case geography includes climate, helps to determine it, and in that and other ways helps to determine culture. To put it another way, situation is not simply terrestrial. Here, while elsewhere describing Europe

---

[21] John Pocock notes that Ferguson's 'history of savagery and barbarism' has a continental setting (*Barbarism and Religion, volume II* pp. 333–5). Ferguson does not, however, say that this stage exhibits '"all the diversities" of human society' (ibid. p. 334). He says that such an 'extensive tract of the earth, containing so great a variety of situation, climate and soil, should' do so, but that at this stage of his discussion 'Every question on this subject is premature' (quoted in ibid.). What will be discovered is that on continents the actual diversity is limited by the factors discussed here.

[22] Ferguson, *An Essay* p. 112.   [23] Ibid. p. 117.

[24] Pocock, *Barbarism and Religion, volume II* p. 342.

as 'the promontory of a continent', Pocock takes Ferguson's point about its 'insular and peninsular configuration'.[25]

Thus for Ferguson, as for Defoe, if island geography was unnecessary, a coast was essential. As for Defoe, one of the things that this made possible was commerce. However, for Ferguson all such considerations were subservient to the objective of an independent and vigorous political culture. In relation to this, as for others writing after the Seven Years War, he could imagine the ocean serving, like rivers and mountains, as a defensible frontier.

This perspective may be compared with that of the Frenchman Guillaume Raynal, translated into English in 1776, and, like Montesquieu, widely read in Britain.[26] Like Defoe's, Raynal's *History of Settlements and Trade*, compiled with collaborators including Denis Diderot, located the origin of its subject in Tyre and then Carthage.[27] While, therefore, its account of the origins of civilization was maritime, it was not anti-continental, nor pro-European, but drew upon the idea of these cities as a global human crossroads.

The commercial states have civilized all others. The Phoenicians, whose extent of country and influence were extremely limited, by their genius of naval enterprises, acquired an importance which ranked them foremost in the history of ancient nations ... they seem to have been destined by nature for the dominion of the sea, Fishing taught them the art of navigation ... By inhabiting, as it were, the confines of Africa, Asia, and Europe, if they could not unite the inhabitants of the globe in one common interest, they at least had it in their power, by a commercial intercourse, to communicate to every nation the enjoyments of all climates.[28]

The same was true of Raynal's treatment of

GREECE, intersected on all sides by seas, must necessarily flourish by commerce. Its situation in the Archipelago, and its distance from any large continent, seemed to make it unlikely that it should either conquer or be conquered. Situated between Asia and Europe, it contributed to civilize both the one and the other, and enjoyed a deserved share of prosperity, as the reward for its services.[29]

---

[25] Ibid. and see the end of chapter 9 below.
[26] Raynal's was the sixth most popular book borrowed from the Bristol Library between 1773 and 1784 (137 times). John Hawkesworth's *Voyages* of Cook was first (201); William Robertson's *History of the Reign of Charles V* 7th (131). Paul Kaufman, *Borrowings from the Bristol Library, 1773–1784* discussed in Brian Richardson, *Longitude and Empire: How Captain Cook's Voyages Changed the World* (Vancouver, 2005) pp. 13–14.
[27] Pocock, *Barbarism and Religion, volume IV: Barbarians, Savages and Empires* (Cambridge, 2005) ch. 13.
[28] Raynal, *A Philosophical and Political History* vol. I pp. 2–3.   [29] Ibid. p. 4.

Raynal identified Greece, led by the Athenians, as an Asiatic colony populated by Egyptians and Phoenicians which had 'elevated human reason to a degree of perfection, which has been reduced so low by the subsequent revolutions of empires, that in all probability it will never rise again to the same standard. Their admirable institutions were superior to the best we have at this day.'[30]

Nor, though he juxtaposed this achievement to the plight of 'The Persians, living under an arbitrary government', was Raynal's account of the effects of climate anti-continental. When treating of Europe he lamented that the superiority of the French to the British climate had not been exploited by a comparable excellence (by which he meant liberty) of French government.[31] When, discussing human migration, he wrote that 'it should seem reasonable to conclude, that a climate the best adapted to the human species, would be peopled the earliest; and that the first men would fix their abode in a delicious climate, pure air, and a soil too fertile to require much cultivation', he was speaking about 'the banks of the Ganges ...':

The air is perfumed with the most delicious fruits, and affords a wholesome and refreshing nourishment; the trees form a shade impenetrable to the rays of the sun; while the living animals ... share in India, in common with their master, the sweets of plenty and security. Even at this day ... Indostan ... is still the most fruitful country in the world.[32]

As in Defoe's *History*, and more sharply, Raynal's praise of Carthage and Athens was accompanied by hostility to Rome. That power 'brought into subjection and destroyed the known world'.

The Romans ... though they dazzled the world with an appearance of grandeur, fell short of the Greeks in their improvements in philosophy, and the arts. They promoted an intercourse between different nations, not by uniting them by ties of commerce, but by imposing upon them the same yoke of subordination ... Their despotism and military government oppressed the people, extinguished the powers of genius, and degraded the human race.[33]

It is possible to see Raynal's anti-Romanism within a French tradition extending back (at least) to François Hotman's *Francogallia* (1573). We may see his maritime equation of civility with commerce as characteristic of European Enlightenment Atlanticism. But his openness to continental geography, and civility, along with his ranking of the Greeks above the present, identified him and his collaborators as radical critics of the predominant mode of European self-praise discussed here.

---

[30] Ibid. p. 5.   [31] Ibid. vol. IV pp. 529–30.   [32] Ibid. vol. I pp. 31–2.
[33] Ibid. pp. 6–7.

Publishing his *History of America* a year after this translation of Raynal appeared, the Scot William Robertson dealt the same cards differently. The navigational and therefore commercial accomplishments of the ancients were limited; their geographical knowledge (perfected by Ptolemy) even more so. For navigation and commerce nobody compared to the Phoenicians and then Carthaginians, who spanned the Mediterranean, traded with India and east Africa, west Africa and the Canaries, Spain, Gaul and Britain.[34] The Greeks, 'notwithstanding such a favourable situation ... almost encompassed by the sea, which formed many spacious bays and commodious harbours ... surrounded by a vast number of fertile islands', remained astonishingly ignorant even of the geography of the Mediterranean, and possessed naval vessels of 'small force'.

Robertson attributed the Athenian naval victory in the Persian War to 'that courage which the enjoyment of liberty inspires', rather than to maritime dexterity. The heroic and then tragic stature of the Persian and Peloponnesian conflicts respectively was a product of 'the eloquence of Greek historians'.[35] The outstanding progress in geographical discovery made in the ancient world was not Carthaginian or Greek, but Roman. Most of this was overland, and opened up western, northern and eastern Europe, and western Asia around the Black Sea. Within the empire 'The trade of Greece, Egypt, and the other conquered countries, continued to be carried on ... the spirit of the Roman government, no less intelligent than active, gave such additional security to commerce, as animated it with new vigour.'[36]

More obviously in the tradition of Ferguson was another Scottish contemporary, James Dunbar. Like Falconer, Montesquieu and Raynal, Dunbar was interested in the political and moral impact of geography and climate. As for Ferguson, this meant not only the role of geography – especially latitude and topography – within a climatic theory inherited largely from Bodin. It also meant extent of space, nature of frontiers and neighbours, and other features capable of having a cultural or political consequence. 'The division of a country by mountains, by lakes, or rivers, the vicinity or distance of the sea, insular or continental situation, and the relative condition of the surrounding nations, are causes which affect, in an eminent degree, the nature and success of public enterprise.'[37]

---

[34] William Robertson, *The History of America* (2 vols., Dublin, 1777) vol. I pp. 3–11.
[35] Ibid. p. 13.   [36] Ibid. p. 18.
[37] James Dunbar, *Essays on the History of Mankind in Rude and Cultivated Ages*, reprint of 1781 edition, (ed.) James Dunbar (Bristol, 1995) 'Essay VII. Of the Farther Tendency of Local Circumstances to Affect the Proceedings of Nations' pp. 257–8; also 318.

Dunbar was not a geographical determinist. He recognized relativities of time as well as space. Although the 'divisions of the terraqueous globe, the consequences arising from the magnitude of states and empires may often be referred ultimately to a geographical source' (what Dunbar was inclined to term a 'Local circumstance'), the role played by these circumstances varied according to their relationship to many features of human history and culture.[38] 'The different ages of society, like the different ages of man, require different discipline and culture. The maxims of policy applicable to one part of the world, are not always applicable to another; nor are the full advantages of any local oeconomy reconcilable, perhaps, with subordination to a general system.'[39] What this meant was that the impact of an island situation (for instance) would depend upon its cultural and historical context.

Before the aera of navigation, a settlement on an island, or the command of an extensive and commodious coast, might have conferred no advantages on the possessors; or rather circumstances, of such inestimable account in a commercial age, might, by cutting off all communication with the rest of the species, have proved, in every former era, invincible obstacles to the civil arts.[40]

In the absence of vessels, water was not a bridge. Dunbar did not concern himself with the question of how, under such circumstances, an island might initially have been populated. Nor could he, from the vantage point of 1781, imagine insularity, or the ocean, as a source of insecurity. Rather, in pre-navigational times 'Our insular situation ... rendered us long an uncultivated and sequestered people ... And the neglect with which Britons were once treated in the society of nations, is compensated only by that attention which their posterity command.' Publishing the third volume of his *Decline and Fall* in the same year as Dunbar's *History*, Edward Gibbon offered a comparable account of an isolated post-Roman Britain:

By the revolution of Britain, the limits of science, as well as of empire, were contracted. The dark cloud, which had been cleared by the Phoenician discoveries and finally dispelled by the arms of Caesar, again settled on the shores of the Atlantic, and a Roman province was again lost among the fabulous islands of the Ocean ... The arts of navigation, by which ... [the Anglo-Saxons] had acquired the empire of Britain and of the sea, were soon neglected by the indolent Barbarians, who supinely renounced all the commercial advantages of their insular situation.[41]

---

[38] Ibid. p. 266.   [39] Ibid. p. 267.   [40] Ibid., Essay VIII pp. 297–8.
[41] Gibbon, *Decline and Fall* vol. IV p. 158.

Comparable, but less historically sensitive, because as Dunbar had explained, and Gibbon's friend Robertson agreed, the commercial advantages of an insular situation were relative to its navigational context. Nor would highly developed navigational culture appear to have been necessary to acquire the empire of an island to which inhabitants of a continent could swim.[42]

According to Dunbar, the current position of Britain at the centre of the world's affairs had two causes. To the first, trade, he, like Defoe and Raynal, assigned a Phoenician pedigree.

In the territory of the Phoenicians, neither large nor fertile, yet lying along a commodious coast, we observe sources of opulence and renown ... it was the glory of the Phoenicians to venture beyond the boundaries of antient navigation, and by commercial enterprise, to diffuse arts and civility over the western regions ... The commodities of every country were embarked on Phoenician bottoms; and as merchants, or factors or navigators, they created a sort of universal dependence, and conducted, almost exclusively, the traffic of the world.

What the Phoenicians were, in early times, relatively to the nations on the Mediterranean coast; what the Hanse Towns and the Dutch lately were, relatively to the other European states; the commercial towns of all Europe are, at this day, relatively to the rest of the earth. The maritime efforts of the Greeks lessened the importance of Phoenicia. The maritime efforts of the English, and of other powers, have sunk the importance of the Dutch commonwealth.[43]

However, it was not only commerce which was responsible for Britain's current power. Only by military command of the ocean had that bridge become a barrier, and thus Britain's insular situation 'so fertile a source of national security, opulence, and grandeur'.

While nations on the continent of Europe maintain their barriers with difficulty, and at an enormous expence, and, if they will consult their security, must often court alliances, and observe, with jealous attention, the minutest variations in the balance of power, Great Britain is exempted from such anxious solicitude. By collecting her forces within herself, by avoiding continental wars, which exhaust, to little purpose, her treasure and her blood, and by rendering the improvement of her maritime strength the fixed and steady object of her policy, she may maintain, in defiance of powerful confederacies, that post of honour and distinction, which seems to have drawn upon her the envy of nations, who now take advantage of internal calamities to insult her fortune.[44]

This was, on the one hand, the underpinning of maritime orientalism by familiar blue-water strategy. As Samuel Johnson had put it on another occasion: 'nature has stationed us in an island inaccessible but by sea,

---

[42] This is not a hypothesis to the effect that the Anglo-Saxons arrived by dog paddle. It is a reminder that the channel was narrow.
[43] Dunbar, *Essays on the History* pp. 298–301.   [44] Ibid. p. 299.

and we are now at war with an enemy, whose naval power is inferior to our own, and from whom therefore we are in no danger of invasion.'[45] In fact Britain was not exempt from 'anxious solicitude' about the balance of power, or 'enormous expence' (as Ferguson had inferred, naval supremacy did not come cheap). In the event of such supremacy, however, Dunbar agreed with Gibson that a commercial global system combined with insular geography had the potential to confer a unique independence. Only if Britannia did rule the waves would Britons be free.

However, while Gibson had been writing a prescription for such a maritime supremacy, Dunbar lived to see it. Moreover, while Gibson had seen England's American colonies as crucial to that global self-sufficiency, Dunbar was writing during the crisis involving secession of the thirteen colonies. These were the 'internal calamities' to which the last quoted passage referred. Thus, when Dunbar campaigned against involvement in 'continental wars', he was not referring, as Johnson was, only, or even mainly, to Eurasia. It was in America, no less than in Europe, that British policy, having attracted the 'envy of nations', could lead the country into disaster. Empire constituted not only an opportunity, but a potentially deadly liability.

David Armitage has analysed the thirteen colonies' Declaration of Independence (1776) as a new kind of political document, and therefore idea, in world history. It became one of a series marking 'the transition from subordination within an empire to independence alongside other states'.[46] What was new was its 'appeal to the tribunal of the world', and specifically that world of independent modern states to membership of which it laid claim.[47] It was thus not simply a claim to rights, individual or collective, against a previous colonial master, let alone a justification of rebellion. It was an announcement of the creation of a new state, directed to the existing community of states, a declaration of independence and interdependence.

All these claims may be correct. However, Armitage recognizes that one possible precedent was the creation of the United Provinces. This, too, had had its context in the secession of several provinces from an empire. This, too, resulted in that rarity in early modern history: the creation (and successful military defence) of a new state. In the Netherlands, as later in America, 'A great revolution ... happened – a revolution made, not by chopping and changing of power in any one of the existing states, but by the appearance of a new state, of a new species.'[48] The document which founded the United Provinces allowed for the incorporation, by

---

[45] Quoted in Simms, *Three Victories* p. 405.   [46] Armitage, *Declaration* p. 104.
[47] Ibid. pp. 17, 19–21, 106.   [48] Edmund Burke, quoted in ibid. p. 87.

unanimous agreement, of other provinces which should seek to join the union, just as the United States eventually incorporated other states (for instance, Vermont).[49] Like the United States, the United Provinces was not only a federation, but a republic. Thus it was free, both religiously and politically, and as Armitage notes, was sometimes in English called 'the united States of the Low Countries'.[50]

It is possible to argue that the American Declaration was innovative in ways not apparent to contemporaries. As Armitage explains: 'No document's meaning can be entirely constrained by the intentions of its creators. This is especially true of a document, like the Declaration, that comes to be seen as the beginning of a genre.'[51] But alongside what comes to be seen as the case, a historian must be interested in what was the case, and also what was seen to be the case at the time. Armitage's textual basis for distinguishing between the two revolutions is to show the difference between the American Declaration of Independence and the Dutch Act of Abjuration of 1581, which renounced allegiance to Philip II, to offer it to the Duke of Anjou (and, as we have seen, both previously and subsequently to Elizabeth I). In light of this effort to replace one prince (who had become a tyrant) with another, we may say that the United Provinces had not yet become a republic, and on that basis, perhaps, that it was not independent and/or not declaring its independence. Thus the Abjuration does not furnish a 'specific generic precedent' for the Declaration.[52] But two related issues are worth considering.

One is the possibility that the foundational agreement of the new Dutch state was not the Act of Abjuration but the Treaty of Utrecht (1579). William Temple certainly believed that this '*Union* ... was the Original Constitution and Frame of that Common-wealth, which has since been so well known in the World by the Name of *The United Provinces*'.[53] Like the Declaration of Independence the Treaty agreed articles of confederation, mutual defence, and aspects of the internal government of the seven provinces which came to constitute the new state of the United Provinces. Concerning the Abjuration Ernst Kossmann and A. F. Mellink remark that

it adds nothing new to what had already been said many times before ... There is an intentional flatness in the resolution ... Of course Philip II did not forfeit his sovereignty on 26 July 1581; he had clearly lost it well before that date. On 26 July the States General confined themselves to stating this as a fact; they did not proclaim independence, they did not decide on any

---

[49] Armitage, *Declaration* pp. 91–2.   [50] Ibid. p. 47.
[51] Ibid. p. 140.   [52] Ibid. pp. 42–4.
[53] Temple, *Observations Upon the United Provinces* p. 50.

revolutionary innovation, they passed the resolution ... by way of a mere formality.[54]

This was because the basis of independence had already been declared by 'The Union signed at Utrecht ... It was a formal alliance of provinces acting as if they were independent states, and deciding to integrate their foreign policies and war efforts through a fairly loose federation in order to defend their individual independence and traditional customs.'[55] It is true that the Treaty of the Union did not declare independence from the 'General Union' of the Netherlands.[56] That is, however, because the military struggle to incorporate the rest of those provinces had not yet been abandoned, not because an independent United Provinces of the Netherlands had not yet been conceived. It is also true that independence was not recognized by Spain or, therefore, the rest of the international community, until 1648. But this may be simply to say, not only that the Dutch military struggle for independence took longer than the American, but that if it was actually the first in a modern succession of such struggles, it is that much less surprising that it was incremental. Nevertheless, without the extraordinary actions by which seven provinces progressed from treaty of union (1579) to act of abjuration (1581) to the fact of an independent republic led by Holland (1590s) to an international treaty recognizing that independence (1648), the possibility of such an achievement might never have been entertained, let alone repeated later.

All this is to say that the establishment of such a new and independent state was a question of actions as well as words. It is presumably on this basis that John Adams claimed that 'The Origins of the two Republicks are so much alike, that the History of the one seems but a Transcript from that of the other,' and Abigail Adams spoke of 'an indissoluble bond of union between the united States of America and the united Provinces who from a similarity of circumstances have each arrived at Independence disdaining the Bondage and oppression of a Philip and a G[e]orge'.[57]

Thus it is possible that the United Provinces played a key role in the creation of both the United Kingdom (1688–1707) and the United States (1776–83). Meanwhile there was, during the 1770s and 1780s, no shortage of criticism of British policy in America. Dunbar opined: 'to recal American allegiance by the power of our arms, if not an impracticable, is certainly a most hazardous attempt'.[58] While counselling against American independence, Raynal also described it as inevitable. 'The

---

[54] E.H. Kossmann and A.F. Mellink (eds.), *Texts Concerning the Revolt of the Netherlands* (Cambridge, 1974) 'Introduction' p. 37.

[55] Ibid. p. 32.   [56] *Treaty of the Union*, in ibid. p. 166.

[57] Quoted by Armitage, *Declaration* pp. 47, 50 (and see 66).   [58] Ibid. p. 284.

foundations of our tottering empires are sapped; materials are hourly collecting and preparing for their destruction, composed of the ruins of our laws ... the subversion of our rights ... the luxury of our courts, and the miseries of the country.'[59]

Of Gibbon's analysis of the loss of Rome's western empire published in 1781, Boyd Hilton writes: 'None of Gibbon's readers could have failed to draw the message. Since 1763 Britain had been the world's most powerful nation, with a dominion stretching from the eastern seaboard of India to the Great Lakes of North America. But now a large part of its western empire was in revolt, leaving the imperial State traumatized. In 1783 the Treaty of Paris formally ceded independence to the thirteen rebel colonies of the new United States of America.'[60]

However – partly perhaps to deflect such an interpretation – Gibbon included some 'General Observations' on the Roman case ruling out their contemporary applicability. Europe was now protected from internal tyranny by a system of many law-governed and competitive states. Even should some 'savage conqueror' overwhelm its modern military might, 'ten thousand vessels would transport beyond their pursuit the remains of civilized society; and Europe would revive and flourish in the American world, which is already filled with her colonies and institutions'.[61] Earlier, in 1778, commissioned by the government, Gibbon had denounced 'the dark agents of the English Colonies, who founded their pretended independence on nothing but the boldness of their revolt'.[62]

Very different was the analysis of Dunbar. For him the target was not this or that empire, but empire itself. To be imperial was to be continental; and to be continental was to be uncivilized and unfree. According to Dunbar, as earlier to Ferguson, in the ancient Near East, the Arabic and Ottoman Middle East, and Tartary, the open spaces of Asia had set the scene for despotism.

The voice of liberty will be heard no more. She can no longer arm her associates in the cause of humanity. The monarch of a great empire sits secure upon the throne, and sets at defiance the murmuring of the people ... Such consequences then may be traced to a geographical source ... The torrent which covered the plains rolls on with increasing violence, and the best fenced territories are no longer able to resist its progress. Nations ... whose frontiers seem little exposed to external annoyance, may have these advantages more than balanced by a dangerous vicinity to a growing empire.[63]

---

[59] Raynal, *Philosophical and Political History* vol. IV p. 390.
[60] Hilton, *A Mad, Bad, and Dangerous People?* p. 1 (discussing a different passage of the same text).
[61] Gibbon, *Decline and Fall* 'General Observations' pp. 165–6.
[62] Quoted by Armitage, *Declaration* p. 83.
[63] Dunbar, *Essays on the History* pp. 261–2.

Dunbar took empire and civilization ('refinement and the liberal arts') to be 'repugnant' to one another.[64] For their cultural achievements civilized nations could thank their limited territorial scope. 'Happy, in this respect, were the governments of antient Greece. Happy, on a larger scale, the governments of modern Europe.'[65] Thus Dunbar agreed with Ferguson and Gibbon that 'The division of Europe into a number of independent states ... is productive of the most beneficial consequences to the liberty of mankind.'[66] According to Dunbar, however, as earlier to Raynal, the question to be asked was not: What had destroyed Rome's empire? It was: What had that empire destroyed? The answer was Rome's liberty, its political culture, and eventually its power.

This was an analysis for which there was a rich classical source base, and which had also come to colour English republican thinking in the aftermath of Cromwell's Protectorate.[67] Nevertheless, as we have seen, in Periclean Athens and Elizabethan England insularity and empire were perfectly compatible. The Athenian empire was emblematic of the city's liberty and its greatness. Among these Enlightenment writers Ferguson and Dunbar were anti-continental; Raynal and Robertson were not. Raynal and Dunbar were anti-imperial; but Ferguson and Robertson were not. For Dunbar, Europe's American empires posed a grave danger. 'The discovery of America has opened an immense field to the ambition of the states of Europe. Instead of augmenting their territorial possessions at home, they began, from that aera, to form distant establishments by conquest or colonization, and to erect, in another hemisphere, a new species of empire.'[68]

These empires, which were despotisms, undermined liberty and civility. Colonies were 'regarded in the light of subordinate provinces, as appendages to government', when in fact the 'relation of a colony to the antient country, rightly understood, is a relation of perfect equality ... The one country is no more the mother, than it is the daughter. They are both the children of the same political parent, and that parent is the government to which they owe equal allegiance.'[69]

In such colonies, denied the appropriate political status, 'Jealousies ripen into disaffection. Political independency figures in the imagination, and is aspired after as an elevation of rank.' At that point European imperial governors encountered three serious problems. The first was that

---

[64] Ibid. p. 271.   [65] Ibid. p. 287.

[66] Quoted by Hugh Trevor-Roper, 'Introduction', in Edward Gibbon, *The Decline and Fall of the Roman Empire* (3 vols., New York, 1993) vol. I p. lxxxix.

[67] David Armitage, 'John Milton: Poet against Empire', in David Armitage, Armand Himy and Quentin Skinner (eds.), *Milton and Republicanism* (Cambridge, 1995); Scott, *Commonwealth Principles* ch. 10.

[68] Dunbar, *Essays on the History* p. 280.   [69] Ibid. p. 281.

across the Atlantic 'distance from the seat of government affords singular advantages to provinces that meditate revolt'. Second, since the American continent had now become a theatre of European rivalry, attempts to mend relations were undermined by external enemies. Finally, divided into so many independent colonies, the outlook for American liberty was as good as had once been the case in Europe. 'The geographical divisions of the American continent are certainly auspicious to civil liberty; and seem to oppose the establishment of such extended governments as have proved, in the antient hemisphere, a source of the most destructive and debasing servitude.'[70]

Thus, in arguing for a maritime rather than continental military policy, Dunbar was not advocating a seaborne empire. He was arguing against empire. And in writing so optimistically about America's federal constitution he departed from Ferguson who asked: 'Is Great Britain then to be sacrificed to America ... and a state which has attained high measures of natural felicity, for one that is yet only in expectation, and which, by attempting such extravagant plans of Continental Republic, is probably laying the seeds of anarchy, of civil wars, and at last of a military government?'[71]

Like Dunbar, Raynal emphasized the damage done by Europe's empires to its liberty. 'The new world was discovered, and the passion for conquest seized upon every nation. That spirit was not to be reconciled with the slowness of popular assemblies; and sovereigns succeeded without much trouble in appropriating to themselves more rights than they had ever enjoyed.' The problem, however, was not continents but empires. For this reason the outlook for American independence was bright, under a government not 'divided' but 'single'. 'When the ties subsisting between old and new Britain are once broken, the northern colonies will have more power when single, than when united with the mother country. This great continent, freed from all connections with Europe, will have the full command of all its motions.'[72] Nor was bluewater anti-continentalism absent from American colonial discourse. This might be directed, as it was in England, against entanglements 'with ... disputes between powers of the [European] continent'.[73]

If America is to be secure at home and respected abroad, it must be by a naval force. Nature and experience instruct us that a maritime strength is the best

[70] Ibid. p. 284.
[71] Adam Ferguson, *Remarks on a Pamphlet lately published by Dr Price*, quoted by Fania Oz-Salzberger, 'Introduction', in Ferguson, *An Essay* p. xxiii.
[72] Raynal, *Philosophical and Political History* vol. IV pp. 390, 513.
[73] James Burgh (1775) quoted by Simms, *Three Victories* p. 588.

defence to an insular situation ... [and] is not the situation of the United States insular with respect to the power of the Old World: the quarter from which alone we are to apprehend danger? Have not the maritime states the greatest influence upon the affairs of the universe?[74]

Insularity had always been a geopolitical rather than geographic claim. Geography informed, but culture completed the work. It was during this Enlightenment discussion, with vigorous British, and especially Scottish, participation, that Europeans sharpened their understanding of a maritime geography and climate which appeared distinct. This offered a new context for considering the potentialities of nations. It clarified the same context for considering the nature and perils of the empires by which those nations were now embedded in the world.

---

[74] William Henry Drayton quoted in Simms, *Three Victories* p. 605.

9 What continent?

> Spider, clever and fragile, Cook showed how
> To spring a trap for islands, turning from planets
> His measuring mission, showed what the musket could do,
> Made his Christmas goose of the wild gannets.
> Still as the collier steered
> No continent appeared;
> It was something different, something
> Nobody counted on.
>
> Allen Curnow, 'The Unhistoric Story'[1]

Recently John Pocock has presented the history of the British empire 'as that of an archipelago, situated in oceans and expanding across them to the Antipodes'.[2] As partly directed to New Zealanders, this is a useful attempt to remind them that their history, both Polynesian and European, has been part of something much larger and more complex than the nation-state. Yet from the perspective of British history this image of empire appears to depict the outcome of a process of geographical redescription, rather than the process itself.

We have seen Britain define itself as an island nation by contradistinction to 'continental' France (or China). We have seen western Europe, and Britain within it, constructed as a maritime alternative to 'continental' Asia (and America). We have seen English-speaking Americans claim an insular independence from the affairs of Europe. In this chapter we encounter a maritime redescription (rather than critique) of the British empire. This was an empire not only held together by, but in some sense composed of, water. When Andrew Fletcher said, 'The sea is the only empire which can naturally belong to us,' he echoed claims by Halifax and Sheres about the natural national sphere of the ocean. He also recalled English republican experience by reference to which liberty might be associated with naval power, and autocracy with armies. Fletcher's denunciations of standing armies as supports of tyranny applied

---

[1] In Curnow, *Early Days Yet* p. 235.   [2] Pocock, *Discovery of Islands*, back cover copy.

as well to Cromwellian as Williamite, and French, cases.[3] To depict a sea 'belong[ing]' to Britain also followed the history of the English republic beyond its initial Dutch maritime model to its embrace of the argument of Selden against Grotius that the sea could be owned.[4]

Britain's empire of the sea might be associated with those of the Athenians, Phoenicians and Dutch (Free States) and distinguished from those of Persia, Rome and France. Peter Marshall and David Armitage have described the depiction during the first half of the eighteenth century of an 'empire over the seas as distinct from the territorial empires of conquest established by imperial Rome or by Spain and to which France was alleged now to be aspiring'.[5] It was a Dutch writer quoted by an English one who observed: 'Such as Desire Empire & Liberty says Aristotle let Them Encourage the Art of Ship-building.'[6]

Such 'blue-water' depictions of the empire overlooked or sought to supplant its European geopolitical centre.[7] Even after the Seven Years War there remained a 'territorial' British empire, 'a tract of continent of immense extent' in both the Americas and India.[8] More broadly, all western European global empires were accomplishments of seafaring. Given that 'virtually every country that bordered on the Atlantic seaboard – Portugal, Spain, France, the Netherlands, Belgium, Denmark – became an imperial nation with a maritime empire ... there was nothing particularly unique about the British ... experience, except that it happened rather late'.[9] Second, all these empires were predominantly continental. This describes the centre of gravity of European empire-building in western Eurasia, South and North America, south and east Asia, and eventually Africa.[10]

John Ogilby's maps of America (1671), like Heylyn's earlier analysis, and Robertson's later, depict a continent, larger than Africa and Europe to the east, and perhaps connected to Asia to the north-west. Oldmixon's

---

[3] Andrew Fletcher, *A Discourse of Government With relation to Militias* (Edinburgh, 1698), in Fletcher, *Political Works*. Fletcher had no problem with free land armies (militias).

[4] Ibid. ch. 4.

[5] P.J. Marshall, 'Britain and the World in the Eighteenth Century: I, Reshaping the Empire', in Marshall, *'A Free though Conquering People'* p. 5.

[6] Nicolaes Witsen, quoted by Sir William Petty, quoted by David Armitage, *Ideological Origins* p. 124.

[7] Simms, *Three Victories*.

[8] *Annual Register for the Year 1763* quoted in Marshall, 'Britain and the World' p. 9.

[9] David Cannadine, 'Introduction', in Cannadine (ed.), *Empire* pp. 2–3.

[10] Studies of the 'continental' or territorial mapping practices deployed include Matthew H. Edney, *Mapping an Empire: the Geographical Construction of British India, 1765–1843* (Chicago, 1997); Burnett, *Masters of All They Surveyed*. On India see also Sudipta Sen, *Distant Sovereignty: National Imperialism and the Origins of British India* (New York, 2002) ch. 3.

British Empire (1741) described *the Continent and Islands of America*. In 1725–6 Defoe exclaimed: '*New England, New York, New Jersey ... New York ... Virginia ...* What then are these Colonies, tho' Great in themselves, and Powerful and Potent ... compar'd to the vast Continent of *North America?* Whose extent North I have describ'd a little, and whose Western Coast is not yet discover'd? neither do we yet know whether ... it is bounded by the Sea *yea* or *no*.'[11] The fact that, by Montesquieu and his successors, empire was theorized as continental helped Thomas Paine to blow this revolutionary raspberry from the other side of the Atlantic: 'there is something absurd in supposing a continent to be perpetually governed by an island. In no instance hath nature made the satellite larger than its primary planet ... [therefore] it is evident that they belong to different systems. England to Europe: America to itself.'[12]

Brian Richardson makes a parallel argument about European geographic thought more generally. Until the chronometer, allowing accurate location of longitude, all long-range navigation was a development from coasting. Within this system the place of the islands was 'marginal ... positioned in the narrative in terms of the nearest point of the main line ... they ... can only be intelligible as points close to a continental line'. Within this schema 'the oceanic island can have no place at all'.[13] This changed during the voyages, and especially the second voyage, of Cook.

[C]oasting is not the only thing that Cook does in the first voyage, and he does much less of it in the second and third voyages. Rather, for most of his time at sea he is exploring the South Seas or the Pacific Ocean, where he encountered an immense number of dispersed islands, separated by large expanses of open water. In the South Seas, the islands were no longer tied to a coast. They were points on a coordinate grid of latitude and longitude, a grid that came to dominate the narrative ... [that] does not imprison Cook's narrative; it makes his particular kind of narrative possible.[14]

That it became possible to see the empire not as continental but as archipelagic was partly a matter of scale. Since continents and islands were relational categories, from a sufficiently general perspective the world was an archipelago. As Greg Dening put it: '[T]he Europeans of the sixteenth century discovered that the world is an ocean and all its continents are islands.'[15] From the invention of the Indies to the search for a north-west passage archipelagic conceptions of empire were not new.[16] However, this development also had everything to do with the transformation of

---

[11] [Defoe], *A General History of Discoveries* pp. 285–6.
[12] Thomas Paine, *Common Sense*, in Thomas Paine, *Political Writings: Revised Student Edition*, (ed.) Bruce Kuklick (Cambridge, 2004) p. 23.
[13] Richardson, *Longitude and Empire* p. 27.   [14] Ibid. p. 31.
[15] Dening, *Islands and Beaches* p. 23.   [16] Gillis, *Islands* p. 59.

perspective which Richardson describes, and to which Cook contributed. What this made possible – as always – was a redescription not only of empire, but of nation. From appendage to a continent, an archipelago might become its own centre, inhabiting the open ocean. Only by means of the new co-ordinate grid, constructed by accurate lines of longitude as well as latitude, could Britain make itself supra-continental and extra-European.

This was not a discovery of islands, in that these had always been fundamental to European geography. It was the discovery of an island-centred view of global political space. Nor did this island now replace local or European with oceanic identity. Rather, these were combined. No longer simply Camden's local stepping stone, Britain was now gateway to the world.[17]

Thus Churchill's vow in 1940 to 'defend our Island, whatever the cost may be' had a global context. For

even if, which I do not for a moment believe, this Island or a large part of it were subjugated and starving, then our Empire beyond the seas, armed and guarded by the British Fleet, would carry on the struggle until, in God's good time, the New World, with all its power and might, steps forth to the rescue and liberation of the Old.[18]

Like every other feature of Britain's empire this development of perspective had a context in Anglo-French rivalry. By the 1760s one regional focus for that rivalry had become the South Pacific. European continent-mindedness also applied, and perhaps especially applied, to this part of the world.[19] Although the central and northern Pacific were first linked by Spain, to the south came the United Provinces, England and France looking for *Terra Australis Incognita*.

When, in 1669, Charles II commissioned a secret voyage to sail through the Straits of Magellan and up the Pacific coast of Chile, John Narborough took with him observations made during the 1577–80 circumnavigation by Drake.[20] His instructions to 'make a Discovery ... of the Sea and Coasts of that part of the World, and if possible to lay the foundation of a Trade there', recalling the aristocratic and mercantile collaboration of Elizabethan voyages, had not changed greatly by 1769 except that Narborough's voyage was for 'the Honour of our Prince

[17] Games, *Web of Empire*; Richard J. Evans, *Cosmopolitan Islanders: British Historians and the European Continent* (Cambridge, 2009).
[18] Churchill, *The Second World War* quoted in Sobecki, *The Sea* p. 1.
[19] Frost, *The Global Reach of Empire* pp. 43–85.
[20] For Drake's initial intention to cross the Pacific at a high southerly latitude see Taylor, *Tudor Geography* pp. 117–18.

and Nation' and Cook's for 'the Honour of this Nation as a Maritime Power'.[21]

Narborough was ordered to avoid the Spanish and therefore not to touch the Atlantic coast of South America north of the Rio de la Plata, and after that to make the '*Indian* Inhabitants ... sensible of the great Power and Wealth of the Prince and Nation to whom you belong'. In fact the Patagonians showed a distinct disinclination to interact with Narborough's crew, who failed to navigate the Straits before the southern winter (despite leaving in May) and so overwintered in St Julien, on the Atlantic coast, where both Magellan and Drake had anchored. Narborough's record of his excursions inland from there later inspired a proposal for Patagonian plantation. According to Daniel Defoe, Narborough had confirmed that the climate was temperate (unlike Spanish America); the earth covered in grass (unlike North America); the grass fed wild sheep and cows; there were no snakes or crocodiles; few Indians; few Spaniards; and if there was gold on one side of the Andes there must be gold on the other ('Sir *John Narborough* ... found several small pieces').[22]

In truth, however, despite making it through the straits to Chile the following year, and aside from the suspiciously English-sounding claim that penguins would queue in order to be clubbed to death (perhaps a moral effect of the temperate climate), Narborough reported relatively little of interest save finding a plaque of 'Sheet-Lead' left by the 1615 circumnavigation of Jacques Le Maire.[23] These voyages were tough on penguins, and on the causes of penguins. Drake had reported 'fowl that could not fly, as big as geese, whereof they killed three thousand, which was good provision'.[24] In 1772 a member of Cook's crew recorded ninety penguins on an iceberg 'set erect on their Leggs ranged in regular lines, which with their Breasts forms a very Whimsical appearance we fired two 4 pounders at them but Mist them after which they wheeld off three deep and March down to ye water in a Rank'.[25]

[21] John Narborough, 'A Journal kept by Captain John Narborough', in *An Account of Several Late Voyages & Discoveries to the South and North ... by Sir John Narborough, Captain Jasmen Tasman, Captain John Wood, and Frederick Marten* (London, 1694) pp. 10–11; James Cook, *The Journals of Captain James Cook on His Voyages of Discovery: the Voyage of the Endeavour 1768–1771*, (ed.) J.C. Beaglehole (Cambridge, 1955) pp. cclxxxii–cclxxxiii, 11. For Cook's secret instructions see below and p. cclxxx.

[22] Defoe, *A General History of Discoveries* pp. 287–98.

[23] Narborough, 'A Journal' pp. 10–11, 30, 36. A manuscript with colour illustrations is in the British Library, Sloane MS 3833.

[24] Awnsham and John Churchill, 'An Introductory Discourse, Containing, The whole History of Navigation from its Original to this time', in *A Collection of Voyages and Travels, Some Now Printed from Original Manuscripts* (6 vols., London, 1632) vol. I p. lxiv.

[25] James Cook, *The Voyage of the Resolution and Adventure 1772–1775*, (ed.) J.C. Beaglehole (Cambridge, 1961) pp. 68–9.

Seeking a route into the south sea alternative to that of the Dutch East India Company, Le Maire had discovered the straits which bear his name and was the first to enter the Pacific by rounding Cape Horn. He then crossed the Pacific, becoming the first European to encounter Tonga and Futuna (between Samoa and Fiji) before arriving in Batavia in October.[26] Leaving Batavia twenty-seven years later, the Dutch commander Abel Tasman entered the Pacific via a new route proceeding south of Australia. At 42 degrees southern latitude, after discovering Tasmania (Van Diemen's Land) – 'Too far south for spices'[27] – Tasman chanced upon another place which he called *Staten Landt*. 'This land looks like being a very beautiful land and we trust that this is the mainland coast of the unknown south land.'

To a Maori challenge issued 'in a rough loud voice', Tasman's crew responded by attempting to communicate in the language of Futuna as rendered by Le Maire. When the natives 'blew many times on an instrument which gave a sound like a Moorish trumpet', Tasman 'made one of our sailors (who could play the trumpet a little) play them some tunes in reply'. When the following day Tasman was unwise enough to launch a cockboat, it was attacked with astonishing speed, leaving four dead. After this 'monstrous happening and detestable affair', New Zealand remained untroubled by Europeans for more than another century.[28]

In the second edition of his *America*, published the year after Narborough's voyage, Ogilby added an Appendix on southern South America, including a chapter on 'The unknown South-Land'. Unsurprisingly Narborough's secret mission was not mentioned, but after beginning with Drake, Hawkins, Quiros and Le Maire, Ogilby provided the first substantial English-language account of Tasman's voyage.[29] In 1694 Narborough's own journal was published with Tasman's in a compilation of *Several Late Voyages to the South and North*, dedicated to Pepys.

The Bookseller's Preface set this work within the genre of *Voyages and Itineraries* established by 'Ramusio, *the* De Brys, Hackluit, Purchas'. Like the compilations of Hakluyt and Purchas this summary was organized geographically first (voyages south and then north) and chronologically

[26] William Eisler, *The Furthest Shore: Images of Terra Australis from the Middle Ages to Captain Cook* (Cambridge, 1995) pp. 70–1.
[27] Quoted in Peter Timms, *In Search of Hobart* (Sydney, 2009) p. viii.
[28] Abel Tasman, 'Journal or Description by me, Abel Jans Tasman, Of a Voyage Made From the City of Batavia … December Anno 1642 … For the Discovery of the Unknown South Land', in *Abel Janszoon Tasman and the Discovery of New Zealand*, (ed.) J.C. Beaglehole (Wellington, 1942) pp. 45, 49–52, 53; see also Denoon *et al.* (eds.), *The Cambridge History of the Pacific Islanders* pp. 127–8 and ch. 4.
[29] Ogilby, *America* pp. 654–61.

within these subsections. Commanding most detail, within both the introduction and the book, were voyages and discoveries since Purchas. These included continued attempts to find a north-west passage to Asia, and several overwinterings in Greenland, by whalers and others, yielding unsought-for data on the extreme effects of cold.[30] Concerning the south, the publishers noted:

The Hollanders *have indeed made the greatest Discoveries towards the South* Terra Incognita, *which they have not yet divulg'd.* Dirk Rembrantse *about 15 or 16 years ago published, in* Low Dutch, *a short Relation out of the Journal of Captain* Abel Jansen Tasman *upon his Discoveries of the South* Terra Incognita *in the year 1642, to the Southward of* Nova Hollandia, Vandemen's Land, &c. *'Tis remarkable that all the Circumnavigators of the Globe enter'd into the* East Indies, *either by the* Philippines *or the* Molucco's, *being peradventure hindred from passing round more Southwards by that vast long Chain of Land, which seems to stretch almost from the* Equinoctial *to the 50 degree of* South Lat.[31]

This was to say that, following Narborough's failure to sail further west than Chile, and Tasman's to sail further east than New Zealand, there remained no evidence to contradict the general European belief that there must exist in the Great South Sea a continent to balance Eurasia. Le Maire had been looking for this, but like all others entering the Pacific from the east had been prevented by westerly winds and northerly currents (the Humboldt current) from crossing the Pacific at a southerly latitude. Tasman, coming from the west, had been further south.[32] Narborough's publishers described Tasman's voyage as '*more considerable, in that 'tis the* Discovery *of a* New World, *not yet known to the English*' and speculated from what information was available that New Guinea, New Holland, Van Diemen's Land and New Zealand were one '*vast prodigious Island*'.

A map of the world included in William Dampier's bestselling *New Voyage Round the World* (1697) – a voyage made in 1689–91 – contained the Tasmanian and New Zealand coasts charted by Tasman, but could not say what they were attached to. Dampier completed another circumnavigation in 1699–1701, becoming the first Englishman to visit Australia, and a third from 1708 to 1711.[33] In 1715 a voyage was projected around Cape Horn via the Solomon Islands to 'Nova Guinea, which is the East Side of Nova Hollandia … lying North and South as

[30] 'The Bookseller's Preface', in *An Account of Several Late Voyages*, pp. xvii–xxv.
[31] Ibid. pp. vi–vii, x–xi.
[32] Tasman, 'Journal or Description by me, Abel Jans Tasman' p. 53.
[33] Beaglehole, *The Exploration of the Pacific* pp. 169–76.

Peru dos ... I believe it abounds in Gold and Silver mines, which ... may be of vast advantage to Great Britain.'[34]

The publishers' 'Introductory Discourse' to a six-volume *Collection of Voyages and Travels* published in 1732 was on a much larger scale, addressing 'The whole History of Navigation from its Original to this time'. Beginning with Noah's Ark, it agreed with Aylett Sammes that the Phoenicians had established in Britain 'a settled trade for tin', that the Greeks had learned seafaring from the Phoenicians and the Romans from the Carthaginians.[35] It distinguished ancient seafaring, which had stayed within sight of coasts, from modern, liberated to cross the open ocean by the 'wonderful discovery' of the 'magnetick ... needle' or compass. While this had been discovered by '*John Goia* of *Amalfi*' in Italy in AD 1300, it had not had a practical impact until the sixteenth century.[36] This introduction also recounted modern voyages chronologically, in order of direction: 'northern discoveries ... all taken out of *Hakluyt*'; then Africa and the East Indies; then the West Indies and America; and finally circumnavigations. There followed a '*Catalogue and Character of most Books of Travels*' in Latin, Italian, French, Spanish and English, the latter jumping from Purchas in 1625 to 1689 with no intervening entries.

Elements of Narborough's instructions were still visible in those given by the Admiralty to Samuel Wallis in 1766, at least as far as the Straits of Magellan.[37] What was being transformed, in the context of Anglo-French rivalry, was the ability to fix longitude. This would make it possible not only to make new discoveries, but to return to them.[38] 'Wheras there is reason to believe that Land or Islands of Great extent, hitherto unvisited by any European Power may be found in the Southern Hemisphere', Wallis was ordered to cross the Pacific to the latitude of New Zealand 'losing as little Southing as possible'.[39] Although this proved impossible ('I began now to keep the ship to the northward, as we had no chance of getting westing in this latitude'), when in June 1767 he became the

---

[34] Dampier, *A New Voyage Round the World*; NMM REC/4 Item 86 John Welbe: 'A Scheme of a Voyage Round the Globe for the discovery of Terra Australis Incognita May 27 1715'.

[35] Churchill and Churchill, 'An Introductory Discourse' pp. ix–xiii.

[36] Ibid. p. xvi.

[37] Among Englishmen Wallis' circumnavigation was preceded by those of Drake (1577–80), Dampier (1689–91, 1699–1701, 1708–11), Shelvocke (1719–22), Anson (1740–4) and Byron (1764–6). On British voyages in the first half of the eighteenth century see 'Introduction' to Part 1 of Jonathan Lamb, Vanessa Smith and Nicholas Thomas (eds.), *Exploration and Exchange: a South Seas Anthology 1680–1900* (Chicago, 2000) pp. 3–7.

[38] Taylor, *Haven-Finding Art* ch. 11.

[39] George Robertson, *The Discovery of Tahiti: A Journal of the Second Voyage of HMS Dolphin Round the World, Under the Command of Captain Wallis ... written by her Master George Robertson*, (ed.) Hugh Carrington (London, 1948), Introduction pp. xx, xxii–xxvi.

first European to visit Tahiti ('we now suposed we saw the long wishd for Southern Continent ... never before seen by any Europeans') Wallis was able to record its location.[40]

A few months later, struggling with the winds, currents and complexity of the Straits of Magellan, Louis de Bougainville observed 'how often have we regretted that we had not got the Journals of Narborough and Beauchesne, such as they came from their own hands, and that we were obliged to consult disfigured extracts of them' produced by printers ignorant 'of ... sea-phrases'.[41] This elicited from his translator John Reinhold Forster a note that 'This complaint is applicable only to ... French publications', as 'marine phrases ... are understood by the greater part of this [the English] nation ... [and] have even a run in common life'.[42]

On the Atlantic side of the straits, Bougainville's business had been to give the Falkland Islands (Malvinas) to Spain before Britain could take possession of them. In the Pacific Bougainville arrived in Tahiti ('New Cytherea') a few months after Wallis, claiming this island for France, and speculating that the visit of the English might explain the presence among the natives of venereal disease.[43] A decade later James Dunbar concluded:

The vices of Europe have already contaminated the Otaheitan blood. Whether the English or French navigators have been first authors of the dreadful calamity which now afflicts that race, it is of little importance to decide. While so odious a charge is retorted on each other by those nations, the natives of the happy island, so cruelly abused, will have cause to lament for ages, that any European vessel ever touched their shores.[44]

It is as well that he didn't know about French (or British, or American) nuclear testing.

Wallis' discovery provided a destination for the British expedition planned for the following year to observe the transit of Venus from the south sea. In fact astronomical observation (though conscientiously

[40] Ibid. pp. 106, 135; Cook praised the accuracy of Wallis' record in July 1769, *Endeavour* p. 118. On the visits of Wallis, Bougainville and Cook to Tahiti see Anne Salmond, *Aphrodite's Island: the European Discovery of Tahiti* (Auckland, 2009).
[41] Bougainville, *A Voyage Round the World* p. 196.   [42] Ibid. p. 197.
[43] Ibid. pp. 218–19, 273–4. The irascible Forster, chief naturalist on Cook's second voyage, gave as one reason for this translation its testimony that 'the honour of the greatest discoveries made within two centuries, in these remote seas is entirely reserved to the British nation' (Translator's Preface p. vi). For Cook's own more generous assessment of Bougainville's accomplishments see *Resolution and Adventure* p. 235. For his worry about Anglo-French conflict for possession of Tahiti see *Endeavour* p. 479.
[44] Dunbar, *Essays* p. 374. On European writing about Tahiti see Rod Edmond, 'The Pacific/Tahiti: Queen of the South Sea Isles', in Peter Hulme and Tim Youngs (eds.), *The Cambridge Companion to Travel Writing* (Cambridge, 2000).

performed) was not the real purpose of James Cook's journey. The Admiralty's choice of Tahiti was informed by Wallis' report of a high land visible to the south.[45] Cook was instructed that

Wheras there is reason to imagine that a Continent or Land of great extent, may be found to the Southward of the Tract lately made by Captn Wallis ... You are to proceed to the southward in order to make discovery of the Continent until you arrive in the Latitude of 40 degrees ... [and then] proceed in search of it to the Westward ... until you discover it, or fall in with the Eastern side of the Land discover'd by Tasman and now called New Zealand.[46]

Hence the dramatic jag south from Tahiti which caused such consternation to Tupia, the ship's Raiatean passenger, 'a very intelligent person' who knew 'more of the Geography of the Islands situated in these seas ... then any one we had met' and who implored his European colleagues to go west.[47] Development of the capacity to determine longitude as accurately as latitude is strikingly illustrated by the vigour of Cook's movements north and south as well as east and west. On board the *Endeavour* Cook and Joseph Banks had the extract from 'Tasmens Journal published by *Dirk Rembrantse*' along with the rest of *Several Late Voyages* (1694) which Banks owned.[48] Upon arrival Banks referred to New Zealand's North Island as 'the Continent', either in hope, or in relation to the 'many [smaller] Islands' by which it was surrounded.[49]

As captain, Cook could have been designed from scratch by Richard Gibson. He was a tarpaulin, a 'man who has not the advantage of Education ... but has been constantly at sea from his youth, and who ... [has] gone through all the Stations of a Seaman, from prentice boy in the Coal Trade to a Commander in the Navy'.[50] He was raised by Quakers and he chose as vessels for his first two circumnavigations (the *Endeavour* and *Resolution*) colliers from Whitby, his home town. When aristocratic accommodation demanded by Banks on the latter compromised its

[45] Carrington, Introduction, in Robertson, *Discovery of Tahiti* p. xxv.
[46] Cook, *Endeavour* p. cclxxxii.
[47] Ibid. pp. 117, 156–7. Banks agreed that while Tupia was 'skilld in the mysteries of their religion ... what makes him more than any thing else desireable is his experience in the navigation of these people and knowledge of the Islands in these seas; he has told us the names of above 70'. *The Endeavour Journal of Joseph Banks 1768–1771*, (ed.) J.C. Beaglehole (2 vols., Sydney, 1962) vol. I p. 312.
[48] Cook, *Endeavour* p. 299 and note 3 (see also p. 274). Banks, *Endeavour Journal* vol. II pp. 1–2 and note 1. The copy of *Several Late Voyages* (1694) reproduced by Early English Books Online from the collection of the British Library carries Banks' signature. Banks donated his library to the British Library. I am grateful to Jacob Pollock for pointing this out to me.
[49] Banks, *Endeavour Journal* vol. I pp. 424, 443.
[50] Cook quoted by Salmond, *Aphrodite's Island* p. 129.

seaworthiness, Cook had it removed. During the first voyage, rounding the South Island to the south-east in early March 1770, Banks recorded the division of the *Endeavour*'s crew into 'Continents' and 'Islanders ... one who wishd that the land in sight might, the other that it might not be a continent; myself have always been most firm for the former tho sorry I am to say that ... the rest begin to sigh for roast beef'.[51] 'A point of land seen this morn ... was supposd by the no Continents the end of the land; towards even however it cleard up and we Continents had the pleasure to see more land to the Southward.' Five days later, however, a fresh wind 'carried us round the Point to the total demolition of our aerial fabrick calld continent'.[52]

Banks suffered mightily as a result of Cook's prudent refusal to put in at one last New Zealand location (Dusky Sound) for him to gather specimens. At least he was fulfilling a larger ambition: 'every blockhead' did the European tour, but 'my Grand Tour shall be one around the whole globe'.[53] Despite 'Proving New Zealand to be an Island ... [and] the land seen by Juan Fernandes, the land seen by the Dutch squadron under Hermite, signs of Continent seen by Quiros, and the same by Roggewein', he continued 'firmly [to] believe' in the existence of a southern continent. This was not to accomplish 'the Balancing of the two poles, which always appeard to me to be a most childish argument'. Indeed, 'if ask'd why I believe so, I confess my reasons are weak'.[54]

Just before crossing the Tasman Sea to New Holland (Australia) Cook made a careful analysis of the geographical knowledge accumulated by his own just-completed Pacific crossing added to those of Quiros, Roggeveen and Le Maire. He concluded that there was now such a reduced space of ocean 'where the grand Object can lay, I think it would be a great pitty that this thing which at times has been the object of many ages and Nations should not now be wholy clear'd up' by one further voyage. Should that reveal that 'after all no Continent was to be found', then its captain 'might turn his thoughts towards the discovery of those multitude of Islands which we are told lay within the Tropical Regions to the South of the line [equator], and this we have from very good Authority'.[55] This authority was Tupia, who had proved

[51] Quoted by Anne Salmond, *The Trial of the Cannibal Dog: the Remarkable Story of Captain Cook's Encounters in the South Seas* (New Haven, 2003) p. 149.
[52] Banks, *Endeavour Journal* vol. I pp. 471, 472.
[53] Quoted in Simon Schaffer, 'Visions of Empire: Afterword', in David Miller and Peter Reill (eds.), *Visions of Empire: Voyages, Botany, and Representations of Nature* (Cambridge, 1996) p. 338.
[54] Banks, *Endeavour Journal* vol. II pp. 38–40.
[55] Cook, *Endeavour* pp. 290–1 (March 1770).

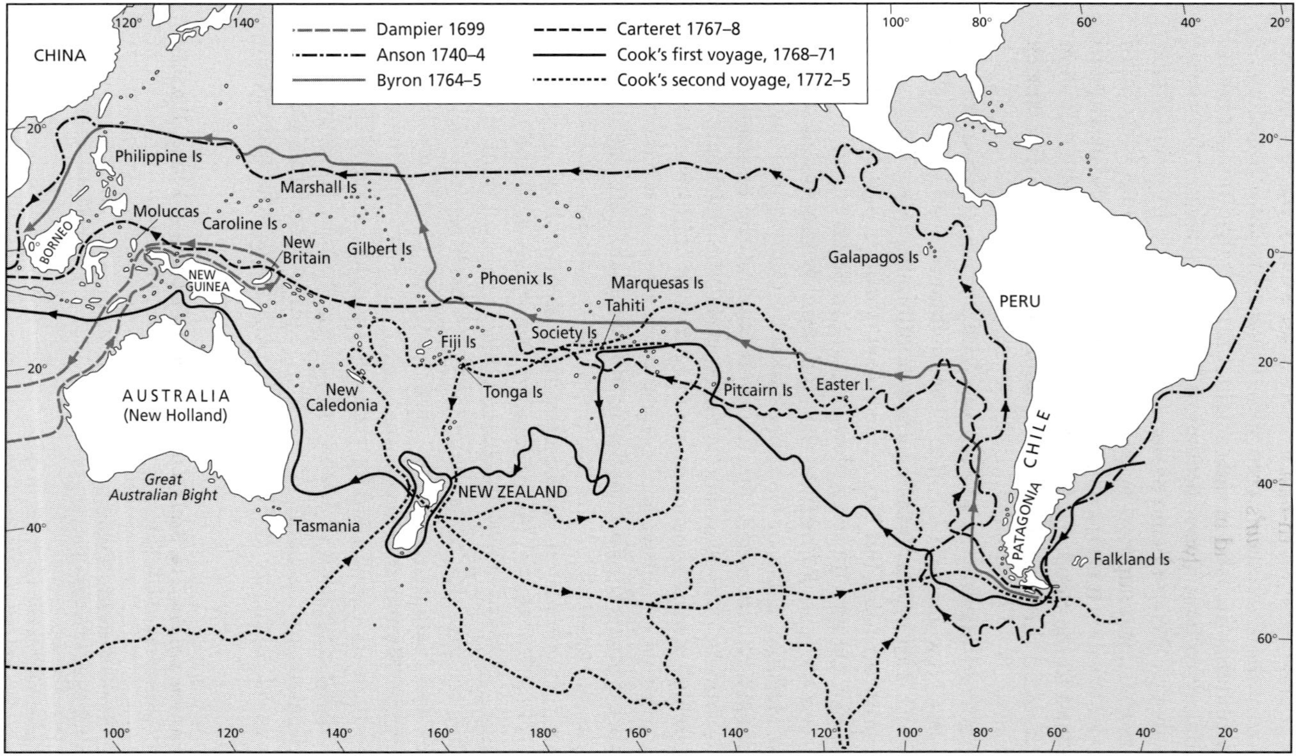
Dampier 1699
Anson 1740–4
Byron 1764–5
Carteret 1767–8
Cook's first voyage, 1768–71
Cook's second voyage, 1772–5
CHINA
Philippine Is
Marshall Is
Moluccas
Caroline Is
BORNEO
NEW GUINEA
New Britain
Gilbert Is
Phoenix Is
Marquesas Is
Tahiti
Society Is
Fiji Is
Tonga Is
New Caledonia
AUSTRALIA
(New Holland)
Great Australian Bight
Tasmania
NEW ZEALAND
Pitcairn Is
Easter I.
Galapagos Is
PERU
CHILE
PATAGONIA
Falkland Is
120°
140°
100°
80°
60°
40°
20°
0°
160°
180°

Map 6 The impact of the chronometer can be seen in the vigour of Cook's movements north and south as well as east and west. Map based on 'British voyages in the South Pacific, 1699–1775', in P.J. Marshall (ed.), *The Oxford History of the British Empire, volume II: The Eighteenth Century* (Oxford, 1998) p. 557.

invaluable in New Zealand where the Maori could understand him (and vice versa).[56] In thus beginning to turn his mind from the shrinking continent to an expanding world of islands, Cook's geographical thought was evolving in a Polynesian direction.[57] To put this differently, new navigational technology had transformed the European capacity to benefit from local knowledge.

On his way home Cook claimed the east coast of Australia for Britain, finding it to be low-lying, though 'indifferently well watered' and 'indifferently fertile'.[58] Later Banks' overly optimistic testimony about Botany Bay (south of modern Sydney) would inform the establishment of a new penal colony. Thereafter, during several hair-raising encounters with the Great Barrier Reef, the *Endeavour* was almost lost, and subsequently many men died of sickness, Tupia included, after reprovisioning in Batavia. The possibility of a southern continent lingered until the astonishing Antarctic sailing of Cook's second voyage, which also proved the accuracy of Harrison's chronometer.[59]

Now circumnavigating the globe in the opposite direction, Cook's two ships, after calling at Cape Town, proceeded south to the edge of the polar ice pack and then east across the southern ocean. After defrosting in New Zealand (where, after defrosting, several of the *Adventure*'s crew had been eaten), the *Resolution* again sailed to the Antarctic, this time in the Pacific, and crossed the entire ocean at extreme southern latitudes. The resulting journals recalled the Elizabethan voyages of Martin Frobisher in encountering islands

of Ice ... some of which were near two Miles in circuit and about 200 feet high ... these dangers ... are in some measure compencated by the very curious and romantick Views many of these Islands exhibit and which are greatly heightned by the foaming and dashing of the waves against them and into the several holes and caverns which are formed in the most of them.[60]

Anders Sparrman recorded: 'On the 26th [December 1772] ... one of the icebergs ... was transformed into the loveliest scene imaginable. The glow of the setting sun fell upon this iceberg, which was as clear as crystal, so that its many thousand crevices and chasms shone like gold, in a

[56] Cook, *Endeavour* pp. 176, 244; Banks, *Endeavour Journal* vol. I pp. 403–5; vol. II p. 30.
[57] Cook had been instructed to 'observe with accuracy the Situation of such Islands as you may discover ... without Suffering yourself however to be thereby diverted from the Object which you are always to have in View, the Discovery of the Southern Continent'. Cook, *Endeavour* p. cclxxxiii.
[58] Ibid. pp. 387, 392–3.
[59] Taylor, *Haven-Finding Art* plate XXIV; Cook, *Resolution and Adventure* pp. 327–8.
[60] Cook, *Resolution and Adventure* pp. 58, 98–9 (and see pp. 304–11, 321–2, 637–46).

clear scintillating yellow, while the rest of the mass reflected a rich pur-
ple colour.'[61] Responding again to the pleas of his crew, Cook repaired
to Tahiti, and then discovered many islands to the west, as Tupia had
intended. Only once he had rounded the Horn and re-entered the temperate Atlantic could it be certainly said that a southern continent did
not exist.[62] The result of perhaps the most spectacular voyage of discovery in the history of humankind was nothing.

Having dined with Cook in London in 1776, prior to his third voyage, James Boswell informed Samuel Johnson that he had 'catched the
enthusiasm of curiosity and adventure, and felt a strong inclination to
go with him'. Johnson replied: 'Why, Sir, a man *does* feel so, till he considers how very little he can learn from such voyages.' Boswell echoed
Banks: 'But one is carried away with the general grand and indistinct
notion of *A Voyage Round the World*.' Johnson: 'Yes, Sir, but a man is to
guard himself against taking a thing in general.'[63] A few years later James
Dunbar recorded his astonishment that Cook 'with a company of 118
men, performed a voyage of three years and eighteen days, throughout
all the climates from 52 degrees north to 71 degrees south latitude, with
the loss of a single man only by disease, a proportion so moderate, that
the bills of mortality, in no climate or condition of society, can furnish
such another example'.[64]

Discussing Cook's voyages, Bernard Smith has illuminated the effect
of exposure to the South Pacific upon the cultural assumptions of British
explorers and artists.[65] This owed much to the role played within these
voyages by precise empirical observation and record-keeping ('collecting, measuring, drawing and painting').[66] Although indebted to English
traditions of maritime log-keeping and Baconian natural philosophy, this

---

[61] Quoted in Bernard William Smith, *European Vision and the South Pacific, 1768–1850: a
    Study in the History of Art and Ideas* (2nd edn, Oxford, 1989) p. 61.
[62] The Tongan archipelago (discovered by Tasman in 1643) elicited praise comparable
    to Tahiti (Cook, *Resolution and Adventure* pp. 260–5). As late as January 1775 South
    Georgia in the South Atlantic was mistaken for 'part of a great Continent' (ibid.
    p. 625).
[63] Quoted in Frost, *Global Reach* p. 7.
[64] Dunbar, *Essays* p. 376. For the perception of Cook's voyages as a model for the main-
    tenance of health at sea see Christopher Lawrence, 'Disciplining Disease: Scurvy, the
    Navy, and Imperial Expansion, 1750–1825', in Miller and Reill (eds.), *Visions of Empire*
    pp. 86–93.
[65] Smith, *European Vision* chs. 2–3.
[66] Michael Bravo, 'Precision and Curiosity in Scientific Travel: James Rennell and the
    Orientalist Geography of the New Imperial Age', in Jas Elsner and Joan-Pau Rubiés
    (eds.), *Voyages and Visions: Towards a Cultural History of Travel* (London, 1999) p. 168;
    David Mackay, *In the Wake of Cook: Exploration, Science and Empire, 1780–1801* (London,
    1985) pp. 5–9, 12–13.

also drew from the example of European rivals.[67] In 1694 *An Account of Several Late Voyages* had

> lamented, *that the* English Nation *have not sent along with their* Navigators *some skilful* Painters, Naturalists, and Mechanists, *under publick* Stipends *and* Encouragement, *as the* Dutch *and* French *have done … We are apt to imitate a certain Prince in every thing, except in the most glorious and best Part of him,* viz. The Encouraging and Rewarding great Men in all Professions, and the promoting Arts and Sciences with his Treasure.[68]

On Cook's first voyage, however, one consequence of a partnership between the Admiralty and the Royal Society was the illustration, by Sidney Parkinson, of new species of flora and fauna. During the second voyage the most striking result was attention, still on display in the ravishing paintings of Hodges, to non-European (both polar and tropical) conditions of atmosphere, colour and light. This owed something to the precise attention to changes in the colour of sea and sky which had long been pivotal to safe long-distance voyaging. It was also indebted, however, to the unprecedented extremes of latitude traversed by the voyage itself.

Whatever the causes, Hodges transcended his classical training. Back in London the resulting exhibition was a failure. 'It is surprising … that a man of Mr Hodges's genius should adopt such a ragged mode of colouring; his pictures all appear as if they were unfinished, and as if the colours were laid on with a skewer.' In Tahiti, and at Dusky Bay, colours were laid on with a skewer (and breezes and scents). Within the metropolis this could not be imagined: Hodges' paintings were outlandish.[69]

A related feature of these voyages was the romantic celebration of a nature apparently untouched by culture. It was not only Hodges' paintings, but their subject which was unfinished. In the words of Banks again, off Iceland in 1772: 'Compared to this what are the cathedrals or palaces built by men! … Nature is here found in her possession, and here it has been for ages undescribed.'[70] At Dusky Bay (Dusky Sound) George Forster recorded: 'we looked upon the country at that

---

[67] Richard Drayton, 'Knowledge and Empire', in P. J. Marshall (ed.), *The Oxford History of the British Empire, volume II: The Eighteenth Century* (Oxford, 1998).

[68] *An Account*, Introduction p. xxix. For the relatively high public and institutional status of geography and cartography in eighteenth-century France see Godlewska, *Geography Unbound* ch. 1.

[69] Quoted by Smith, *European Vision* p. 75. Harriet Guest, however, emphasizes the debt of this aspect of Hodges' style to that of his master Richard Wilson. Guest, *Empire, Barbarism and Civilization: Captain Cook, William Hodges, and the Return to the Pacific* (Cambridge, 2007) pp. 18–19, 23–4.

[70] Quoted by Smith, *European Vision* p. 32.

time, as one of the most beautiful which nature unassisted by art could produce'.[71] A settler in New Zealand wrote in 1842 – the longstanding occupation by Maori notwithstanding – of 'most delightful streams of fresh water ... no traces of mans work, all is natures own ... a sky of unclouded brilliancy'.[72]

Examples of European voyagers mistaking indigenous cultural practices for 'nature' became legion. These perceptions, what J. C. Beaglehole called 'this nonsense on stilts', were themselves Enlightenment cultural constructs.[73] One response by Bougainville's naturalist Commerson to the apparent perfection of Tahiti was (in effect) to reverse Camden's earlier emphasis on migration history in favour of an anti-colonial myth of autochthony. This reflected the new European capacity to imagine islands independent of continents.

> It will doubtless be asked, from what continent, what people have these islanders come? As if it were only from emigration to emigration that the continents and the isles could have been peopled ... [however] I do not see why the good Tahitians might not have sprung from their own soil, I mean, descended from ancestors who have always been Tahitians, going back as far as the people most jealous of its antiquity. Still less do I see to what nation we should ascribe the honour of the colony of Tahiti, always maintained within the bounds of simple nature.[74]

In Simon Schama's environmental history this myth of untouched nature was reversed, the motif supplied by Henry David Thoreau:

> It is in vain to dream of a wildness
> distant from ourselves. There is none such.
> It is the bog in our brains and bowels, the
> Primitive vigour of Nature in us, that inspires
> That dream. I shall never find in the wilds of
> Labrador any greater wildness than in some recess
> Of Concord, i.e than I import into it.[75]

These suggestions, about both human beings (that we carry the 'dream of a wildness' inside ourselves) and the natural environment (that there

---

[71] Quoted by Guest, *Empire* p. 139.

[72] ATL MS 2233, Thomas Parkinson 1842 p. 38.

[73] Cook, *Endeavour 1768–1771* p. clxxiii, quoting Commerson on *Nouvelle Cythère* 'ou habitant des hommes sans vices, sans prejuges, sans besoins, sans dissensions, Nes sous le plus beau ciel, nourris des fruits d'une terre qui est feconde sans culture, Regis par des peres de famille plutot que par des Rois, ils ne coinnoissent d'autre Dieu que l'amour ...' In Tahiti even the preternaturally sane Cook was not immune to similar thoughts (see p. 121).

[74] Quoted in Grove, *Green Imperialism* pp. 242–3.

[75] Thoreau, *Journal*, 30 August 1856, frontispiece in Simon Schama, *Landscape and Memory* (New York, 1996).

is no wilderness, or nature outside culture), are also cultural constructs.[76] Many historians of Europe have accepted, because there 'the impact of human activity over the past two millennia ... has been so conspicuous', that 'landscapes are culture before they are nature'.[77] Thoreau's lines may be understood as criticizing an alternative perspective in North America, where the idea of wilderness as a 'pristine site uncontaminated' by culture remains important.[78] A 1964 Act of Congress defined wilderness as 'an area where the earth and its community of life are untramelled by man'.[79]

In parts of the world less heavily populated and habitable than modern Europe, the idea of nature as a cultural projection has its limits. In the salutary formulation of one Australian: 'Project what you like. If you fail to find water, you will die.'[80] As we have seen in chapter 1, early modern English writers recognized several categories of wilderness. At the other end of the colonial chronology – perhaps not such a great distance – in 1950 a pakeha New Zealander making the mental journey 'from emigrant to native' imagined of the authors of some Maori cave drawings in the South Island:

Their unknown purposes brought them ranging into the wilderness, penetrating the secrets of its water and its natural shelter, in the bitter sun that beat on me now or the cold rain. But now I saw clearly that though they had known and possessed this great and somehow desolate land, and perhaps loved it, that was not all. As perhaps happens to all men in vast and silent places, because of its inscrutability and the narrowness of their way, it had possessed *them*, as no lesser place could.[81]

Oceanic distance between islands in the South Pacific had a profound impact upon the pattern of human settlement. Travelling a series of arcs from east Asia as far as the Marquesas and Easter Island, and then turning north, and eventually south-west, the Austronesian ancestors of Polynesians accomplished the largest-scale maritime migration of pre-modern times.[82] This occurred in multiple voyages

---

[76] Howe, *Nature, Culture and History* pp. 13–14; Caroline Ford, 'Nature's Fortunes: New Directions in the Writing of European Environmental History', *The Journal of Modern History* 79 (March 2007) p. 115.

[77] Mark Cioc and Simon Schama respectively quoted in Lekan, *Imagining the Nation in Nature* pp. 9, 15.

[78] Ibid. p. 14.

[79] 'Where the Wild Things Are', *The Economist* 15 January 2009.

[80] Cathcart, *The Water Dreamers* p. 3.

[81] T.H. Scott, 'South Island Journal', *Landfall* 4, 4 (December 1950) p. 301; Scott, 'From Emigrant to Native' Part 1, *Landfall* 1, 4 (December 1947); Part 2, *Landfall* 2, 2 (June 1948).

[82] Denoon *et al.* (eds.) *Cambridge History of the Pacific Islanders* pp. 56–69.

over a two thousand year period, entailing constant developments in navigation and vessel design. Most of the voyages were into winds blowing and currents setting from the east, furnishing the possibility, in the absence of landfall, of return.[83] The islands of the eastern and southern Pacific were the last habitable parts of the globe to receive human settlement.

Because of its remoteness in the deep southern ocean New Zealand was the very last of these.[84] Voyaging downwind, not into the wind, Maori may have arrived from the Cook Islands as recently as AD 1300 and could not have expected to return. For those who arrived a temperate climate supported few of their tropical crops (only the sweet potato, an import from Peru). Similarly, as we have seen, New Zealand was well south of the usual (east to west) European routes of Pacific crossing. Consequently, the landing by Tasman notwithstanding, it was not until 1769 that the country became accessible to Europeans.[85]

Thereafter New Zealand's oceanic geography did not persuade its British settlers to consider themselves non-Europeans. On the contrary, having burned most of the trees, planted grass and erected the nearest thing possible in place of cold-climate rain forest to an antipodean Derbyshire or Devon, these colonists congratulated themselves on being a better type of Briton.[86] They did so despite the unfamiliarity of their physical surroundings. In the earliest accounts of New Zealand the dominant theme was not sea or coast but mountains.[87] Drawing upon the testimony of Tasman and Cook, Thomas Bankes described 'this high mountainous country ... [the South Island as] mostly hilly, and, to appearance, barren and thinly inhabited ... [the North Island] though very mountainous ... [is] tolerably fertile ... with a rivulet running through every valley'.[88] 'The Character of the land appeared very rugged and bold.'[89] 'It is a bold bluff coast, chiefly sand hills covered with

[83] K.R. Howe, *The Quest for Origins: Who First Discovered and Settled the Pacific Islands?* (Honolulu, 2003) pp. 60–120. Informed by Tupia, Cook reflected usefully upon this process in August 1769: *Endeavour* p. 154; see also Dening, *Islands and Beaches* p. 16.

[84] McNeill, 'Of Rats and Men' p. 73; Howe, *Quest for Origins* ch. 8.

[85] Miles Fairburn, 'Culture and Isolation', J.C. Beaglehole Lecture delivered at the University of Canterbury, December 2001; James Belich, *Making Peoples: a History of the New Zealanders from Polynesian Settlement to the End of the Nineteenth Century* (Auckland, 1996).

[86] James Belich, *Paradise Reforged: a History of the New Zealanders from the 1880s to the Year 2000* (Auckland, 2001); Kerry Howe, 'Two Worlds?', *New Zealand Journal of History* 37, 1 (2003) pp. 50–1.

[87] Cf., however, Banks' rave about New Zealand fish: Banks, *Endeavour Journal* vol. II pp. 6–8.

[88] Bankes, *Universal Geography* p. 12.

[89] ATL MS 2053, Letters and Journals of Samuel Stephens, Surveyor of the NZ Co. at Nelson 1841–54 p. 15.

herbage.'[90] '[T]he shores have not a promising appearance ... hill rising among hill till they are lost in the clouds.'[91] '[T]he land is well wooded and watered, but rather mountainous.'[92] '[T]he land appeared very high covered with a thick bush ... two or three high Mountains ... covered with snow.'[93]

There was, it was agreed, far less level land in the colony than in the south and midlands of England, a source of both scenic sublimity and agricultural worry. For one writer the effect was 'more similar ... to Scotland, than it is to any other European country'; for another, 'this country has some similarity to the northern parts of Italy, and to Switzerland ... Like Switzerland and the Caucasus mountains, it will doubtless give birth to a race of freemen, and its government must necessarily be framed upon a similar plan to that of the Swiss.'[94]

Where archipelagic imagery reappeared suddenly, however, was in comparisons with that scarlet hussy, or Persia of the South Pacific, Australia. Thus Presbyterian minister John Dunmore Lang, a member of the Legislative Council of New South Wales, wrote after visiting New Zealand in 1839: 'The territorial extent, insular form ... numerous harbours, its relative position to the Australian Continent, and to the Pacific and Southern Oceans, its natural fertility ... and its evident adaptation to all purposes of maritime and commercial enterprise, have obtained for [New Zealand] ... the common appellation of the "Britain of the South".'[95] In the words of another:

New Zealand differs, then, from Australia in nearly every leading characteristic. The result is already a different type of the Anglo-Saxon race. The imagination of the Australian is nurtured upon mystery and change; it feeds on the immense distances of his continent ... The New Zealander dwells in a land of light and beauty ... the sea for ever close at hand ... Already the islands have been called the 'Fortunate Isles'; and ... the historian Froude wrote of them: '... I can well believe that it will be in the unexhausted soil and spiritual capabilities of New Zealand that the great English poets,

---

[90] ATL MS 8012, Diary of William M. Baines 1850 p. 11.

[91] ATL MS 2233, Thomas Parkinson 1842 p. 35.

[92] *Latest Information from the Settlement of NEW PLYMOUTH ... NEW ZEALAND* (London, 1842), p. 38, Letter from Peter Hoskin, 21 June 1841.

[93] ATL MS 2812, Robert Jenkins. Cook agreed: *Endeavour* pp. 176, 180, 251, 256, 269–70, 276: 'No country upon earth can appear with a more ruged ... aspect than this doth from the sea' (270).

[94] ATL MS N.24.1: 'Narrative of a Residence in New Zealand' 1839–40 pp. 1–2, 27; Letter from John Wallace, Wellington, to Mr Drake 6 April 1842 in *Letters from Settlers and Labouring Emigrants ... From Feb 1842, to June, 1843* (London, 1843) p. 12.

[95] Revd John Dunmore Lang, *New Zealand: A Lecture, By a Young Missionary* (London, 1849) Appendix II p. 26. On Lang see Cathcart, *The Water Dreamers* pp. 59, 71.

artists, philosophers, statesman, and soldiers of the future will be born and nurtured.'[96]

In time New Zealand/Aotearoa would become a sea of islands, Polynesian, European and more recently Asian.

> And again I see the long pouring headland,
> And smoking coast with the sea high on the rocks,
> The gulls flung from the sea, the wooded hills
> Swarming with mist, and mist low on the sea.
> And on the surf-loud beach the long spent hulks,
> The mats and splintered masts, the fires kindled
> On the wet sand, and men moving between the fires,
> Standing or crouching with backs to the sea.[97]

Within the archipelagic mindset explored by Allen Curnow, Charles Brasch and Alistair Campbell insularity stood not necessarily for uniqueness – this could be argued either way – but for remoteness.[98] In the words of one contributor to *Distance Looks Our Way*:

New Zealand is isolated from South America, its nearest neighbour to the east, by some 4500 miles of ocean, while to the south there are 1600 miles of sea to the Antarctic continent; Australia lies 1230 miles to the west and 2500 miles to the north-west is New Guinea … This … degree of remoteness … [has] lasted for … 70 million years.[99]

These were Curnow's 'two islands not in narrow seas'.[100] The oceanic setting of New Zealand was decisively different from that of Britain. Within it post-colonial independence could be imagined. That independence remains culturally incomplete. Today New Zealanders consider the country a better type of island nation: more beaches, better sailors, warmer weather, tastier fish. New Zealand's water is wider, bluer and deeper. That may not be how the political theory of water ends, but it is the current state of play.

It was from this perspective 'Formed partly in an archipelago of the Southern Ocean' that John Pocock wrote about 'the islands including

[96] *The New Zealand Colony: Its Geography and History* (London, 1903) pp. 11–12.
[97] Alistair Campbell, *The Return*, part of the extract read at the Memorial Service for D. F. McKenzie (1931–99) at the Chapel of Magdalen College, Oxford, 5 June 1999.
[98] Francis Pound, *The Invention of New Zealand: Art and National Identity 1930–1970* (Auckland, 2009) pp. 38–50.
[99] E. J. Godley, 'Fauna and Flora', in Sinclair (ed.), *Distance Looks Our Way* p. 1. In his own essay Sinclair remarked: 'When Dr Harry Scott first planned this series of lectures … he decided that, though New Zealand was physically remote, whether or not it was isolated was a thing to be determined' (p. 27). For Scott's thinking about New Zealand's relation to the world see Jonathan Scott, *Harry's Absence* chs. 3, 5, 7, 11, 13, 17.
[100] Quoted in Pound, *Invention* p. 41.

Britain as another archipelago ... *not* the promontory of a continent ... [this study] presupposes histories "*not* in narrow seas"'.[101]

Pocock used this oceanic setting to contextualize the shared history of Britain and its former colonies. Even so Britain does have two coasts in narrow seas. Notwithstanding the arguments of Aylett Sammes, it was until recently a promontory.

Pocock has added: 'Europhiles and Europhobes at present share a bad habit of placing "England" and "Europe" in a zero-sum relation, so that any attention to the one entails a diminution of the other.'[102] This is not, presumably, habitual among historians who take England to be a part of Europe and therefore any attention to either to be attention to both. The history of Europe, to which New Zealand has made some contribution, is one of islands and peninsulas, of plains and mountains, of globe-spanning oceans and inland seas.

[101] Ibid. p. 23; Colin Kidd, 'Europe, What Europe?', *London Review of Books*, 6 November 2008 p. 17.
[102] J.G.A. Pocock, *Barbarism and Religion, volume I: The Enlightenments of Edward Gibbon, 1737–1764* (Cambridge, 1999) p. 308.

Conclusion: floating islands

> Our islands lost again, all earth one island,
> And all our travel circumnavigation.
>
> Allen Curnow, *Discovery*[1]

By the early nineteenth century the British empire included many islands in the Mediterranean and Asia as well as the Caribbean and Pacific. In 1808 this drew from G. F. Leckie another rumination upon Britain's accomplishment in emulating the maritime achievements of Athens and Rhodes.[2] If maritime empire was not new, after 1815 the scale of British naval power was.[3] We should thus not be surprised to see the imperial archipelago further reimagined as a fleet. This floating archipelago had a specific genesis in English republican experience and its intellectual and cultural anticipations. In 1627–8 it was a swarm of bees. Under the republic it was 'Of floting Islands a new Hatched Nest; A Fleet of Worlds, of other Worlds in quest.'[4] Acts 10 and 11 of the reign of William and Mary referred to Newfoundland as 'a great English ship moored near the Banks'.[5]

To describe the empire as a fleet was not simply to emphasize its global – the equivalent today would be planetary – reach ('A Fleet of Worlds'). It was to set it again, against the empire of Sparta, and with that of Athens, as a thing in motion. Michel Foucault captured this mobile universality thus: 'The boat is a floating piece of space, a place without a place, that exists by itself, that is closed in on itself and at the same time is given over to the infinity of the sea.'[6] When Wallis' *Dolphin* appeared in 1767, Tahitians 'thought that this might be a floating island, just as Tahiti itself had once been, driven by ancestral power'.[7] When

---

[1] In Curnow, *Early Days Yet* p. 217.   [2] Bayly, *Imperial Meridian* p. 103.
[3] Tim Clayton, *Tars: the Men Who Made Britain Rule the Waves* (London, 2007) pp. 300–1.
[4] Marvell, *The First Anniversary*, in *Poems and Letters* vol. I p. 112.
[5] Gerald S. Graham, 'Fisheries and Sea Power', in G.A. Rawlyk (ed.), *Historical Essays on the Atlantic Provinces* (Toronto, 1967) p. 10.
[6] M. Foucault, 'Of Other Spaces', *Diacritics* 16 (1986) p. 27, quoted in O'Hara, '"The Sea is Swinging into View"' p. 1125.
[7] Salmond, *Aphrodite's Island* p. 39. This study (particularly chapter 1) relates ancient Greek to Polynesian maritime mythologies, including the theme of floating islands.

Cook's *Endeavour* arrived in New Zealand in October 1769, local Maori recorded: 'When the old men and women saw Captain Cook's ship, they called out "It is an island, an island floating from afar. Here it is, coming towards us!" When they saw its sails, they cried out "Aha, ha! The sails of this traveling island are like clouds in the sky!"'[8]

This study has encountered floating islands in three contexts. First they described the religiously and politically contested status of island geography in its relationship to an adjacent continent, to other islands, and to that island's internal component parts. Then there was the constructed image of an island nation and empire. Finally there were the floating islands by passage within which not only the British, but other Europeans acquired and extended their experience and power. All of these images, gesturing at unity, dynamism and universality, amounted to more than a geographical description. Although borrowed from Greece – from Homer, Aeschylus and Thucydides – they were the packaging, in three successive layers, of one national claim to modernity.

In its components this imagery was as European as the flight path of Defoe's decoy ducks. Over time its English and then British usage acquired national, regional, Atlantic and global functions. Thus Diana Loxley's claim that by the nineteenth century the motif of the island was *the* theme of British colonialism is anchored in the European ubiquity of the island as a metaphor for contained and penetrable exotic space. In Britain in 1882 Instructions to School Inspectors recommended that 'More than three set books are not necessary in any standard … in Standard V, VI and VII … works such as *Robinson Crusoe*, Voyages and Travels or Biographies of eminent men … are to be preferred.'[9] Two years later a British survey of reading in 1884 'among 790 boys … gathered from widely different sources … showed the dominance of island adventures, with *Robinson Crusoe* and *Swiss Family Robinson* topping the list'.[10]

The same year appeared the most successful Robinsonnade (Stevenson had to instruct William Gladstone to stop reading *Treasure Island* and attend to affairs of state).[11] Robert Louis Stevenson analysed the plain style by means of which Defoe had prioritized doing over describing. Since, while it 'reaches into the highest abstraction of the ideal, it does not refuse the most pedestrian realism, *Robinson Crusoe* is as realistic as it is romantic: both qualities are pushed to an extreme'. Readers praised

---

[8] Quoted in Salmond, *The Trial of the Cannibal Dog* p. 113.
[9] Quoted in Loxley, *Problematic Shores* pp. 83–4.   [10] Ibid. p. 32.
[11] Ibid. p. 135.

just those features of *Treasure Island* which had earlier excited Rousseau about Defoe: 'timelessness, immediacy, transparency of perception'.[12]

Stevenson set *Treasure Island* in the eighteenth century, drawing on Defoe's *History of the Pirates* (1724).[13] Like those of Crusoe, the adventures of Jim Hawkins began under English circumstances of 'domesticity and confinement' in realistic style and on a specific date.[14] In piracy Stevenson invoked a major theme of English maritime experience from the Elizabethan period onwards. By placing at the centre of his island (and its map) a fabulous hoard of treasure he invoked the dream of European empire from its inception. It was after reading *Treasure Island*, *Coral Island* and *The Swiss Family Robinson* to his children at bedtime that the idea came to William Golding in 1951 to make an island the site for the dystopian *Lord of the Flies*.[15]

Contemporaneously with Stevenson, who eventually moved to Samoa, Samuel McFarlane of the London Missionary Society struggled to bring the Gospel to eastern Papua. Unlike Polynesia, New Guinea was malarial. The native people were linguistically diverse, politically divided, and often at war.[16] As violence and disease took their toll, McFarlane moved from the mainland to offshore islands. As the problems persisted he became a peripatetic inhabitant of his ship. 'Mr McFarlane', sniped the *Brisbane Courier*, 'is an able man who from the deck of the *Ellengowan* writes interesting reports of the ... natives, with whom his intercourse is, we believe, limited to cruising around their coasts.'[17]

McFarlane had called his islands 'cities of refuge'. Then he trusted to his wooden walls. This had been the advice of the oracle at Delphi to Themistocles, repeated by Richard Gibson during the 1690s. In November 1906, after witnessing the first European aeroplane flight in France, Lord Northcliffe, proprietor of the *Daily Mail*, reported: 'The news is ... that England is no longer an island. There will be no more sleeping safely behind the wooden walls of old England with the Channel our safety moat. It means the aerial chariots of a foe descending on British soil if war comes.'[18] Those walls had always been a myth. In two world wars to come, as well as those of the eighteenth and nineteenth centuries

---

[12] Quoted in ibid. pp. 137, 141.   [13] Ibid. p. 133.   [14] Ibid. pp. 147, 149.
[15] John Carey, *William Golding, the Man Who Wrote Lord of the Flies* (London, 2009) p. 149.
[16] ATL LMS Papua Letters 1872–85, Micro MS Coll. 2 Reels 91–3; LMS Papua Journals 1871–1901, Micro MS Coll. 2 Reel 11.
[17] Jonathan Scott, 'Samuel McFarlane, William Lawes and James Chalmers in New Guinea 1872–1885', unpublished BA (Hons) research essay, Victoria University of Wellington, 1980, p. 41.
[18] Quoted in Peter Fitzsimons, *Charles Kingsford Smith and Those Magnificent Men* (Sydney, 2009) p. 21.

passed, Britain's wars were fought on land – and eventually in the air – as well as at sea. But they were an oracular inspiration.

Britain's island idea, while connecting the component parts of the United Kingdom, made a claim about Britain's relationship to the rest of Europe. It drew upon the literature of the ancient Mediterranean, and contemporary Dutch and other European example. Finally, like Cook's ships, it became a vehicle whereby the nation located itself outside Europe, inhabiting the world.[19] It was these claims about the national achievement which the island idea was developed to express, and which it still expresses, even now that the empire is gone.

[19] Williams, *The Great South Sea*.

Appendix: Duck Language (1724)

[In] these Fens of *Lincolnshire* ... are ... an infinite Number of wild Fowl, such as Duck and Mallard, Teal and Widgeon, Brand Geese, wild Geese ... and for the taking of the four first Kinds, here are a great Number of *Decoys* or *Duckoys* ... from all which the vast Number of Fowls they take are sent to *London*; the Quantity indeed is incredible ... [so] that some of these Decoys ... are let for great Sums of Money by the Year, *Viz.* from 100 *l.* to 3, 4, and 500 *l.* a Year Rent.

The Art of Taking the Fowls, and especially of Breeding up a Set of Creatures, called *Decoy Ducks*, to entice and then betray their Fellow-Ducks ... is very admirable ... and deserves a Description ...

The Decoy Ducks are first naturalized to the Place, for they are hatch'd and bred up in the Decoy Ponds ... where they are constantly fed, and where being made tame, they are used to come even to the Decoy Man's Hand for their Food.

When they ... are sent abroad, they go none knows where; but tis believ'd by some they fly quite over the Seas into *Holland* and *Germany*; There they meet with others of ... their own Kind, where sorting with them, and observing how poorly they live, how all the Rivers are frozen up, and the Lands cover'd with Snow, and that they are almost starv'd, they fail not to let them know, (in Language that they make one another understand) that in *England*, from whence they came, the Case is quite alter'd; that the *English* Ducks live much better than they do in these cold Climates; *that they* have open Lakes, and Sea Shores full of Food, the Tides flowing freely into every Creek; *that they* have also within the Land, large Lakes, refreshing Springs of Water, open Ponds, covered and secured from human Eyes, with large Rows of grown Trees and impenetrable Groves; that the Lands are full of Food; the stubbles yielding constant Supplies of Corn, left by the negligent Husbandmen ... that 'tis not once in a wild Duck's Age, that they have any long Frosts or deep Snows, and that when they have, yet the Sea is never frozen, or the Shores void of Food; and that if they will please but to go with them into *England*, that they shall share with them in all these good Things.

By these Representations, made in their own Duck Language ... they draw together a vast Number of the Fowls, and, in a Word, *Kidnap* them from their own Country; for being once brought out of their Knowledge, they follow the Decoys, as a Dog follows the Huntsman; and 'tis frequent to see these subtle Creatures return with a vast Flight of Fowls with them ...

When they have brought them over, the first Thing they do is to settle with them in the Decoy Ponds, to which they ... belong: Here they chatter and gabble to them, in their own Language, as if they were telling them, that these are the Ponds they told them of, and here they should soon see how well they should live, how secure and how safe a Retreat they had here ...

Here the Decoy-man keeping unseen, behind the Hedges of Reeds ... goes forward, throwing Corn over the Reeds into the Water; the Decoy Ducks greedily fall upon it, and calling their foreign Guests, seem to tell them, that now they may find their Words good, and how well the Ducks live in *England* ... wheedling them forward, 'till by Degrees they are all gotten under the Arch or Sweep of the Net, which is on the Trees, and which by Degrees, imperceptibly to them, declines lower and lower, and also narrower and narrower ...

When the whole Quantity are thus greedily following the Leading Ducks or Decoys, and feeding plentifully as they go ... on a sudden a Dog ... who is perfectly taught his Business, rushes from behind the Reeds, and jumps into the Water, swimming directly after the Ducks, and (terribly to them) Barking as he swims.

Immediately the Ducks ... rise upon the Wing ... but to their great Surprize, are beaten down again by the arched Net ... and thus they crowd on ... the Net growing lower and narrower ... where another Decoy-man stands ready to receive them, and who takes them out alive with his Hands.

As for the Traytors, that drew the poor Ducks into this Snare, they are taught to rise but a little Way, and so not reaching the Net, they fly back to the Ponds ... or else ... are taken out as the rest; but instead of being kill'd with them, are strok'd ... fed and made much of for their Services.

Daniel Defoe, *A Tour Thro' the Whole Island of Great Britain*
vol. II pp. 496–9

Bibliography

MANUSCRIPTS

ALEXANDER TURNBULL LIBRARY (ATL), WELLINGTON

Letters and Journals 1840–60
LMS Papua Letters 1872–85, Micro MS Coll. 2 Reels 91–3
LMS Papua Journals 1871–1901, Micro MS Coll. 2 Reel 11
MS 1730 Thornton family
MS 2053 Stephens, Samuel, Surveyor to the New Zealand Company, Letters
    and Journals at Nelson, 1841–54
MS 2233 Parkinson, Thomas, 1642
MS 2812 Jenkins, Robert
MS 3205 Conway, Rose
MS 4282 Wright, S. E. L., Journal, 1842–4
MS 5694 Daniell, Henry Cooper
MS 8012 Baines, William M., Diary, 9 Aug.–30 Dec. 1850
MS N.24.1 'Narrative of a Residence in New Zealand' 1839–40
MS Papers 0495, Diary of George Darling, 1842
MS TUL 138, 762 Tully, J., Diaries, 1841–6
Ref 89–084 Murray, John, Journal, 1839–43

BODLEIAN LIBRARY, OXFORD

Rawlinson MSS
D 147 Navall Essays written by Sir Hen[ry] Shere[s] Whilst a Prison[e]r in ye
    Gate-House Anno 1691
A 195 A–B Correspondence and Papers of Samuel Pepys
A 342 Letters to Sir Henry Shere 1676–9
A 464 Papers on the State of the Navy 1684–6

BRITISH LIBRARY (BL), LONDON

Add MS 9302 Navy Papers 1618–87
Add MSS 9307 9316 Naval Papers 1618–1707
Add MS 11602 'One Hundred and Twenty Different Treatises, Principally
    Relating to the Navy, Collected by Richard Gibson'

Add MS 11684 Another volume of Gibson's collections
Add MS 15643 Committee of Intelligence 1679–83
Add MS 18986 Navy Committee 1651–2
Add MS 19872 Letters to Sir Henry Sheres
Add MS 21239 Ship King George in Voyage round the world 1785–8
Add MS 22546 Navy Committee correspondence 1649–53
Add MS 30369 'A Voyage for Whaling and Discovery … in the Rattler'
    1793–4
Add MS 32094 Papers relating to the second Anglo-Dutch War (1665–7)
Add MS 51511 Notebook kept by George Savile, Marquis of Halifax
Egerton MSS 2618, 3383 Naval Papers
Harleian MSS 6277, 6287 Naval Tracts
Harleian MS 6843 'How the Coast of yor Ma[je]sties Kingdome may be
    defended against any enemie' [Elizabethan?]
Sloane MS 54 Voyage of Abraham Cowley around the World 1683–6
Sloane MS 2572 'A Survey of ye 17 provinces' [Elizabethan]
Sloane MS 3820 'A Journall into the South Sea by Basil Ringrose' 1680
Sloane MS 3833 Voyage of the Sweepstake to America 1669–70

MINISTÈRE DES AFFAIRES ETRANGÈRES, PARIS

Archives Diplomatique, Correspondence Politique Angleterre vol. VC

NATIONAL ARCHIVES, KEW

PRO 30/24 Shaftesbury Papers
SP 84 State Papers Foreign, Holland

NATIONAL MARITIME MUSEUM (NMM), GREENWICH, LONDON

ADM/L/D/95 Journals of the Diamond
CAD/D/18–20 Naval Papers
CLU/7 Naval Letters and Papers
JOD/1/2 Guard of the Narrow Seas: Admiral Sir John Penington's Journal
    1631–6
JOD/58 Byron's Journal 1764–6
JOD/173 Journal of Samuel Atkins 1680–4
LBK/1 Letter Book of Sir John Narborough 1687–8
REC/1 Naval Papers, early seventeenth century
REC/3 Naval Documents
REC/4 Naval Miscellanies
REC/5 Naval Treaties
REC/6 Admiralty and Sea Manuscripts 1660–1700
REC/28/1 History of the Navy
REC/36 Historical Description of Dunkirk
SER/1 Navy Board Minutes 1673–4

PEPYS LIBRARY (PL), MAGDALENE COLLEGE, CAMBRIDGE

MS 2141 Papers relating to Charles II's Escape from Worcester
MS 2142 Character of Charles II by the Marquess of Normanby
MS 2184, 'April 21 1697 Mr Flamsteed's Acct of ye Beginning, Progress + present State … in ye Doctrine + Practice of Navigation'
MS 2349 John Cox his Travils over the Land into the South Seas
MS 2581 Pepys' Navy White Book
MS 2888 'The political grounds and maxims of the Republic of Holland and West Friesland', translation by Toby Bonnell of *Aanwysing der heilsam politike Gronden en Maximen van de Republicke van Holland en West-Vriesland* (Leiden and Rotterdam, 1669)

MANUSCRIPT ESSAYS

'Arguments to prove that it is necessary for the restoring of the Navie of England to have more ffish eaten' [1563] NMM REC/3.
'A Discourse on the Necessity of Maintaining Freedom of the Seas by Keeping Shipping in an efficient state', 35pp, NMM REC/1 Item 56.
Gibson, Richard, 'Defects and Remedies in the present management of the royal navy', BL Add MS 11602 ff. 57–61. Another version possibly in Gibson's hand dated 25 July 1693 and addressed to John Trenchard Add MS 11684 ff. 37–42.
'Discourse on our Naval Conduct', NMM REC/6 Item 16. Another two copies in BL Add MS 11602 ff. 37–41 and 43–9. Published as *Reflections On Our Naval Strength*, in J. Knox Laughton (ed.), *The Naval Miscellany*, vol. II (London, 1912) pp. 149–68.
'Dr Richard Lower his proposal for the better Cureing Sick + Wounded Seamen … Wrot by Richard Gibson', 9 December 1690 NMM REC/4 Item 59. Another version BL Add MS 11684 ff. 96–101.
'The Dutch Action at Chatham Examined', BL Add MS 11684 ff. 31–3.
'A few Instances of English Courage and Conduct at Sea within the Memory of Richard Gibson', BL Add MS 11684 ff. 2–21. Published in S. R. Gardiner and C. T. Atkinson (eds.), *Letters and Papers Relating to the First Dutch War, 1652–4* (2 vols., London, 1899) vol. I pp. 2–30.
'Gibson to Admiral Russell against Victualling the Royall Navy by Contract', BL Sloane MS 2572 ff. 88–91. Another version possibly in Gibson's hand dated London 27 February 1693/4 BL Add MS 11684 ff. 59–62.
'Gibson to Pepys about Victualling 23 August 1686', BL Add MS 11684 ff. 65–73.
'Heads of a Discourse between an English and Dutch Sea Captain how ye English came to Beate the Dutch at Sea in Anno 1652 + 1653', BL Add MS 11602 ff. 90–1. Another version possibly in Gibson's hand: 'A Discourse then between an English Sea-Captaine and a Dutch-Skipper how the English came to Beate the Dutch at Sea', April 1654 BL Add MS 11684 ff. 30–2. The latter published in S. R. Gardiner and C. T. Atkinson (ed.), *Letters and Papers Relating to the First Dutch War, 1652–4* (2 vols., London, 1899) vol. I pp. 31–3.

'Memorials for the King About the Fleet, Flagg-Officers, Admiralty, Navy-Bord, Victualling, and Sick and Wounded Comissioners. Wrot at the Command of Sr John Trenchard the Secretary of State; by Richard Gibson', London 5 October 1693 BL Add MS 11684 ff. 51–7.

'Mr Gibson to Sam Pepys upon the present Method of Victualling', 1 October 1686 NMM REC/4 Item 99 (Item 49 another copy dated 26 August 1686). Another copy in REC/6 Item 12.

'Observations Upon Islands in Generall and England in particular relating to safety and strength at Sea', NMM REC/6 Item 17 (ff. 271–82). Another version possibly in Gibson's hand: 'Enquirys touching Islands in General + England in perticuler, relating to Safety + Strength at Sea', BL Add MS 11684 ff. 22–9. The latter published in S. R. Gardiner and C. T. Atkinson (eds.), *Letters and Papers Relating to the First Dutch War, 1652–4* (2 vols., London, 1899) vol. I pp. 33–47.

'Observations on Queen Elizabeth's gentlemen sea captains' ill-conduct', BL Add MS 11602 Item XVI.

'Petition to the King concerning the mismanagement of the navy', BL 11602 ff. 125–30.

'Reasons to prove There hath been Negligence, Ignorance, or Treachery in ye Lds of Admiralty and Commissioners of the Navy ... October 1693', NMM CAD/D/20.

'A Reformation in ye Royall Navy most Humbly Proposed to his Majesty King George by Richard Gibsen Gent.', BL Add MS 11602 ff. 66–89.

'How a State may the best provide itself for a Warr', NMM REC/3 ff. 240–2.

Manwaring, Sir Henry, 'A Discourse written by Sr Henry Manwaringe and by him presented to the Kings Matie An. Dni 1618 Wherein are discovered the beginnings practises and Proceedings of the Pyrates', NMM CAD/D/19.

Monson, Sir William, 'Concerning the Abuses of our Seamen', 1623, NMM REC/4 Item 18. Published in *The Naval Tracts of Sir William Monson*, (ed.) M. Oppenheim (5 vols., London, 1902–14) vol. I pp. 237–52.

'How to imploy our ffleet against Spain', NMM REC/4 Item 12.

'Observacons touchinge the Royal Navy and Sea Service', NMM CAD/D/19 Item 2.

'Observations Concerning Dominion of the Sea', NMM REC/6 Item 30b.

'Relating to ye Fishery', NMM REC/4 Item 13. Published in *The Naval Tracts of Sir William Monson*, (ed.) M. Oppenheim (5 vols., London, 1902–14) vol. V pp. 223–302. See also *An Addition* in ibid. pp. 303–27.

Pepys, Samuel, 'The State of the Royall Navy of England at the Dissolution of the late Comission of the Admiralty', 31 December 1684 NMM REC/6 Item 14.

Sheres, Sir Henry, 'A Discourse touching ye decay of our Naval Discipline by Sir H Sheers' [1694], NMM REC/4 Item 4. There is another copy in BL Egerton 3383 ff. 116–37.

Navall Essays written by Sir Hen[ry] Shere[s] Whilst a Prison[e]r in ye Gate-House Anno 1691', Bodleian Rawl MS D 147.

'Of Fortifying Ports +c', Bodleian Rawl MS D 147.

'Of Navall Architecture', Bodleian Rawl MS D 147.

'Of Navall Warr', Bodleian Rawl MS D 147.
'Of Navigation + ye Benefit of Nav[igationa]ll Science', Rawl MS D 147.
'Of Ports and Havens', Bodleian Rawl MS D 147.
'A Scheme + Model of a Marit[i]me Monarchy', Bodleian Rawl MS D 147.
'Sir H Shere's proposal to King James for preserving the Naval Royal in Port from any Insult', 4 May 1688 NMM REC/6 Item 24.
Slingsbie, Sir Robert, 'A Discourse touching the Past and Present state of ye Navy', NMM REC/4 Item 10.

PRINTED PRIMARY SOURCES

An Account of Several Late Voyages & Discoveries to the South and North ... by Sir John Narborough, Captain Jasmen Tasman, Captain John Wood, and Frederick Marten (London, 1694), 'The Bookseller's Preface'.
An Agreement of the People for a firm and present peace (1647), in J. P. Kenyon, *The Stuart Constitution 1603–1688: Documents and Commentary* (2nd edn, Cambridge, 1993).
An Inquiry into the Causes of our Naval Miscarriages (2nd edn, London, 1707).
Andrews, Kenneth (ed.), *English Privateering Voyages to the West Indies 1588–1595* (Cambridge, 1959).
Anson, George, *Voyage Round the World, 1740–44*, comp. Richard Walter, extract in Jonathan Lamb, Vanessa Smith and Nicholas Thomas (eds.), *Exploration and Exchange: a South Seas Anthology 1680–1900* (Chicago, 2000) pp. 39–45.
Antiquity Reviv'd: or the Government of a Certain Island Antiently call'd Astreada (1693).
Aubrey, John, *Aubrey's Brief Lives*, (ed.) Oliver Lawson Dick (London, 1958).
Bacon, Francis, *Bacon's Essays*, (ed.) Edwin A. Abbott (2 vols., London, 1889).
    The New Organon, (eds.) Lisa Jardine and Michael Silverthorne (Cambridge, 2000).
    'On the Ebb and Flow of the Sea', in James Spedding, Robert Leslie Ellis and Douglas Denon Heath (eds.), *The Works of Francis Bacon, volume V. Translations of the Philosophical Works, volume II* (London, 1877).
Bankes, Thomas, *A New Royal Authentic and Complete System of Universal Geography Antient and Modern* (London, ?1790).
Banks, Joseph, *The Endeavour Journal of Joseph Banks 1768–1771*, (ed.) J. C. Beaglehole (2 vols., Cambridge, 1968).
Bethel, Slingsby, *The World's Mistake in Oliver Cromwell ... shewing, That Cromwell's Mal-administration ... layed the Foundation of Our present ... Decay of Trade* (London, 1668).
Bodin, Jean, *Six Bookes of a Commonweale*, a facsimile reprint of the English translation of 1606, (ed.) K. D. McRae (Cambridge, Mass., 1962).
Bougainville, Lewis [Louis Antoine] de, *A Voyage Round The World ... In the Years 1766, 1767, 1768, and 1769 by Lewis de Bougainville*, trans. by John Reinhold Forster (London, 1772).
Bourne, William, *A Regiment for the Sea and other writings on Navigation*, (ed.) E. G. R. Taylor (Cambridge, 1963).

Brasch, Charles, *Collected Poems*, (ed.) Alan Roddick (Auckland, 1984).

Burke, Edmund, *Reflections on the Revolution in France* (1790), in Iain Hampsher-Monk, *The Political Philosophy of Edmund Burke* (Harlow, 1987).

[Burton, Robert] Democritus Junior, *The Anatomy of Melancholy: What it is* (Oxford, 1624).

Calendar of State Papers and Manuscripts relating to English Affairs ... in the archives ... of Venice (London, 1927) vol. XXVIII.

Camden, William, *Britain, Or A Chorographicall Description of the Most flourishing Kingdomes, England, Scotland, and Ireland*, trans. Philemon Holland (London, 1610).

Charnock, John, *Biographia Navalis* (6 vols., London, 1794–8).

An History of Marine Architecture (3 vols., London, 1800–2).

Churchill, Awnsham and John, 'An Introductory Discourse, Containing, The whole History of Navigation from its Original to this time', in *A Collection of Voyages and Travels, Some Now Printed from Original Manuscripts* (6 vols., London, 1732).

Cook, James, *The Journals of Captain James Cook on His Voyages of Discovery: the Voyage of the Endeavour 1768–1771*, (ed.) J. C. Beaglehole (Cambridge, 1955).

The Voyage of The Resolution and Adventure 1772–1775, (ed.) J. C. Beaglehole (Cambridge, 1961).

Curnow, Allen, *Early Days Yet: New and Collected Poems 1941–1997* (Manchester, 1997).

Dampier, William, *A New Voyage Round the World. Describing particularly, The Isthmus of America* (London, 1697).

Darwin, Charles, *The Voyage of the Beagle*, (ed.) James H. Brix (New York, 2000).

Day, Robert Adams, 'Introduction', in Tobias Smollett, *The History and Adventures of an Atom* (Athens, Ga., 1989).

Dee, John, *General and Rare Memorials pertaining to the Perfecte Arte of Navigation* (London, 1577).

The Limits of the British Empire, (ed.) Ken MacMillan, with Jennifer Abeles (Westport, Conn., 2004).

Defoe, Daniel, *Robinson Crusoe: an Authoritative Text Contexts Criticism*, (ed.) Michael Shinagel (2nd edn, London, 1994).

A Tour Thro' the Whole Island of Great Britain, (ed.) G. D. H. Cole (2 vols., New York, 1968).

[Defoe, Daniel], *An Essay at Removing National Prejudices Against a Union with Scotland* (London, 1706).

[Defoe, Daniel], *A General History of Discoveries and Improvements in Useful Arts, Particularly in the great Branches of Commerce, Navigation, and Plantation* (London, 1725–6).

Donne, John, *The Complete English Poems*, (ed.) A. J. Smith (Harmondsworth, 1986).

Devotions Upon Emergent Occasions, Meditation XVII, (ed.) with commentary by Anthony Raspa (Montreal, 1975).

Drury, Robert, *Madagascar; Or, Robert Drury's Journal, During Fifteen Years' Captivity On That Island*, (ed.) Capt. Pasfield Oliver (New York, 1969).

Dunbar, James, *Essays on the History of Mankind in Rude and Cultivated Ages*, reprint of 1781 edition, (ed.) James Dunbar (Bristol, 1995).

Erasmus, *The Education of a Christian Prince*, (ed.) Lisa Jardine (Cambridge, 1997).

Evelyn, John, *Navigation and Commerce, Their Original and Progress* (London, 1674).

   Pomona, or an Appendix Concerning Fruit-Trees, In relation to Cider, The Making and several ways of Ordering it (London, 1664).

   Sylva, Or A Discourse of Forest-Trees, and the Propogation of Timber (London, 1664).

Falconer, William, *Remarks on the influence of climate, situation, nature of country … on the disposition and temper* (London, 1781).

Ferguson, Adam, *An Essay on the History of Civil Society* (1767), (ed.) Fania Oz-Salzberger (Cambridge, 1995).

Fletcher, Andrew, *A Discourse concerning the Affairs of Spain: written in the month of July, 1698*, in *Political Works*, (ed.) J. Robertson (Cambridge, 1997).

   A Discourse of Government With relation to Militias (Edinburgh, 1698), in *Political Works*, (ed.) J. Robertson (Cambridge, 1997).

Frisch, Hartvig (ed.), *The Constitution of the Athenians: a Philological Analysis of Pseudo-Xenefon's Treatise De Re Publica Atheniensium* (Copenhagen, 1942).

Gardiner, S. R. and Atkinson, C. T. (eds.), *Letters and Papers Relating to the First Dutch War, 1652–4, volume I* (London, 1899).

Gates, Sir Thomas, *A true repertory of the wracke, and redemption of Sir Thomas Gates Knight; upon, and from the Ilands of the Bermudas*, in Samuel Purchas, *Hakluytus Posthumus or Purchas His Pilgrimes. Contayning a History of the World, in Sea voyages & lande-Travells, by Englishmen & others* (4 vols., London, 1625).

Gentleman, Tobias, *The Best Way to Make England the Richest and Wealthiest Kingdome in Europe, By Advancing the Fishing Trade … [and] Building … Busses and Pinks after the Holland Manner* (London, 1660).

Gibbon, Edward, *The History of the Decline and Fall of the Roman Empire*, (ed.) J. B. Bury (7 vols., London, 1896).

Gregory, Francis, *David's Returne From His Banishment* (Oxford, 1660).

Hakluyt, Richard, 'Discourse of Western Planting, 1584', in E. G. R. Taylor (ed.), *The Original Writings and Correspondence of the Two Richard Hakluyts, volume II* (London, 1935).

   The Principall Navigations, Voiages and Discoveries of the English Nation (2 vols., London, 1589; facsimile edn, Cambridge, 1965).

H[akluyt], R[ichard] the Younger, *Divers Voyages Touching the Discoverie of America and the Ilands adiacent unto the same* (London, 1582; facsimile, Ann Arbor, 1966).

Harrington, James, *The Common-Wealth of Oceana* (London, 1656).

   The Commonwealth of Oceana, (ed.) J. G. A. Pocock (Cambridge, 1992).

   The Political Works of James Harrington, (ed.) J. G. A. Pocock (Cambridge, 1977).

The Hartlib Papers: a Complete Text and Image Database of the Papers of Samuel Hartlib c.1600–1662 (second edition, University of Sheffield, 2002).

[Head, Richard], *The Floating Island: Or, A New Discovery Relating the Strange Adventure on a late Voyage, From Lambethana to Villa Franca* (London, 1673).

Herbert, George, *The Poems of George Herbert* (2nd edn, Oxford, 1961)

Herodotus, *The Histories*, trans. Aubrey De Selincourt (Harmondsworth, 1996).

Heylyn, Peter, *Cosmography in Four Books. Containing the Chorography and History of the Whole World: And All the Principal Kingdoms, Provinces, Seas, and Isles thereof* (London, 1677).

Microcosmus, Or, A Little Description of the Great World (Oxford, 1621).

Hobbes, Thomas, *Leviathan*, (ed.) Richard Tuck (Cambridge, 1996).

'On the Life and History of Thucydides' and 'To the Reader', in R. B. Schlatter (ed.), *Hobbes' Thucydides* (New Brunswick, N.J., 1975).

The Holy Bible, King James Version, facsimile reprint of the edition of 1611 (Peabody, Mass., 2003).

Homer, *The Odyssey of Homer*, trans. Edward McCrorie (Baltimore, 1975).

Hume, David, *Political Essays*, (ed.) Knud Haakonssen (Cambridge, 1994).

Kenyon, J.P., *The Stuart Constitution 1603–1688: Documents and Commentary* (2nd edn, Cambridge, 1993).

Knighton, C.S., *Catalogue of the Pepys Library at Magdalene College, Cambridge* (Woodbridge, 1981).

Knox Laughton, J. (ed.), *The Naval Miscellany, volume II* (London, 1912).

Kossman, E.H. and Mellink, A.F. (eds.), *Texts Concerning the Revolt of the Netherlands* (Cambridge, 1974).

Lamb, Jonathan, Smith, Vanessa and Thomas, Nicholas (eds.), *Exploration and Exchange: a South Seas Anthology 1680–1900* (Chicago, 2000).

Lang, Revd John Dunmore, *New Zealand: A Lecture, By A Young Missionary* (London, 1849).

Latest Information from the Settlement of NEW PLYMOUTH, on the coast of Taranake, NEW ZEALAND (London, 1842).

Latham, Robert (ed.), *Samuel Pepys and the Second Dutch War* (Navy Records Society, 1995).

Letters from Settlers and Labouring Emigrants in the New Zealand Company's Settlements of Wellington, Nelson and New Plymouth. From February, 1842, to January, 1843 (London, 1843).

Locke, John, *Locke's Two Treatises of Government*, (ed.) Peter Laslett (2nd edn, Cambridge, 1967).

Machiavelli, Niccolò, *Discourses*, (ed.) B. Crick (Harmondsworth, 1985).

Marvell, Andrew, *The Character of Holland* (London, 1672).

The Poems and Letters of Andrew Marvell, (ed.) H.M. Margoliouth (2 vols., Oxford, 1927).

The Prose Works of Andrew Marvell, (eds.) Annabel Patterson, Martin Dzelzainis, N.H. Keeble and Nicholas von Maltzahn (2 vols., New Haven, 2003).

Milton, John, *Complete Prose Works*, (ed.) D.M. Wolfe *et al.* (8 vols., New Haven, Conn., 1953–82).

Second Defence of the English People (1654), in *Complete Prose Works*, (ed.) D.M. Wolfe *et al.* (New Haven, Conn., 1953–82) vol. IV.

The Tenure of Kings and Magistrates (1649), in *Complete Prose Works* vol. III.

Monson, Sir William, *The Naval Tracts of Sir William Monson*, (ed.) M. Oppenheim (5 vols. London, 1902–14).

Montesquieu, Charles-Louis de Secondat, Baron, *The Spirit of the Laws*, (eds.) Anne Cohler, Basia Carolyn Miller and Harold Samuel Stone (Cambridge, 1989).

More, Thomas, *Utopia*, (eds.) George Logan and Robert Adams (Cambridge, 2000).

Narborough, John, 'A Journal kept by Captain John Narborough', in *An Account of Several Late Voyages* … (London, 1694).

Nedham, Marchamont, Epistle Dedicatorie, in John Selden, *Of the Dominion, Or, Ownership of the Sea* (London, 1652).

[Nedham, Marchamont], *The Case Stated Between England and the United Provinces* (London, 1652).

[Neville, Henry], *The Isle of Pines, Or, A late Discovery of a fourth ISLAND near Terra Australis, Incognita* (London, 1668), reprinted in Onofrio Nicastro (ed.), *Henry Neville e l'isola di Pines* (Pisa, 1988).

The New Zealand Colony: Its Geography and History (London, 1903).

Ogilby, John, *America: Being the Latest, and Most Accurate Description of the New World* (London, 1671).

[Oldmixon, John], *The British Empire in America, Containing The History of the Discovery, Settlement, Progress and State of the British Colonies on the Continent and Islands of America* (London, 1741).

Orgel, Stephen and Goldberg, Jonathan (eds.), *John Milton: a Critical Edition of the Major Works* (Oxford, 1991).

Paine, Thomas, *Common Sense*, in Thomas Paine, *Political Writings: Revised Student Edition*, (ed.) Bruce Kuklick (Cambridge, 2004).

[Penn, William], *England's Present Interest Discover'd With Honour to the Prince and Safety to the People* (London, 1675).

Pepys, Samuel, *The Diary of Samuel Pepys 1660–1669*, (eds.) R. C. Latham and W. Mathews (11 vols., London, 1971–83).

　Samuel Pepys' Naval Minutes, (ed.) J. R. Tanner (London, 1926).

　Samuel Pepys and the Second Dutch War: Pepys' Navy White Book and Brooke House Papers, (ed.) Robert Latham (London, 1996).

　The Tangier Papers of Samuel Pepys, (ed.) Edwin Chappell (London, 1935).

Plato, *The Republic*, (ed.) F. M. Cornford (Oxford, 1941).

Ptolemy's Geography: An Annotated Translation of the Theoretical Chapters, (eds. and trans.) J. Lennart Berggren and Alexander Jones (Princeton, 2000).

Purchas, Samuel, *Hakluytus Posthumus or Purchas His Pilgrimes. Contayning a History of the World, in Sea voyages & lande-Travells, by Englishmen & others* (4 vols., London, 1625).

　Purchas his Pilgrimage. Or Relations of the World (4th edn, London, 1626).

Raban, Jonathan, *The Oxford Book of the Sea* (Oxford, 2001).

Ralegh, Sir Walter, *Excellent Observations and Notes, Concerning the Royall Navy and Sea-Service* (London, 1650).

　History of the World (London, 1614).

Raleigh [Ralegh], Sir Walter, *A Discourse of Seaports; Principally of the Port and Haven of Dover* (London, 1700).

Raynal, Guillaume, *A Philosophical and Political History of the Settlements and Trade of the Europeans in the East and West Indies*, trans. J. Justamond (4 vols., Dublin, 1776).

Reasons for Giving Encouragement To The Sea-Faring People of Great Britain, In Times of Peace or War (London, 1739).

Robertson, George, *The Discovery of Tahiti: A Journal of the Second Voyage of HMS Dolphin Round the World, Under the Command of Captain Wallis*, (ed.) Hugh Carrington (London, 1948).

Robertson, William, *The History of America* (2 vols., Dublin, 1777).

Sammes, Aylett, *Britannia Antiqua Illustrata: Or, The Antiquities of Ancient Britain, Derived from the Phoenicians* (London, 1676).

Savile, George, *The Works of George Savile Marquis of Halifax*, (ed.) Mark N. Brown (3 vols., Oxford, 1989).

Scott, Thomas, *The Belgicke Pismire: Stinging the slothfull SLEEPER* (London, 1622).

Shakespeare, William, *The Oxford Shakespeare: the Complete Works of William Shakespeare* (London, 1914).

The Tempest, (ed.) David Lindley (Cambridge, 2002).

The Tempest, (eds.) Alden T. Vaughan and Virginia Mason Vaughan, *The Arden Shakespeare*, series 3 (New York, 2005).

Shelvocke, Capt. George, *A Voyage Round the World By Way of the Great South Sea* (London, 1726).

Sheres, Sir Henry, *Sir Henry Sheere's Discourse of the Mediteranian Sea, And the Streights of Gibraltar*, in *Miscellanies Historical and Philological: Being a Curious Collection of Private Papers* (London, 1703).

Useful Remarks ... on that Subject, by Command of his late Majesty K. Charles the Second. Never before made Publick, appended to Sir Walter Raleigh, *A Discourse of Seaports; Principally of the Port and Haven of Dover* (London, 1700), pp. 9–16.

[Sheres, Sir Henry], *A Discourse Touching Tanger* (London, 1680).

Sidney, Algernon, *Court Maxims*, (eds.) Hans W. Blom, Eco Haitsma-Mulier and Ronald Janse (Cambridge, 1996).

Discourses Concerning Government, in *Sydney on Government: the Works of Algernon Sydney*, (ed.) J. Robertson (London, 1772).

Discourses Concerning Government, (ed.) Thomas West (Indianapolis, Ind., 1992).

Sidney, Sir Philip, *Selected Writings*, (ed.) Richard Dutton (Manchester, 1987).

Smith, Adam, *An Inquiry into the Nature and Causes of the Wealth of Nations* (2 vols., Homewood, Ill., 1963).

Smollett, Tobias, *The History and Adventures of an Atom* (London, 1786).

Speed, John, *The Theatre of the Empire of Great Britaine* (London, 1650).

Spenser, Edmund, *The Faerie Queene*, (ed.) A.C. Hamilton (London, 1977; 2nd edn, Harlow, 2001).

Stevenson, Robert Louis, *Tales of the South Seas* (Edinburgh, 1996).

Streater, John, *Observations Historical, Political and Philosophical, Upon Aristotle's first Book of Political Government* (London, 1654).

Strode, William, *The Floating Island: a Tragi-Comedy, Acted before his Majesty at Oxford, Aug. 29. 1636* (London, 1655).
Swift, Jonathan, *Gulliver's Travels: a Facsimile Reproduction of a Large-Paper Copy of the First Edition* [Lemuel Gulliver, *Travels into Several Remote Nations of the World* (London, 1726)], (ed.) Colin McKelvie (New York, 1976).
Tasman, Abel, 'Journal or Description by me, Abel Jans Tasman, Of a Voyage Made From the City of Batavia ... December Anno 1642 ... For the Discovery of the Unknown South Land', in *Abel Janszoon Tasman and the Discovery of New Zealand*, (ed.) J. C. Beaglehole (Wellington, 1942).
Temple, Sir William, *Observations Upon the United Provinces of the Netherlands* (London, 1673).
Of Popular Discontents, in *Miscellanea. The Third Part* (London, 1701).
Thucydides, *History of the Peloponnesian War*, trans. Rex Warner (Harmondsworth, 1972).

UNPUBLISHED SECONDARY SOURCES

Davis, J. C., ' "Concerning the Best State of a Commonwealth": Thomas More's *Utopia*: Sources, Legacy and Interpretation', draft essay.
Emiralioglu, Pinar M., 'Cognizance of the Ottoman World: Visual and Textual Representations in the Sixteenth Century Ottoman Empire (1514–96)', PhD dissertation, University of Chicago, 2006.
Fairburn, Miles, 'Culture and Isolation', J. C. Beaglehole Lecture delivered at the University of Canterbury, December 2001.
Scott, Jonathan, 'Samuel McFarlane, William Lawes and James Chalmers in New Guinea, 1872–1885', BA (Hons) research essay, Victoria University of Wellington, 1980.
Witmore, Michael, 'An Island of One: Spinoza and Shakespeare's *Tempest*', talk given at Duquesne University, Pittsburgh, 2007.

PUBLISHED SECONDARY SOURCES

Adamson, John, *The Noble Revolt: the Overthrow of Charles I* (London, 2007).
'An Artist Sets Sail, but South Pacific Pulls Him Home', *New York Times*, 22 April 2006.
Anderson, Benedict, *Imagined Communities: Reflections on the Origin and Spread of Nationalism* (rev. edn, London, 1991).
'And Sometimes, the Island is Marooned on You', *New York Times Sunday*, 6 November 2005.
Andrews, Kenneth R., *Trade, Plunder and Settlement: Maritime Enterprise and the Genesis of the British Empire, 1480–1630* (Cambridge, 1984).
Appleby, John C., 'War, Politics and Colonization 1558–1625', in Nicholas Canny (ed.), *The Oxford History of the British Empire, volume I: The Origins of Empire* (Oxford, 1998).
Armitage, David, 'The Cromwellian Protectorate and the Languages of Empire', *The Historical Journal* 35, 3 (1992).
The Declaration of Independence: a Global History (Cambridge, Mass., 2007).

The Ideological Origins of the British Empire (Cambridge, 2000).

'John Milton: Poet against Empire', in David Armitage, Armand Himy and Quentin Skinner (eds.), *Milton and Republicanism* (Cambridge, 1995).

'Literature and Empire', in Nicholas Canny (ed.), *The Oxford History of the British Empire, volume I: The Origins of Empire* (Oxford, 1998).

Baker, Alan R.H., *Geography and History: Bridging the Divide* (Cambridge, 2003).

Ballantyne, Tony, *Orientalism and Race: Aryanism in the British Empire* (Houndmills, 2002).

Bayly, C.A. *The Birth of the Modern World 1780–1914* (Oxford, 2004).

Imperial Meridian: the British Empire and the World 1780–1830 (London, 1989).

Beaglehole, J.C., *The Exploration of the Pacific* (3rd edn, London, 1966).

'The New Zealand Scholar', in Peter Munz (ed.), *The Feel of Truth: Essays in New Zealand and Pacific History* (Wellington, 1969).

'On the Place of Tasman's Voyage in History', in J.C. Beaglehole (ed.), *Abel Janszoon Tasman and the Discovery of New Zealand* (Wellington, 1942).

Beaglehole, Tim, *A Life of J. C. Beaglehole: New Zealand Scholar* (Wellington, 2006).

Beckles, Hilary, 'The "Hub of Empire": the Caribbean and Britain in the Seventeenth Century', in Canny (ed.), *The Origins of Empire*.

Beddard, Robert, 'The Unexpected Whig Revolution of 1688', in Robert Beddard (ed.), *The Revolutions of 1688* (Oxford, 1991).

'Belgians Invented the Game of Cricket', *Television New Zealand News*, 4 March 2009 (online resource).

Belich, James, *Making Peoples: a History of the New Zealanders from Polynesian Settlement to the End of the Nineteenth Century* (Auckland, 1996).

Paradise Reforged: a History of the New Zealanders from the 1880s to the Year 2000 (Auckland, 2001).

Benitez-Rojo, Antonio, 'The Repeating Island', in Julie Rivkin and Michael Ryan (eds.), *Literary Theory: an Anthology* (Oxford, 1998).

Black, Jeremy, *The British Seaborne Empire* (New Haven, 2004).

Blackbourn, David, *The Conquest of Nature: Water, Landscape and the Making of Modern Germany* (New York, 2006).

Bliss, Robert, *Revolution and Empire: English Politics and the American Colonies in the Seventeenth Century* (Manchester, 1990).

Braddick, Michael, *State Formation in Early Modern England c.1550–1700* (Cambridge, 2000).

Braudel, Fernand, *Civilisation and Capitalism, 15th–18th Century, volume III: The Perspective of the World*, trans. Sian Reynolds (London, 1984).

The Mediterranean and the Mediterranean World in the Age of Philip II, trans. Sian Reynolds (Berkeley and Los Angeles, 1995).

Bravo, Michael, 'Precision and Curiosity in Scientific Travel: James Rennell and the Orientalist Geography of the New Imperial Age', in Jas Elsner and Joan-Pau Rubiés (eds.), *Voyages and Visions: Towards a Cultural History of Travel* (London, 1999).

Brenner, Robert, *Merchants and Revolution: Commercial Change, Political Conflict, and London's Overseas Traders 1550–1653* (Princeton, 1993).

Brewer, John, *Sinews of Power: War, Money and the English State 1688–1783* (London, 1989).

Bridges, R. C. and Hair, P. E. H. (eds.), *Compassing the Vaste Globe of the Earth: Studies in the History of the Hakluyt Society 1846–1996 with a Complete List of the Society's Publications* (London, 1996).

Burnett, D. Graham, *Masters of All They Surveyed: Exploration, Geography, and a British El Dorado* (Chicago, 2000).

Burrow, Colin, 'New Model Criticism', *London Review of Books*, 19 June 2008.

Burrow, John, *A History of Histories: Epics, Chronicles, Romances and Inquiries from Herodotus and Thucydides to the Twentieth Century* (New York, 2008).

Calder, Angus, *The Myth of the Blitz* (London, 1991).

Cannadine, David (ed.), *Empire, the Sea and Global History: Britain's Maritime World, c.1760–c.1840* (Houndmills, 2007).

Canny, Nicholas, *Making Ireland British 1580–1650* (Oxford, 2001).

Canny, Nicholas (ed.), *The Oxford History of the British Empire, volume I: The Origins of Empire* (Oxford, 1998).

Capp, Bernard, *Cromwell's Navy: the Fleet and the English Revolution 1648–60* (Oxford, 1989).

'Naval Operations', in John Kenyon and Jane Ohlmeyer (eds.), *The Civil Wars: a Military History of England, Scotland and Ireland 1638–1660* (Oxford, 1998).

Carey, John, *William Golding, the Man Who Wrote Lord of the Flies* (London, 2009).

Cathcart, Michael, *The Water Dreamers: the Remarkable History of our Dry Continent* (Melbourne, 2009).

Churchill, Winston S., *The Island Race* (New York, 1964).

Clarke, Peter, *Hope and Glory: Britain 1900–2000* (London, 2004).

Clayton, Tim, *Tars: the Men Who Made Britain Rule the Waves* (London, 2007).

Coclanis, Peter, 'Drang nach Osten: Bernard Bailyn, the World-Island, and the Idea of Atlantic History', *Journal of World History* 13, 1 (2002).

Colley, Linda, *Britons: Forging the Nation 1707–1837* (New Haven, 1992).

Captives: Britain, Empire and the World, 1600–1850 (New York, 2002).

The Ordeal of Elizabeth Marsh: a Woman in World History (New York, 2007).

Collini, Stefan, 'Our Island Story', *London Review of Books*, 20 January 2005.

Cormack, Lesley, ' "Good Fences Make Good Neighbours": Geography as Self-Definition in Early Modern England', *Isis* 82 (1991).

Crosby, Alfred, *Ecological Imperialism: the Biological Expansion of Europe, 900–1900* (Cambridge, 1986).

Curtin, Philip, *The Atlantic Slave Trade, a Census* (Madison, Wisc., 1969).

Cust, Richard, *The Forced Loan and English Politics 1626–28* (Oxford, 1987).

Daniels, Stephen, *Fields of Vision: Landscape Imagery and National Identity in England and the United States* (Princeton, 1993).

Dash, Mike, *Batavia's Graveyard: the True Story of the Mad Heretic who Led History's Bloodiest Mutiny* (New York, 2002).

Davies, J. D., *Gentlemen and Tarpaulins: the Officers and Men of the Restoration Navy* (Oxford, 1991).

'Sheres, Sir Henry 1641–1710, Military Engineer and Author', in *Oxford Dictionary of National Biography* (Oxford, 2004) vol. L pp. 289–90.

Davies, Norman, *The Isles: a History* (Oxford, 1999).

Dening, Greg, 'Deep Times, Deep Spaces: Civilizing the Sea', in Bernhard Klein and Geesa Mackentun (eds.), *Sea Changes: Historicising the Ocean* (New York, 2004).

Islands and Beaches: Discourse on a Silent Land: Marquesas, 1774–1880 (Honolulu, 1980).

Denoon, Donald with Stewart Firth, Jocelyn Linnekin, Malama Meleisa and Karen Neno (eds.), *The Cambridge History of the Pacific Islanders* (Cambridge, 1997).

De Vries, Jan and van der Woude, A., *The First Modern Economy: Success, Failure, and the Perseverance of the Dutch Economy, 1500–1815* (Cambridge, 1997).

Dickinson, H. T., *Liberty and Property: Political Ideology in Eighteenth-Century Britain* (New York, 1977).

Drayton, Richard, 'Knowledge and Empire', in P. J. Marshall (ed.), *The Oxford History of the British Empire, volume II: The Eighteenth Century* (Oxford, 1998).

Nature's Government: Science, Imperial Britain, and the 'Improvement' of the World (New Haven, 2000).

Edmond, Rod, 'The Pacific/Tahiti: Queen of the South Sea Isles', in Peter Hulme and Tim Youngs (eds.), *The Cambridge Companion to Travel Writing* (Cambridge, 2000).

Edmond, Rod and Smith, Vanessa (eds.), *Islands in History and Representation* (London, 2003).

Edney, Matthew H., *Mapping an Empire: the Geographical Construction of British India, 1765–1843* (Chicago, 1997).

Eisler, William, *The Furthest Shore: Images of Terra Australis from the Middle Ages to Captain Cook* (Cambridge, 1995).

Elliott, J. H., *Empires of the Atlantic World: Britain and Spain in America 1492–1830* (New Haven, 2007).

Elsner, J. and Rubiés, Joan-Pau (eds.), *Voyages and Visions: Towards a Cultural History of Travel* (London, 1999).

Elton, G. R., 'Piscatorial Politics in the Early Parliaments of Elizabeth I', in N. McKendrick and R. B. Outhwaite (eds.), *Business Life and Public Policy: Essays in Honour of D. C. Coleman* (Cambridge, 1986).

Evans, Richard J., *Cosmopolitan Islanders: British Historians and the European Continent* (Cambridge, 2009).

Fernandez-Armesto, Filipe, 'Britain, the Sea, the Empire, the World', in David Cannadine (ed.), *Empire, the Sea and Global History: Britain's Maritime World, c.1760–c.1840* (Houndmills, 2007).

Fitzsimons, Peter, *Charles Kingsford Smith and Those Magnificent Men* (Sydney, 2009).

Flynn, Dennis O. and Giraldez, Arturo, 'General Editors' Preface', in Tony Ballantyne (ed.), *The Pacific World: Lands, Peoples and History of the Pacific, 1500–1900, volume VI: Science, Empire and the European Exploration of the Pacific* (Aldershot, 2004).

Ford, Caroline, 'Nature's Fortunes: New Directions in the Writing of European Environmental History', *The Journal of Modern History* 79 (March 2007).

Fox, Frank, *Great Ships: the Battlefleet of King Charles II* (Greenwich, 1980).

French, Patrick, *The World is What it is: the Authorized Biography of V. S. Naipaul* (New York, 2008).

Frost, Alan, *The Global Reach of Empire: Britain's Maritime Expansion in the Indian and Pacific Oceans 1764–1815* (Melbourne, 2003).

Games, Alison, *The Web of Empire: English Cosmopolitans in an Age of Expansion* (Oxford, 2008).

Gillis, John R., *Islands of the Mind: How the Human Imagination Created the Atlantic World* (Houndmills, 2004).

Ginzburg, Carlo, *No Island is an Island: Four Glances at English Literature in World Perspective* (New York, 2000).

Glacken, Clarence J., *Traces on the Rhodian Shore: Nature and Culture in Western Thought from Ancient Times to the End of the Eighteenth Century* (Berkeley, 1967).

Glaisyer, Natasha, 'Networking: Trade and Exchange in the Eighteenth-Century British Empire', *The Historical Journal* 47, 2 (2004).

Godlewska, Anne Marie Claire, *Geography Unbound: French Geographic Science from Cassini to Humboldt* (Chicago, 1999).

Godley, E.J., 'Fauna and Flora', in Keith Sinclair (ed.), *Distance Looks our Way: the Effects of Remoteness on New Zealand* (Auckland, 1961).

Grafton, Anthony, *New Worlds, Ancient Texts: the Power of Tradition and the Shock of Discovery* (Cambridge, Mass., 1992).

Graham, Gerald S., 'Fisheries and Sea Power', in G. A. Rawlyk (ed.), *Historical Essays on the Atlantic Provinces* (Toronto, 1967).

Greenblatt, Steven, *Marvelous Possessions: the Wonder of the New World* (Oxford, 1991).

Grove, Richard, *Green Imperialism: Colonial Expansion, Tropical Island Edens and the Origins of Environmentalism 1600–1860* (Cambridge, 1995).

Guest, Harriet, *Empire, Barbarism and Civilization: Captain Cook, William Hodges, and the Return to the Pacific* (Cambridge, 2007).

Hadfield, Andrew, *Literature, Politics and National Identity: Reformation to Renaissance* (Cambridge, 1994).
  Literature, Travel, and Colonial Writing in the English Renaissance 1545–1625 (Oxford, 1998).

Haley, K. H. D., *The British and the Dutch: Political and Cultural Relations through the Ages* (London, 1988).
  The First Earl of Shaftesbury (Oxford, 1968).
  William of Orange and the English Opposition 1672–4 (London, 1953).

Hanson, Neil, *The Confident Hope of a Miracle: the True History of the Spanish Armada* (London, 2003).

Harding, Richard, 'The Royal Navy', in H. T. Dickinson (ed.), *A Companion to Eighteenth-Century Britain* (Oxford, 2002).

Helgerson, Richard, *Forms of Nationhood: the Elizabethan Writing of England* (Chicago, 1992).

Hill, Christopher, *The English Bible and the Seventeenth-Century Revolution* (London, 1993).

Hilton, Boyd, *A Mad, Bad, and Dangerous People? England 1783–1846* (Oxford, 2006).

Hont, Istvan, *Jealousy of Trade: International Competition and the Nation-State in Historical Perspective* (Cambridge, Mass., 2005).

Hornstein, Sari, *The Restoration Navy and English Foreign Trade 1674–1688: a Study in the Peacetime Use of Sea Power* (Aldershot, 1991).

Houston, Alan and Pincus, Steven, *A Nation Transformed?* (Cambridge, 2001).

Howe, K. R., *Nature, Culture and History: the 'Knowing' of Oceania* (Honolulu, 2000).

   The Quest for Origins: Who First Discovered and Settled the Pacific Islands? (Honolulu, 2003).

   'Two Worlds?', *New Zealand Journal of History* 37, 1 (2003).

Hughes, Robert, *The Fatal Shore: the Epic of Australia's Founding* (New York, 1986).

Hulme, Peter and Youngs, Tim (eds.), *The Cambridge Companion to Travel Writing* (Cambridge, 2002).

Israel, Jonathan, *The Dutch Republic: Its Rise, Greatness, and Fall 1477–1806* (Oxford, 1998).

   'The Dutch Role in the Glorious Revolution', in Jonathan Israel (ed.), *The Anglo-Dutch Moment: Essays on the Glorious Revolution and its World Impact* (Cambridge, 1991).

   'The Emerging Empire: the Continental Perspective, 1650–1713', in Nicholas Canny (ed.), *The Oxford History of the British Empire, volume I: The Origins of Empire* (Oxford, 1998).

   'England, the Dutch Republic and Europe in the Seventeenth Century', *Historical Journal* 40, 4 (1997).

   Radical Enlightenment: Philosophy and the Making of Modernity 1650–1750 (Oxford, 2001).

Jardine, Lisa, *Going Dutch: How England Plundered Holland's Glory* (New York, 2008).

Jones, Whitney R. D., *Thomas Rainborowe (c.1610–1648): Civil War Seaman, Siegemaster and Radical* (Woodbridge, 2005).

Keneally, Thomas, *Australians: Origins to Eureka, volume I* (Sydney, 2009).

Kennedy, Paul, *The Rise and Fall of the Great Powers, 1500–2000* (New York, 1987).

Kerrigan, John, *Archipelagic English: Literature, History and Politics 1603–1707* (Oxford, 2008).

Kidd, Colin, *British Identities before Nationalism: Ethnicity and Nationhood in the Atlantic World 1600–1800* (Cambridge, 1999).

   'Europe, What Europe?', *London Review of Books*, 6 November 2008.

Kishlansky, Mark, 'The Army and the Levellers: the Roads to Putney', *Historical Journal* **22**, 4 (1979).

Klein, Bernhard and Mackentun, Gesa (eds.), *Sea Changes: Historicizing the Ocean* (New York, 2004).

Knowles, Ronald, *Gulliver's Travels: the Politics of Satire* (New York, 1996).

Langford, Paul, *A Polite and Commercial People: England 1727–1783* (Oxford, 1989).

Lawrence, Christopher, 'Disciplining Disease: Scurvy, the Navy, and Imperial Expansion, 1750–1825', in David Miller and Peter Reill (eds.), *Visions of Empire: Voyages, Botany, and Representations of Nature* (Cambridge, 1996).

Lekan, Thomas M., *Imagining the Nation in Nature: Landscape Preservation and German Identity, 1885–1945* (Cambridge, Mass., 2004).

Levack, Brian P., *The Formation of the British State: England, Scotland and the Union 1603–1707* (Oxford, 1987).

Levillain, Charles-Edouard, 'London Besieged? The City's Vulnerability during the Glorious Revolution', in Jason McElligott (ed.), *Fear, Exclusion and Revolution: Roger Morrice and Britain in the 1680s* (Aldershot, 2006).

Lewis, Martin and Wigen, Karen, *The Myth of Continents: a Critique of Metageography* (Los Angeles, 1997).

Linebaugh, Peter and Rediker, Marcus, *The Many-Headed Hydra: Sailors, Slaves, Commoners, and the Hidden History of the Revolutionary Atlantic* (Boston, 2000).

Loxley, Diana, *Problematic Shores: the Literature of Islands* (New York, 1991).

Lunn, Ken and Day, Ann, 'Britain as Island: National Identity and the Sea', in Helen Brocklehurst and Robert Phillips (eds.), *History, Nationhood and the Question of Britain* (Houndmills, 2004).

McCalman, Iain, *Darwin's Armada* (Melbourne, 2009).

McDermott, James, *England and the Spanish Armada: the Necessary Quarrel* (New Haven, 2005).

McElligott, Jason, 'Introduction: Stabilizing and Destabilizing Britain in the 1680s', in Jason McElligott (ed.), *Fear, Exclusion and Revolution: Roger Morrice and Britain in the 1680s* (Aldershot, 2006).

Mackay, David, *In the Wake of Cook: Exploration, Science and Empire, 1780–1801* (London, 1985).

McNeill, J. R., 'Of Rats and Men: the Environmental History of the Island Pacific', in J. R. McNeill (ed.), *Environmental History in the Pacific World* (Aldershot, 2001).

McNeill, J. R. and McNeill, William H., *The Human Web: a Bird's-Eye View of World History* (New York, 2003).

McNeill, W. H., *A History of the Human Community: Prehistory to the Present* (4th edn, Englewood Cliffs, N.J., 1993).

Mahlberg, Gaby, 'Republicanism as Anti-patriarchalism in Henry Neville's *The Isle of Pines*', in John Morrow and Jonathan Scott (eds.), *Liberty, Authority, Formality: Political Ideas and Culture, 1600–1900* (Exeter, 2008).

Manwaring, G. E. and Dobree, Bonamy, *The Floating Republic: an Account of the Mutinies at Spithead and the Nore in 1797* (Edinburgh, 1935).

Marshall, P. J., *'A Free though Conquering People': Eighteenth-Century Britain and its Empire* (Aldershot, 2003).

'A Nation Defined by Empire, 1755–1776', reprinted in P. J. Marshall, *'A Free though Conquering People': Eighteenth-Century Britain and its Empire* (Aldershot, 2003).

'Britain and the World in the Eighteenth Century: I, Reshaping the Empire', in P. J. Marshall, *'A Free though Conquering People': Eighteenth-Century Britain and its Empire* (Aldershot, 2003).

Marshall, P.J. (ed.), *The Oxford History of the British Empire, volume II: The Eighteenth Century* (Oxford, 1998).

Marshall, P.J. and Williams, G., *The Great Map of Mankind: British Perceptions of the World in the Age of Enlightenment* (London, 1982).

Mayhew, Robert J., *Enlightenment Geography: the Political Languages of British Geography, 1650–1850* (Houndmills, 2000).

'Geography, Print Culture and the Renaissance: "The Road Less Travelled By"', *History of European Ideas* 27 (2001).

'Geography's English Revolutions: Oxford Geography and the War of Ideas', in D. Livingstone and C. Withers (eds.), *Geography and Revolution* (Chicago, 2005).

Miller, David and Reill, Peter (eds.), *Visions of Empire: Voyages, Botany and Representations of Nature* (Cambridge, 1996).

Miller, Leo, *John Milton and the Oldenburg Safeguard* (New York, 1985).

John Milton's Writings in the Anglo-Dutch Negotiations 1651–1654 (Pittsburgh, n.d.).

Moir, Esther, *The Discovery of Britain: the English Tourists 1540–1840* (London, n.d.).

Morrow, John and Scott, Jonathan (eds.), *Liberty, Authority, Formality: Political Ideas and Culture, 1600–1900* (Exeter, 2008).

Murray, John J., 'The Cultural Impact of the Flemish Low Countries on Sixteenth- and Seventeenth-Century England', *The American Historical Review* 62, 4 (July 1957).

Nelson, Eric, 'Greek Nonsense in More's Utopia', *Historical Journal* 44, 4 (2001).

The Greek Tradition in Republican Thought (Cambridge, 2004).

Norbrook, David, 'What Cares These Roarers for the Name of King?: Language and Utopia in *The Tempest*', in R. S. White (ed.), *The Tempest* (Basingstoke, 1999).

'Notes on a Small Island: an Old Approach to History is New Again', *The Economist*, 20 August 2005.

O'Hara, Glen, '"The Sea is Swinging into View": Modern British Maritime History in a Globalised World', *English Historical Review* 124, 510 (October 2009).

Ollard, Richard, *Pepys: a Biography* (London, 1974).

Olwig, Kenneth R., *Landscape, Nature and the Body Politic: From Britain's Renaissance to America's New World* (Madison, Wisc., 2002).

Oppenheim, H., *A History of the Administration of the Royal Navy and of Merchant Shipping in Relation to the Navy* (repr., London, 1961).

Ormrod, David, *The Rise of Commercial Empires: England and the Netherlands in the Age of Mercantilism 1650–1770* (Cambridge, 2003).

Ovenden, Keith, *A Fighting Withdrawal: the Life of Dan Davin* (Oxford, 1996).

Pagden, Anthony, *European Encounters with the New World* (New Haven, 1993).

The Fall of Natural Man: the American Indian and the Origins of Comparative Ethnology (Cambridge, 1982).

Parry, Glyn, 'John Dee and the Elizabethan British Empire in its European Context', *Historical Journal* 49, 3 (2006).

Parry, Graham, *The Trophies of Time: English Antiquarians of the Seventeenth Century* (Oxford, 2007).

Pincus, Steven, *England's Glorious Revolution 1688–1689: a Brief History with Documents* (Houndmills, 2005).

Protestantism and Patriotism: Ideologies and the Making of English Foreign Policy, 1650–1668 (Cambridge, 1996).

Pocock, J. G. A., *Barbarism and Religion, volume I: The Enlightenments of Edward Gibbon, 1737–1764* (Cambridge, 1999).

Barbarism and Religion, volume II: Narratives of Civil Government (Cambridge, 1999).

Barbarism and Religion, volume IV: Barbarians, Savages and Empires (Cambridge, 2005).

The Discovery of Islands: Essays in British History (Cambridge, 2005).

Porter, Roy, *The Creation of the Modern World: the Untold Story of the British Enlightenment* (New York, 2000).

Pound, Francis, *The Invention of New Zealand: Art and National Identity 1930–1970* (Auckland, 2009).

Pounds, N. J. G., *An Historical Geography of Europe 1500–1840* (Cambridge, 1979).

Powell, David, *Nationhood and Identity: the British State since 1800* (London, 2002).

Rainsford, Dominic, *Literature, Identity and the English Channel: Narrow Seas Expanded* (Houndmills, 2002).

Reeve, John, 'Britain or Europe? The Context of Early Modern English History: Political and Cultural, Economic and Social, Naval and Military', in Glenn Burgess (ed.), *The New British History: Founding a Modern State 1603–1715* (London, 1999).

Charles I and the Road to Personal Rule (Cambridge, 1989).

Rennie, Neil, *Far-Fetched Facts: the Literature of Travel and the Idea of the South Seas* (Oxford, 1995).

Richardson, Brian, *Longitude and Empire: How Captain Cook's Voyages Changed the World* (Vancouver, 2005).

Roberts, Clayton, 'The Impeachment of the Earl of Clarendon', *Cambridge Historical Journal* 13, 1 (1957).

Rodger, N. A. M., *The Command of the Ocean: a Naval History of Britain, 1649–1815* (London, 2005).

The Safeguard of the Sea: a Naval History of Britain 660–1649 (New York, 1998).

Said, Edward W., *Orientalism* (New York, 1979).

Salmond, Anne, *Aphrodite's Island: the European Discovery of Tahiti* (Auckland, 2009).

The Trial of the Cannibal Dog: the Remarkable Story of Captain Cook's Encounters in the South Seas (New Haven, 2003).

Sawday, Jonathan, *Engines of the Imagination: Renaissance Culture and the Rise of the Machine* (New York, 2007).

Schaffer, Simon, 'Visions of Empire: Afterword', in David Miller and Peter Reill (eds.), *Visions of Empire: Voyages, Botany, and Representations of Nature* (Cambridge, 1996).

Schama, Simon, *Landscape and Memory* (New York, 1996).
Scott, Jonathan, *Algernon Sidney and the English Republic 1623–1677* (Cambridge, 1988).
  Algernon Sidney and the Restoration Crisis 1677–1683 (Cambridge, 1991).
  Commonwealth Principles: Republican Writing of the English Revolution (Cambridge, 2004).
  'England's Houdini: Charles II's Escape from Worcester as a Metaphor for his Reign (1660–1685)', in John Morrow and Jonathan Scott (eds.), *Liberty, Authority, Formality: Political Ideas and Culture, 1600–1900* (Exeter, 2008).
  England's Troubles: Seventeenth-Century English Political Instability in European Context (Cambridge, 2000).
  ' "Good Night Amsterdam": Sir George Downing and Anglo-Dutch Statebuilding', *English Historical Review* 118, 176 (April 2003).
  Harry's Absence: Looking for my Father on the Mountain (Wellington, 1997).
  'James Harrington's Prescription for Healing and Settling', in Michael Braddick and David Smith (eds.), *The Experience of Revolution in Seventeenth Century England* (Cambridge, 2011).
  'The Peace of Silence: Thucydides and the English Civil War', in G. A. J. Rogers and Tom Sorell (eds.), *Hobbes and History* (London, 2000).
  'The Peace of Silence: Thucydides and the English Civil War', in Jeffrey Rusten (ed.), *Oxford Readings in Classical Studies: Thucydides* (Oxford University Press, 2009).
  'The Rapture of Motion: James Harrington's Republicanism', in Nicholas Phillipson and Quentin Skinner (eds.), *Political Discourse in Early Modern Britain* (Cambridge, 1993).
  'What the Dutch Taught Us', *Times Literary Supplement*, 16 March 2001.
Scott, T. H., 'From Emigrant to Native' Part 1, *Landfall* 1, 4 (December 1947); Part 2, *Landfall* 2, 2 (June 1948).
  'South Island Journal', *Landfall* 4, 4 (December 1950).
Sell, Jonathan P. A., *Rhetoric and Wonder in English Travel Writing, 1560–1613* (Aldershot, 2006).
Sen, Sudipta, *Distant Sovereignty: National Imperialism and the Origins of British India* (New York, 2002).
Sharpe, Kevin, *Sir Robert Cotton 1586–1631: History and Politics in Early Modern England* (Oxford, 1979).
Sherman, William, 'Stirrings and Searchings (1500–1720)', in Peter Hulme and Tim Youngs (eds.), *The Cambridge Companion to Travel Writing* (Cambridge, 2002).
Shigehisa, Kuriyama, ' "Between Mind and Eye": Japanese Anatomy in the Eighteenth Century', in Charles Leslie and Allan Young (eds.), *Paths to Asian Medical Knowledge* (Berkeley, 1992).
Simms, Brendan, *Three Victories and a Defeat: the Rise and Fall of the First British Empire, 1714–1783* (London, 2007).
Sinclair, Keith (ed.), *Distance Looks our Way: the Effects of Remoteness on New Zealand* (Auckland, 1961).
Smith, Bernard William, *European Vision and the South Pacific 1768–1850: a Study in the History of Art and Ideas* (2nd edn, Oxford, 1989).
  Imagining the Pacific: In the Wake of the Cook Voyages (Melbourne, 1992).

Smyth, William J., *Map-making, Landscapes and Memory: a Geography of Colonial and Early Modern Ireland c.1530–1750* (Notre Dame, Ind., 2006).

Sobecki, Sebastian I., *The Sea and Medieval English Literature* (Cambridge, 2008).

Spufford, Peter, 'Access to Credit and Capital in the Commercial Centres of Europe', in Karel Davids and Jan Lucassen (eds.), *A Miracle Mirrored: the Dutch Republic in European Perspective* (Cambridge, 1995).

Spurr, John, *England in the 1670s: 'This Masquerading Age'* (Oxford, 2000).

Steensgaard, Niels, 'The Growth and Composition of the Long-Distance Trade of England and the Dutch Republic before 1750', in James Tracy (ed.), *The Rise of Merchant Empires: Long Distance Trade in the Early Modern World* (Cambridge, 1990).

Steinberg, Philip, *The Social Construction of the Ocean* (Cambridge, 2001).

Stern, Philip J., ' "A Politie of Civill & Military Power": Political Thought and the Late Seventeenth-Century Foundations of the East India Company-State', *Journal of British Studies* 47 (April 2008).

Suranyi, Anna, *The Genius of the English Nation: Travel Writing and National Identity in Early Modern England* (Cranbury, N.J., 2008).

Taylor, E. G. R., *The Haven-Finding Art: a History of Navigation from Odysseus to Captain Cook* (New York, 1957).

Late Tudor and Early Stuart Geography, 1583–1650 (London, 1934).

Tudor Geography, 1485–1583 (London, 1932).

Thomas, Keith, *Man and the Natural World: Changing Attitudes in England 1500–1800* (London, 1983).

Thompson, Martin, 'Images of an Expanding World', *Cam: Cambridge Alumni Magazine* 50 (Lent Term 2007).

Timms, Peter, *In Search of Hobart* (Sydney, 2009).

Trevelyan, G. M., *History of England* (2nd edn, London, 1937).

Trevor-Roper, Hugh, 'Introduction', in Edward Gibbon, *The Decline and Fall of the Roman Empire*, (3 vols., New York, 1993).

Wevers, Lydia, *Country of Writing: Travel Writing and New Zealand 1809–1900* (Auckland, 2002).

Williams, Glyndwr, *The Great South Sea: English Voyages and Encounters 1570–1750* (New Haven, 1997).

Wilson, Charles, *Anglo-Dutch Commerce and Finance in the Eighteenth Century* (Cambridge, 1966).

England's Apprenticeship 1603–1763 (2nd edn, London, 1984).

Profit and Power: a Study of England and the Dutch Wars (1957).

Wilson, Kathleen, 'Introduction: Histories, Empires, Modernities', in Kathleen Wilson (ed.), *A New Imperial History: Culture, Identity and Modernity in Britain and the Empire 1660–1840* (Cambridge, 2004).

The Island Race: Englishness, Empire, and Gender in the Eighteenth Century (London, 2003).

Withington, Phil, *The Politics of Commonwealth: Citizens and Freemen in Early Modern England* (Cambridge, 2005).

Woolf, Virginia, *The Common Reader* (1925).

Woolrych, Austin, 'Historical Introduction', in John Milton, *Complete Prose Works, volume VII: 1659–1660* (rev. edn, New Haven, Conn., 1980).

Wrightson, Keith, *Earthly Necessities: Economic Lives in Early Modern Britain* (New Haven, 2000).

Wrigley, E. A., Davies, R. S., Oeppen, J. E. and Schofield, R. S., *English Population History from Family Reconstitution 1580–1837* (Cambridge, 1997).

Index

Albion, 13, 19
ale, established in Britain by Phoenicians,
    109
America, North
    Carthaginian settlement of, 131
    indigenous inhabitants, 27–8
    natural resources, 50
Anglo-Dutch
    geographic proximity (maritime), 98
    government, 117
    political proximity, moments of, 4, 39,
        78, 120
    union proposal, 1651, 77–80
    war, 1652–4, 75, 76, 80, 82
    war, 1665–7, 96–7
    war, 1672–3, 104
Anglo-French rivalry, 177
Anglo-Scottish union, 121–2
Armitage, David, 10, 166–7
Ashley Cooper, Anthony, Earl of
    Shaftesbury, 96, 104
Athenians compared with Spartans,
    47, 60
Athens, 29
    maritime empire of, 45
    as model for England, 5
    naval power of, 2, 46–7
    see also orientalism
Atkins, Samuel, 76
Australia, 149, 191; see also Botany Bay

Bacon, Francis, 15, 19, 20, 21
Banks, Joseph, 183, 184, 187
Bankes, Thomas, Universal Geography, 28
Barillon, Paul, French ambassador, 113
Bermuda, storm preceding shipwreck on,
    43, 70–1
Bible and the sea, 17
Blake, Admiral, 84, 150
Bodin, Jean, 157–9
Boswell, James, 186
Botany Bay, 137, 185

Bougainville, Louis de, 182
Bourne, William, 48
Braudel, Fernand, 38
Britain
    a European power, 13, 38
    free because an island, 155
    geography characteristically European,
        10, 20
    purported origins as a Phoenician
        mining colony, 109
    see also England
Buckingham, Lord Admiral, 68
Burton, Robert, 40

Cabot, Sebastian, 51
Cadiz, naval disaster at, 63–4
Camden, William
    Britain, 22–4, 29
    criticized, 109, 110
    on European migration,
        22–4
Canny, Nicholas, 26
Capp, Bernard, 69
Carthaginians 29, 130–1; see also Phoenicia
Caspian Sea, 11
channel, English, 13
Charles I, 54, 63, 67
Charles II, 92, 101, 113, 115, 177
    allows liberty of conscience
        in America, 96
    lazy government of, 127
    memory of Chatham raid, 103
Chatham, Dutch raid on, 97
    political impact of, 96, 102–3
China compared to France, 152
Churchill, Winston, 7, 8, 177
commonwealth as a ship, 87, 89, 90, 116
commonwealth of a ship see ship as a
        commonwealth
compass, invention of, 181
continentalism, anti-, 154, 155, 156;
        see also orientalism, maritime

Cook, James
  first circumnavigation, 183, 185
  planning of second voyage, 184
  second circumnavigation, 185–6
  a tarpaulin captain, 183–4
Coventry, Sir William, 69, 103
Crete, 9, 19, 24
Cromwell, Oliver, 76, 87, 88

Dampier, William, 149, 180
Darwin, Charles, 15, 43
Dee, John, 44, 45, 48
Defoe, Daniel, 6, 17, 176
  on Anglo-Scottish union, 121–2
  History of Discoveries, 130–1
  Robinson Crusoe, 143–5, 195
    captivity of, 144
    impact of, 144–5
    internal voyage of, 144
    terror in a storm, 143
  Tour Thro' the Whole Island, 131–6
    divided into coastal circuits, 131
    on fish, 133–4
    focus on improvement, 131
    on Greenwich 132
    lack of interest in antiquity, 131
    maritime preoccupations, 132
    on the Scilly Isles, 132
    on wilderness, 18
    on Yarmouth, 132
discipline of a ship, undistinguishing, 129, 136
discipline of the sea, 65, 66, 72, 114, 127
Donne, John, 11, 92
Dover, Treaties of, 102, 105
Downing, Sir George, 27, 93
Drake, Sir Francis, 33, 63
Drury, Robert, *Madagascar*, 148
duck language, 6, 199
ducks, decoy, 198–9
Dunbar, James, *History of Mankind*, 163–4
  against empire, 169–70, 171
  on Britain's insular situation, 164
  on Britain's need to avoid continental wars, 165
  on Cook's second circumnavigation, 186
  on the danger to Britain from its American empire, 166, 170–1
  on the Phoenicians, 165
  on the relationship of geography to culture, 164
Dunkirk, sale of, 113
Dusky Bay, New Zealand, 184, 187

Dutch, 61
  engrossing of English trade, 65
  invasion of England, 9, 117, 139
  religious toleration, brought to England, 125
  see also United Provinces

East India Company, English, 34
Elizabethan maritime activity, 33–4, 36, 149
Elizabeth I, 40, 50, 53
Elliott, John, 26
empire, British, 117, 123, 153
  argument against, 155–56;
    see also Dunbar
  predominantly continental, 175–6
  redescription as archipelagic, 176–7
  redescription as a fleet, 194
  redescription as maritime, 174–5
  redescription as oceanic and extra-European, 177, 197
empire, English, 10, 13, 26, 50–1, 54, 85
  English republican, 78, 79
  Roman, 23, 29, 106–7;
    see also Robertson
  Spanish, 26, 39, 50, 123–4
England
  acquisition of maritime culture, 3–4
  advantages towards naval power, 129–30, 138
  advantages for trade, 139, 143
  maritime geography, 4–5
  not an island, 10
  'Paramount Power by Sea', 138
  a rural society, 31
  strategic location in relation to Dutch trade, 82, 143
  vulnerability to invasion, 140
  see also Britain
English courage, 137, 143
English state formation, 25
English timber for shipbuilding, 129–30
Erasmus, 42
Eurasian history, 1
Europe
  geography of, 20–1
  not a continent, 14
Evelyn, John, 5, 30
  on the beauty of a ship, 130
  on the Mediterranean, 105
  Navigation and Commerce, 105–7
excise, 62–3, 73, 93

Falconer, William, 154, 156–57
Ferguson, Adam, *History of Civil Society*
    all of Europe temperate, 159
    continents climatically extreme, 159–60
    Europe temperate because maritime, 160
    interaction of situation and climate, 157
    more to temperature than latitude, 159–60
fishing
    foreign in British waters, 48, 51–2, 105
    obstacles to British, 52
    potential of British, 52–3
Flamsteed, John, 142
Fletcher, Andrew
    on the British empire, 174
    on the Spanish empire, 123–4, 125
France, 104, 107
    fear of invasion by, 122–3
frugality, 62, 76, 77

Games, Alison, 2
gentleman captains
    before 1660, 65, 67–8, 69, 91
    after 1660, 92, 126
    see also Gibson
Germany, 18
Gibbon, Edward
    defends England's empire in America, 169
    on the Saxon neglect of navigation, 164
Gibson, Richard, 70
    'Advantages and Disadvantages ariseing to an Island', 139–42
    advice on the navy, 119–20
    on the Chatham raid, 98–9
    on collier masters as captains, 80
    'Discourse between an English and Dutch Sea Captain', 82–3
    on election of naval officers, 128
    on Elizabethan navy, 83
    on gentleman captains, 81, 83, 85, 92, 113, 114
    scheme for maritime cultural reform, 140
    on victualling, 80
    on war of 1652–4, 80, 84
    on war of 1672–3, 80
Gilbert, Sir Humphrey, 26, 43
Gomerians, 23
Greece, ancient, 2

Hakluyt, Richard, 15, 17, 31, 48
    'Discourse of Western Planting', 50–1
    Principall Navigations, 49
Harrington, James
    Commonwealth of Oceana

    absence of maritime reference in, 86, 87
    agrarian political economy of, 86
    debt to Hobbes, 87
    A Discourse upon this saying, 89
    on empire, 87–8
    gentry leadership in, 86
    doctrine of constitutional navigation, 89, 90
    a gentleman, 86
havens (harbours)
    decay of English, 142
    English and Dutch compared, 5, 138
    English and French compared, 112, 138
Head, Richard, *The Floating Island*, 102
Heylyn, Peter, 20
    Cosmography, 21, 26, 27
    on islands, 21–2
    Microcosmus, 19
    on the ocean, 22
Hilton, Boyd, 35, 169
Hobbes, Thomas, 54, 57, 60–1
Hodges, William, painting on Cook's second voyage, 187
Holland, 31, 54; *see also* United Provinces
Homer's *Odyssey*, 40, 137
Hume, David, 91

Ireland, 88
    attempted English conquest of, 24–6
    as site for imperial expropriation, 26
islanders
    Athenians as, 44, 48
    English as, 48
island nation
    idea of Britain as an, 6, 7–8, 139, 140, 142, 154
islands
    advantages attending, 141
    divinely wrought stepping stones, 23
    European, 14
    floating, 40, 41, 66, 71–2, 73, 194, 195
    of ice, 185–6
    inclined to liberty, 153–54
    myth of, 155
    oceanic, 176, 189
    a sea of, 16, 156, 192
    understood in relation to continental line, 176
    versus continents, 137, 139, 153–4;
        see also orientalism, maritime
    as a world, 145, 147
    see also Gibson

Jamaica, 150
James II, 116
James VI and I, 54

James, Duke of York, 92
Japan compared to Britain, 151–52
Jenkinson, Anthony, 15
Johnson, Samuel, 165, 186

Kishlansky, Mark, 69

laws, government of, 119
Le Maire, Jacques, 179, 180
Linebaugh and Rediker, *The Many-Headed Hydra*, 72, 75–6
lobsters, 147
Locke, John, 124
London
  Defoe's admiration of, 134–6
  fire of, 97
  fiscal and political dominance of, 79, 119
  growth of, 35
  locus of naval power, 103
  military occupation of, 118
  plague in, 96
Loxley, Diana, 195

McFarlane, Samuel, 196
Madagascar, 68, 148; *see also* Drury
mariners, English, 64
maritime
  civilizations, 1–2
  and commercial power, republican approval of, 87
  ideology, 70
  systems, 28, 29, 30
Marvell, Andrew, 31
  Last Instructions, 99–100, 101–2
Mayhew, Robert, 22
merchant marine, English, 64–5
military government, social transformation of, 85
Mongols, 14
Monson, Sir William, 51, 61, 99
Montagu, Edward, Earl of Sandwich, 92
Montaigne, Michel de, 15
Montesquieu, Baron de, 154, 155, 157
More, Thomas, *Utopia*, 36–7
Mylius, Hermann, 77

Naipaul, V. S., 8
Narborough, Sir John, 18
  expedition to Chile, 177–8
Navigation Act (1651), 65, 75
Navigation Act (1660), 93
navigational science, English neglect of, 125
navy, under
  Augustus, 106–7
  Charles I, 68

Charles II, 92–3
Elizabeth I, 34, 50, 56
the English republic, 3, 73, 75, 76, 81–2, 85, 149
James VI and I, 56, 57
parliament, 69
William and Mary, 126
Neville, Henry, 89
  Isle of Pines, 100–1
New Model Army, 3, 84
New Model Navy, 84
New Zealand, 15, 193, 195
  geographical remoteness, 190, 192
  mountainous appearance, 190–1
  oceanic geography, 190, 192
New Zealanders, 9
nobles, revolt against, 72
north-west passage, 34, 48
Norwich, 61

Ogilby, John, 16, 20, 138
  America, 27–8, 179
Oldmixon, John, 141
Oppenheim, H., 57, 69
orientalism, maritime
  Athenian, 46, 47–8
  Elizabethan, 46, 48
  Enlightenment, 154, 155, 156
Ortelius, Abraham, 23, 51

Pacific Ocean
  immensity of, 15
Paine, Thomas, 176
Patagonia, proposal for plantation of, 63, 178
penguin-bashing, 18, 178
Penn, William, 124, 125
Pepys, Samuel, 5, 33, 57, 93, 103, 115
  and Gibson, 97, 98
  on Gibson, 80
  report on the navy, 114–15
  to Sheres on the navy, 115
Pericles, 44
Persia, 136
Peter, Hugh, 68, 69, 81
Phoenicia/Carthage, 104
  as model for England, 5
  Phoenicians first settlers of Britain, 109
  see also Sammes
Phoenix (ship), 82
Plantation Act of 1650, 75
Plantation Act of 1673, 96
plantations, English 141; *see also* empire, English
Plato, 36–7
Pocock, J. G. A., 160–1, 174, 192–3
Polybius, 109

'Pseudo-Xenophon', 2
Ptolemy, 11, 13, 19, 151
Purchas, Samuel, 15

Quianlong, Chinese emperor, 16

Rainsborough, Thomas, 69–70
Ralegh, Sir Walter, 45, 131
Raynal, Guillaume, 146
    History of Settlements, 161–2
        against European empires, 168, 171
        criticism of Roman empire, 162
        on Greece, 159
        maritime but not orientalist 161, 162
reformation and counter-reformation,
        struggle between, 25
Rhodians, 31
Richardson, Brian, 176
Robertson, William, 125
    History of America, 163
        praise of Rome, 163
        unimpressed by Greeks, 163
Romans, 131; see also empire
Rousseau, Jean-Jacques, 144
Royal African Company, 93

sailors' language, 66
Sammes, Aylett, Britannia Antiqua
        Illustrata, 107–11
    on antiquity of English channel,
        107–8
    Britain first settled by Phoenicians, 109
    deepening the antiquity of Britain,
        110–11
    Phoenician origin of British words and
        names, 109
Savile, George, Earl of Halifax
    England in an island, 137
    England's root in the sea, 128
    England's unfitness for a
        commonwealth, 129
Saxons, 24, 55
Schama, Simon, 188
Scotland, 13, 17, 53, 72, 121, 149;
        see also Defoe
Scott, Thomas, 24, 57–9, 61, 66
sea a leveller, 71
sea, longing to go to, 148–9
sea-lions
    destruction of, 18, 147
    roaring of, 146, 147
Self-Denying Ordinance, 84
Selkirk, Alexander, 146
Seller, John, 5
Seven Years War, 153

Shakespeare, William, The Tempest, 43–4,
        70
Shelvocke, George, 18
    on Juan Fernandes Island, 146–47
    Voyage Round the World. 145
Sheres, Sir Henry, 103, 120, 128
    on Chatham, 103
    A Discourse Touching Tanger, 105, 111
    on the improvement of French harbours
        and coastal defences, 112
    instructed to raze the mole, 111
    'Modell of a Maritime Monarchy', 138
    on naval defence in 1688, 116–17
    Naval Essays, 123
    'Of Navall Discipline', 126–7
    to Pepys on iron, 130
    project for the recovery of Dover haven,
        112–13
    in Tangiers, 104
ship as a commonwealth, 66–7, 127
Sidney, Algernon, 25, 76, 84, 117
Sidney, Sir Philip, 25
Simms, Brendan, 11, 13
sloth and idleness, English, 106, 127
Smith, Bernard, 186
Smollett, Tobias, Adventures of an Atom
    bottom-kicking in, 150–1
    bottom-licking in, 151
    impact of beard colours upon, 151
Solomon, King, 106
southern continent, search for, 177,
        180, 186
Spanish armada, 39, 64, 122, 130
Speed, John, 38, 55
Spenser, Edmund
    The Faerie Queene, 11, 17, 31, 40–1
Steinberg, Philip, 16
Stevenson, Robert Louis, 196
Streater, John, 27
Strode, William, The Floating Island,
        71–2
Swift, Jonathan, Gulliver's Travels, 40, 44,
        148–9, 180

Tahiti, 182, 183, 186, 188
Tangiers, 111
tarpaulin versus gentlemen officers, 126;
        see also gentleman captains
Tasman, Abel, discovery of Tasmania and
        New Zealand, 179, 180
Temple, Sir William, 59, 77, 138, 167
Themistocles, 45
Thucydides, 44, 60
traffique (trade), 62, 75, 93
Trinidad, 8
Tupia, 182, 183, 186, 188

United Provinces of the Netherlands,
  61, 117
  creation of, a precedent for the USA,
    166, 167–8
  a Free State, 78, 79
  geographic advantages for trade, 138
  maritime culture of, 3
  maritime geography of, 4, 59, 60
  as a model for England, 5, 57–9, 61–3,
    77
  near fall of, 104
United States of America, claimed
  insularity, 172

Venice, 65
Vespucius, Americus (Amerigo Vespucci),
  142
Virgil, 22

Wales, 13
Wallis, Samuel, 181–2
walls
  of brass, 64, 67
  bronze, 137
  wooden, 48, 119, 196
war, land versus sea, 128
war, social and political impact of,
  4, 85
water
  fresh, 28–9
  human exploitation of, 1
  political theory of, 192
wilderness, 188–9
  on land, 17–18
  perceptions of the ocean as, 16
Witt, Johann De, 97, 105, 150
Woolf, Virginia, 144